7-2012

1

SCIENCE & HISTORY

public opinion polls and survey research

public affairs and administration
(editor: James S. Bowman)
vol. 24

Garland reference library
of social science
vol. 575

the public affairs and administration series: James S. Bowman, editor

public opinion polls and
survey research
*A selective annotated
bibliography of
U.S. guides and studies
from the 1980s*

Graham R. Walden

Garland Publishing, Inc. • New York & London
1990

Library of Congress Cataloging-in-Publication Data

Walden, Graham R., 1954–
  Public opinion polls and survey research: a selective annotated
bibliography of U.S. guides and studies from the 1980s / Graham R.
Walden.
    p.   cm. — (The Public affairs and administration series; 24)
(Garland reference library of social science; vol. 575)
  ISBN 0–8240–5732–5 (alk. paper)
  1. Public opinion polls—Bibliography. 2. Social surveys—
Bibliography. 3. Public opinion—United States—Bibliography.
4. Social surveys—United States—Bibliography. I. Title.
II. Series. III. Series: Garland reference library of social
science; v. 575.
Z7164.P956W34   1990
[HM261]
016.3033'8'0723—dc20   89–25956
                                                            CIP

Printed on acid-free, 250-year-life paper
Manufactured in the United States of America

To my parents

Ingeborg Strobach Walden

and

Graham Kenneth Walden

Contents

Series Foreword

The twentieth century has seen public administration come of age as a field of study and practice. As a result of the dramatic growth in government, and the accompanying information explosion, many individuals—managers, academicians and their students, researchers—in organizations feel that they do not have ready access to important information. In an increasingly complex world, more and more people need published material to help solve problems.

The scope of the field and the lack of a comprehensive information system has frustrated users, disseminators, and generators of knowledge in public administration, While there have been some initiatives in recent years, the documentation and control of the literature have been generally neglected. Indeed, major gaps in the development of the literature, the bibliographic structure of the discipline, have evolved.

Garland Publishing, Inc., inaugurated the present series as an authoritative guide to information sources in public administration. It seeks to consolidate the gains made in the growth and maturation of the profession.

The Series consists of three tiers:
1. core volumes keyed to the major subfields in public administration such as personnel management, public budgeting, and organizational behavior;
2. bibliographies focusing on substantive areas of administration such as community health; and
3. titles on topical issues in the profession, such as civil service reform, productivity, and ethics.

Each book will be compiled by one or more specialists in the area. The authors—practitioners and scholars—are selected in open competition from across the country. They design their work to include an introductory essay, a wide variety of bibliographic materials, and, where appropriate, an information resource section. Thus each contribution in the collection provides a systematic basis for manager and researchers to make informed judgments in the course of their work.

Since no single volume can adequately encompass such a broad, interdisciplinary subject, the Series is intended as a continuous project that will incorporate new bodies of literature as needed. Its titles represent the initial building blocks in an operating information system for public affairs and administration. As an open-ended endeavor, it is hoped that not only will the Series serve to summarize knowledge in the field but also will contribute to its advancement.

This collection of book-length bibliographies is the product of considerable collaboration on the part of many people. Special appreciation is extended to the editors and staff of Garland Publishing, Inc., to the individual contributors in the Public Affairs and Administration Series, and to the anonymous reviewers of each of the volumes. Inquiries should be made to the Series Editor.

James S. Bowman
Department of Public Administration
Florida State University

Foreword

The use of public opinion polls by policy makers and social researchers has continued to grow in the past decade. Along with this growth there have been significant changes in methodology and technology of which computer-assisted telephone interviewing is probably the most widespread example. The literature describing these changes is found in a broad range of books and professional journals and even experienced poll users and researchers are unlikely to be aware of them all.

Thus, a new annotated bibliography of major works on the topic of polling and survey research is an important addition to the references already available. It is obvious that such a bibliography will have a limited shelf life and that a decade from now a new bibliography will be needed. By that time, it is likely that it will be accessed online by computer.

Although published in a series on Public Affairs and Administration, I would predict that this bibliography will be useful to a broad range of social science researchers. Public opinion research has been a major tool for setting public affairs agendas and evaluating government programs, but it has also become the primary tool of data collection for most social scientists.

Walden has chosen to exclude references prior to 1980. This is probably a sensible decision given that any effort at a complete bibliography would include many out-of-date references and obsolete issues. There is always some cost of ignoring the past. Some references from earlier periods still have contributions to make to our current understanding. Most of these can be located by using the references given in the works discussed in this book.

About half of this book deals with methodological issues and the other half with more general issues such as specific studies related to politics, law, print and electronic media and education. The annotations describing each cited work are prepared with great care and give readers enough details so they can determine if the work will be useful for their purposes.

As is typically the case with bibliographies, this one will probably be of greatest use to students and information specialists who will find it a convenient way of getting an overview of the available literature. Even experienced survey researchers will find references here that are both useful and new. I did.

Seymour Sudman
Walter Stellner Chair of Marketing
University of Illinois at
Urbana–Champaign

Introduction

After more than fifty years of scientific polling and survey research, it is time to begin the process of organizing the literature in this bibliographically neglected field. The first historically recorded poll was on 24 July 1824 by the Harrisburg *Pennsylvanian*, although the sampling approach employed would not be considered scientific today. In the mid-1930s George Gallup, followed by Elmo Roper and Archibald Crossley, conducted the first scientific public policy polls.[1] *Public Opinion Quarterly* was first published in 1937, and is the premier publication for leading researchers and practitioners in the field. Selective subsequent milestones include the founding of the National Opinion Research Center (NORC) in 1941 (a nonprofit organization providing consultation and opinion measuring services), the 1946 establishment of the Survey Research Center (SRC) at the University of Michigan, and the 1947 creation of the American Association for Public Opinion Research (AAPOR). In 1963 Louis Harris began a survey organization bearing his name. The National Council on Published Polls (NCPP) was organized in 1967 and has produced, among other achievements, the *Principles of Disclosure* document.

The development and application of polls and surveys has become a major industry involving over two thousand research organizations, with annual revenues in excess of $4 billion.[2] There are thousands of companies engaged in public opinion research, with the names of some widely known, e.g., Gallup, Harris, and Roper. Research indicates that poll results are even "utilized in the development of opinion."[3] With the significant scope and impact of polls and surveys suggested, it is self-

---

[1]Mildred Parten, *Surveys, Polls, and Samples: Practical Procedures* (New York: Cooper Square Publishers, 1966), 24.

[2] L. John Martin, ed. *Polling and the Democratic Consensus*, Annals of the American Academy of Political and Social Science, vol. 472 (Beverly Hills, CA: Sage Publications, March 1984), 9.

[3]Nadine S. Koch, "Perceptions of Public Opinion Polls," (Ph.D. diss., Ohio State University, 1985), 184.

evident that the opinion research community especially, and the wider public in general, could benefit from access to the methodological research upon which all of these enterprises rest. Additionally, learning the techniques through the instructional literature is both useful for new researchers, and basic for the general population. This annotated bibliography seeks to address both perceived needs, covering the literature of all but the closing months of the decade of the eighties.

The future for this field is very bright. New technologies will extend the reach of researchers. The 1990s promise to usher in an age of much greater communication capabilities through the increased reachability of everyone by telephone in automobiles, planes, and boats, as well as through portable telephones, the regular use of the picture image telephone, much more widespread availability and access to fax machines, and the worldwide computer networking possibilities that already exist will doubtless become commonplace. For the opinion researcher these opportunities suggest both many challenges and the need for new research. Polls and surveys and their results may be able to be generated significantly more quickly, with the need for ready access to past research ever greater. The growth of the research literature in this field may demand an update within five years; certainly by the year 2000, the update will probably be accessible online as Dr. Sudman suggests in the Foreword.

As a starting point for gaining access to the literature, this bibliography is arranged through a detailed table of contents, a thorough chapter overview section, and extensive author and keyword indexes. The volume is divided into twenty chapters. Categorization was determined according to the major focus of each entry; overlapping of subject areas generates many challenges. Even though some items might be found in a number of chapters, each entry appears only once; entries are consecutively numbered. The ordering of the chapters posed options where a variety of possibilities might be equally appropriate depending upon the user's perspective and intended use of the literature.[4]

To compensate for the variety of research orientations, and

---

[4]Chapters 9 through 17 represent the core of the research literature on methodology, and are meant to be viewed as highly interrelated, and hence the arrangement is somewhat artificial in that elements from each chapter may require virtual simultaneous consideration in order to successfully follow through the many stages of a project, i.e., when writing questions response effects must be considered. Logically, a side-by-side presentation is called for, but print limitations call upon authors to place one chapter ahead of another, and so the many issues addressed in the response chapter follow chapters on questions, sampling, and interviewing. Some aspects in the response chapter, such as response effects might be placed ahead of the question chapter, while others could be placed elsewhere.

philosophies of categorization, a very thorough thirty-one page keyword index is included, as well as a detailed chapter overview section. The table of contents, chapter overview, and indexes are designed to provide differing access approaches, which are of course complementary and hierarchical. To aid understanding of this book's intentions and design, a number of sections follow in this introduction, including purpose, scope, coverage, methodology, chapter overview, addendum and appendixes, indexes, and sources of future information.

Purpose

The decade of the 1980s witnessed the ever-increasing use of polls and surveys as well as an expanded research effort into public opinion polls and survey research from the economic, historical, legal, methodological, organizational, and political viewpoints. The purpose of this volume is to provide a timely resource for practitioners, researchers, students, librarians, and others seeking access to this interdisciplinary literature. Prior to this compilation, no annotated bibliographic treatment of public opinion polls or survey research existed.

The volume provides access to the literature from the 1980s. Over 350 citations receive bibliographic reference with lengthy annotations. The annotations (averaging two hundred words) should assist users in determining whether the item is relevant to their work, and if an examination of the full text is merited.

Scope

Instructional guides, handbooks, reference works, textbooks, research studies, and evaluative and critical studies on public opinion polls and survey research published since 1980 are included in the bibliography (the author believes that the literature from the decade of the 1980s will serve the immediate needs of most readers). Studies which deal with poll or survey results are rarely considered, and are discussed only when they highlight or explain a certain research study or finding. Polling and survey research findings are available in a variety of other sources.[5]

A number of items from the literature on market research are considered, i.e., items that this author believes have generalizable value to the areas of polls and surveys, and which do not specifically consider

---

[5]This author's article titled "Public Opinion Polls: A Guide to Accessing the Literature" in *RSR Reference Services Review,* Volume 16, Number 4, 1988, pages 65–74, documents where poll and survey data can be found, including results from Gallup, Harris, NORC, and others. Also discussed is the *Guide to Resources and Services* by the Inter-University Consortium for Political and Social Research (ICPSR), a repository for the work of over 310 colleges and universities located in fourteen countries throughout the world.

"marketing" issues. Although many business indexes and online services were searched, the research conducted in this area was not exhaustive, but nevertheless may represent the core of relevant recent works.

Throughout the annotations this bibliographer has been careful to adhere to the wording and phrasing used by the original authors. The words poll, survey, and questionnaire have differing interpretations both historically and by various users. There is little agreement, standardization, or effort toward unifying the vocabulary of this interdisciplinary research.

A distinction in the field, but not addressed in the literature, is between the words public opinion polling and survey research. The term polling tends to be used by the media; survey research seems to be the choice of academia. Again, there are no uniform rules that govern the terminology, with commercial firms, academia, practitioners, and the media using varying formats. While this bibliography contains some items found under the questionnaire subject heading, it relies primarily on the 1986 Berdie volume to provide broad coverage in this area (Item 1 in this volume).

In three instances (Items 71, 90, and 331), the subject discussed involves private polling. These references have been included (although they are clearly outside the realm of this book) because of their comparative value, and also to provide access to the small body of publicly available literature on private polling.

Coverage
The volume covers public opinion poll and survey research literature from January 1980 through June 1989. There are two specific exceptions to this time period, as well as a group of citations which fall prior to, and within the years covered. The individual exceptions are Items 2 and 46. Item 2, an unannotated bibliography on public opinion polls, is included because it may be the only previous general bibliography published on public opinion polls. The Sharma bibliography, covering the period from 1950 to 1965, could be of historical value to present day users. The other exception is Item 46, House hearings held in 1972 on the "Truth-in-Polling Act." These hearings are included because of their unusual and interesting nature, and because the issues raised remain pertinent today.

The group exception category consists of all relevant U.S. dissertations (beginning with the earliest in 1941 to the present). Dissertations are included to show the historical progression of research in the area, and to permit access to the bibliographies of these works as well as, of course, their substantive contents.

While public opinion polling and survey research exist in other English-speaking countries and elsewhere, a decision was made from the outset of this project to limit consideration to American authors appearing in U.S. publications. As a result, experts in the field will note the absence of some prominent British, Canadian, and Australian contributors, as well as researchers writing in foreign languages. The major concern was over the availability of foreign materials for other than very well known titles, and the language challenges presented by non-English titles. The author believes that separate treatments for non–United States works would be most appropriate.

Newspaper articles, reviews of journals, book reviews, university occasional papers, proceedings (with selective exceptions), master's theses, and mass market periodicals (with some exceptions) have been excluded. American Association for Public Opinion Research (AAPOR) annual proceedings and other regularly issued conference proceedings are not included. The large quantity of these papers awaits review in another volume. Special conferences devoted to relevant subjects have received attention when published proceedings were available. Since the intent of this work is to provide the reader with the record of the scholarly endeavors in public opinion polling and survey research, the abundance of "opinion" pieces in newspapers, magazines, books, and elsewhere is not addressed.

The bibliography does not contain references to technical papers and reports that are not in the public domain, such as those held by private organizations and associations. This literature is substantial but unavailable for review by the general public. Additionally, newsletters, annual reports, technical papers, and so on, emanating from university polling and survey research units are not covered.

Methodology

The research method used employed traditional print indexes and abstracts, bibliographic tools, as well as online and compact disc options. Appendix E provides a list of the basic bibliographic sources searched. The online bibliographic databases included: Online Computer Library Center (OCLC); Research Libraries Information Network (RLIN); and the Washington Library Network (WLN). The online database vendors used were BRS and DIALOG. The author located, verified, examined, annotated, and subject categorized every item in the main body of the bibliography (Items 1–359). The sources annotated, as well as those listed in the addendum, are available from university libraries, medium sized college libraries, and many public libraries.

The *Chicago Manual of Style* (13th edition) was the basis for formatting, grammatical details, and bibliographical form. A footnote explains the format for the entries.[6]

---

[6]Books and monographic citations include author(s) or editor(s); title; edition if other than first; series name if applicable; editor of series if applicable; place of

Chapter Overview

The goal of this work is to bring together the research studies from a number of relevant areas and to provide a useful framework through which the material could be accessed. Chapter 1 (Items 1–7) examines an annotated bibliography on questionnaires, two bibliographies on public opinion polls, and a bibliography on survey and questionnaire design. The directories described review the Roper Center and discuss a Gale Research title designed to cover statistical studies found in surveys, polls, censuses, and forecasts. The chapter closes with an entry which provides a guide to accessing the findings of published public opinion polls. The article includes references to the *Guide to Resources and Services* by the Inter-University Consortium for Political and Social Science Research (ICPSR) and the *Gallup Poll* and *Harris Survey*. The intent of this book is to focus on poll and survey methodology, not on results or findings oriented research; Item 7 should be consulted for a broad spectrum of sources to locate poll and survey data.

Chapter two (Items 8–37) contains instructional material literature, divided into four major categories. While the overall literature may be greater than discussed here, it is felt that the works selected are useful, and serve to illustrate another facet of the overall literature. Items 8–16 contain explanations of how polls and surveys work, and how polls should be interpreted, understood, and evaluated. Items 17–20 include "how-to" volumes for the general user and for the news reporter. Telephone surveying is discussed in another how-to book. Items 21–25 are five handbooks for the general user, citizen advocacy groups, and the professional. Items 26–37 discuss some of the textbooks available, with a considerable range in the type of material included. Single chapters within volumes, as well as specialized volumes for one profession (geographers) are incorporated. Mail and telephone surveys are represented here. (See Chapter 13, Item 279, for a textbook dealing exclusively with interviewing.)

---

publication; publisher; year of publication; and total number of pages. When the entry item is a book chapter, the inclusive page numbers provided are those for the chapter. Journal entries include author(s); title; journal name; volume number; issue number if applicable; month (season, if quarterly); and article page number(s). Dissertation entries include author; title; type of degree (i.e., Ph.D.); awarding institution; year; and total number of pages. All dissertations within the body of the book have been examined and annotated by the author. Book reviews were examined for some addendum items since they assisted in the addendum inclusion decision-making process. Citations to congressional hearings include committee; subcommittee; title; Congress; session; year; place of publication; publisher; publication date; and number of pages.

Chapter 3 (Items 38–46) has entries which range from a book length treatment of survey research from 1890 to 1960, through congressional hearings covering the "Truth-in-Polling-Act." The remaining studies are journal articles and book chapters which either provide a broad overview history or focus more narrowly on a topic such as sampling.

Chapter 4 (Items 47–56) could also have been titled "Miscellaneous." While the studies found usually look at the broad picture, quite a few examine specific issues—ones which do not easily or neatly fit into any of the many other categories in this book. The chapter covers everything from the fundamental attribution error to the power of polls, as well as a conference on polling issues, large-scale surveys, artifacts, and consensuses.

Chapter 5 (Items 57–69) contains items from three subject areas: impact, influence and perceptions. Impact entries deal with the effect of polls and surveys on presidential elections, voting behavior in general, consideration of the bandwagon and underdog effects, the role of polls with respect to public opinion, and whether or not polls affect what people think. The second subject area covers the influence of polls and surveys on the shaping of the news, election campaigns, and the idea of "government by opinion." The perception items deal with a study of a small group to ascertain their views, research on attitudes toward and participation in survey research in general, and finally a study evaluating polls through an examination of poll data.

Chapter 6 (Items 70–126) discusses the studies which focus on a variety of subject areas, such as politics, law, print and electronic media, education, and others. The section covering politics (Items 70–97) deals with a variety of issues, including: the use of public opinion polls in elections, in particular with relationship to presidential elections (and also private polling in this area); the abuses of polls in politics; the top political polling firms; presidential uses of polls in decision making; the relationship between polls and public policy; and especially forecasting and predicting elections. There are three entries in the law section (Items 98–100) which discuss the use of surveys as evidence, how businesses have used surveys to defend themselves, and the use of psychologists and surveys in change of venue cases.

The third section in the chapter (Items 101-120) considers the subject areas of the print and electronic media. Horse race journalism, polls as journalism, the liaison between the press and polling, polling as a news gathering tool, the credibility of polls in the media, network television use of polls, polls as news events, and do-it-yourself newspaper polling are some of the subjects addressed. The fourth section (Items 121–122) considers survey research in higher education and a guide for the local use of polls. The additional studies (Items 123–126) include a review of differing perspectives on the use of polls by some religious leaders, the use of surveys in needs determinations, the Gallup Poll as a psychohistorical tool, and finally, the use of polls by unions as tools to evaluate potential services to be offered to the membership.

Chapter 7 (Items 127–138) on exit polling and election projection considers these topics from many perspectives, including: exit polling restrictions; the time of day and the impact on exit poll results; congressional attacks on exit polling; projections and West Coast turnout as well as projections in general; the performance of election day polls; exit poll influence on voting behavior; congressional hearings on election projections; and alternatives to exit polls.

Chapter 8 (Items 139–144) focuses on the pollster and provides presentations of the following subjects: the 1984 presidential campaign and pollsters; a representative American government textbook illustrating how pollsters are covered in this genre; the answers leading pollsters gave to a series of polling methodology questions; the 1980 presidential elections and wrong poll calls; the role of pollsters in presidential campaigns; and the roots, roles, and practices of pollsters.

Chapter 9 (Items 145–153) examines the administration and design of surveys and questionnaires. The entry (Item 145) which deals with administration covers the management of survey organizations. Entries which follow in the design (Items 146–147) and the instrument length (Items 148–149) sections consider advanced design, question writing and overall design, length, and page length for questionnaires. The incentives section (Items 150–151) examines the issue of charitable contributions and financial incentives, on the part of survey organizations, as means to encourage response in mail surveys. The chapter closes with a section (Items 152–153) on computers in survey research, and a comparison between the use of computers versus scanners in the administration of surveys.

Chapter 10 (Items 154–169) deals with two areas in survey research, namely measurement and scaling. The first section on measurement (Items 154–166) reviews a variety of aspects of this subject, from theory and techniques to handbook treatment of the topic. Also covered are the measurement of values (comparing ratings versus rankings); construct validity using a structural modeling approach; evaluating change through a laboratory investigation; Rasch measurement; measurement error; surveys as social indicators; attitudes versus nonattitudes; causal modeling; and a series of volumes on subjective phenomena. The second part of the chapter (Items 167–169) deals with magnitude scaling and unidimensional scaling.

Chapter 11 (Items 170–209) is divided into a number of parts on form, wording, filter questions and context, order and order effects, and miscellaneous. The form entries (Items 170–182) focus on research across organizations and time; the open versus closed questioning controversy of the 1940s; ranking tasks; open-ended questions; a test of the form resistant correlation hypothesis; alternative question forms for telephone interviews; the use of the Pareto Curve with income distributions; assertion versus interrogation format; problems with survey question format; attitudes versus nonattitudes; and form, wording and context (an item which could equally have been placed in the next chapter section on wording). The second chapter section on wording (Items 183–188) begins with an examination of experiments dealing with the middle response alternative, and continues with the following: a further study on the middle option, studies of specific response categories and what they mean, how to ask the age question, the measurement of the middle position, and the impact of question wording on the responses.

Filter questions and context (Items 189–194) are next, beginning with the effects of filter questions, and followed by research into filtering political opinions. The screening out of uninformed responses with filter questions is considered, as well as the improvement of retrospective reports by using landmark events. Context in questionnaires and bounded recall procedures are also covered. The fourth chapter section on order and order effects (Items 195–203) includes studies on the use of the conditional inference model to explain order and context effects; the impact of question order in electoral contexts; political information processing and question order; order issues in relationship to political campaigns in general and specifically during the 1982 Connecticut election; order effects and presidential popularity; and a number of other broader examinations of question order and order effects. The last section of the chapter includes a range of materials which do not readily fit into any one section, and therefore appear in a miscellaneous section (Items 204–209). Considered are the presentation of one versus two sides of an issue in survey questions; a guide to questions for questionnaires; an index of public opinion questions; the dropping of the "independent" label as a political party affiliation in the National Election Study; a fifty-year review of questions asked in public opinion polls; and retrospective questions on the 1982 General Social Surveys.

Chapter 12 (Items 210–236) divides the literature on sampling into five categories. The first covers respondent selection (Items 210–217) and includes the following subjects: polling and the attentive public; selecting respondents in telephone surveys; an examination into whether it is possible to conduct noninvasive telephone respondent selection; multiplicity sampling; the next-birthday method of respondent selection; applied sampling; persistence in respondent selection and the importance of the practice in preelection surveys; and dual frame designs in telephone surveys. The next section (Items 218–221) on sample size examines how large the sample size should be, along with consideration of the one-sample case, sample size formula for multiple regression studies, and an additional item covering how to determine the sample size. The section on subgroups and special populations (Items 222–226) deals with locating special populations using random digit dialing, using ethnic surnames as a sampling approach, screening methods for the sampling of geographically clustered special populations, and several items on the detection of subgroups. The nonresponse section (Items 227–232) includes considerations of the problem of nonresponse, adjustments for it, tests for potential nonresponse bias, and historical trends in nonresponse from 1952–1979. The other sampling research covered in the last section of the chapter (Items 233–236) compares nonsampling errors with sampling errors, provides a handbook treatment of sampling theory, reviews the sampling practices used for the Social Research Surveys 1947 to 1980 at the Survey Research Center, and closes with an introductory textbook on survey sampling. (Textbooks on specialized subjects appear with the appropriate subject chapter rather than in the textbook section of Chapter 2.)

Chapter 13 (Items 237–279) contains the interviewing literature. There are nine sections in this chapter, the first of which deals with telephone interviewing (Items 237–242). Covered here are items on the impact of advance telephone calls for personal interviews, experimental techniques, interviewers' voices and refusal rates, a reappraisal along with a field experiment, speech characteristics and effectiveness, and ring policies. The next section is on computer-assisted telephone interviewing (CATI). The CATI section (Items 243–249) includes items on costs; errors; organization; the effects of CATI on interviewers and respondents; a comparison with hard copy telephone interviewing; microcomputer-assisted telephone interviewing; the current status and future of CATI; the use of CATI for the California Disability Survey; and technological changes in survey research. Section three on scheduling and forewarning (Items 250–253) discusses how to increase response rates to telephone surveys, the effects of respondent fore-warning, optimal times to find someone age fourteen or older at home, and the development of an optimal call schedule for telephone surveys.

The fourth section of the chapter (Items 254–258) concerns interviewer effects and training, and considers how to increase response quality through interviewer training, the use of practice interviews as predictors of interviewer behavior, measuring and explaining interviewer effects in centralized telephone surveys, the effect of interviewer characteristics and expectations on the responses, and a study of eleven polls conducted by CBS and the *New York Times* to determine the size of the interviewer effects in telephone surveys. Section five on ethnicity and race of interviewer (Items 259–265) covers the effects of the race of the interviewer on self-reported voting; actual voting and attitudes of black respondents; the effects of the race of the interviewer on race-related attitudes; the race of interviewer effects among Southern adolescents; the race of interviewer effects in telephone interviews; ethnicity-of-interviewer effects among Mexican Americans and Anglos; evaluating race of interviewer effects in a national survey; and ethnicity of interviewer effects on ethnic respondents. Section six (Items 266–268) concerns confidentiality. Two entries deal with telephone surveys, one dealing with experiments using a confidentiality reminder, the other concerning response privacy. Another entry deals with survey research on drugs and issues of informed consent. Section seven on informed and parental consent (Items 269–273) covers written parental consent and the sample bias that occurs as a consequence, informed consent procedures for use with telephone surveys, survey introductions content analysis in relation to the informed consent issue, methodological consequences of informed consent, and a comparison of methods used to increase parental consent rates. The comparative studies section (Items 274–278) includes items on the tracking of respondents in a telephone interview panel, interviewing older adults with comparisons between face-to-face and telephone modes, response styles in telephone and household interviewing, and finally, a comparison of different modes of surveying, including secret ballots, open ballots, and personal interviews. The last section in the chapter (Item 279) is a textbook on interviewing. (Other textbooks can be found in Chapter 2, section four, but these deal with the overall subject of public opinion polls or survey research—as elsewhere, textbooks on specific elements of the subject are found in their respective chapters.)

Chapter 14 (Items 280–309) examines responses. Response effects are the subject of the first section (Items 280–283). Considered here are a handbook treatment of response effects, response effects in electronic surveys, a cognitive theory of response-order effects, and experiments with form, wording, and order effects in relation to attitude intensity. The second section examines no opinion/don't know responses (Items 284–287), and considers the pressure to answer survey questions, whether or not different kinds of noncommittal responses are interchangeable, "don't know" item nonresponse and the issue of question form, and the "don't know" option in mail questionnaires. The third section (Items 288–292) deals with randomized response and covers the randomized response model, the use of randomized response in sensitive surveys, telephone interviews, mail questionnaires, and studies on the use of randomized response techniques for multiple sensitive attributes, as well as the validity of randomized response for sensitive measures. Section four on lying, nonattitudes and uninformed responses (Items 293–297) deals with uninformed response error, the issue as to whether the public lies to pollsters, the use of fictitious or obscure issues to study uninformed response, uninformed response rates, and nonattitudes, a review and evaluation. Respondent anonymity (Items 298–300) is covered in section five and contains articles on anonymity and the influence of public opinion polls, a method for anonymous collection of longitudinal questionnaire data, and a study comparing anonymous with identifiable reports on adolescent drug use. The final section covers additional studies (Items 301–309), including black–white response styles, pseudo-opinions on public affairs, social desirability and response bias, response errors, mail survey response rate and methods to increase it, the Mushiness Index, assessing respondent comprehension, respondent burden, and the internal stability of opinion as measured through the Mushiness Index.

Chapter 15 (Items 310–312) on data collection covers issues and methods in a textbook format, a comparison of three approaches to the collection of sensitive data, and a handbook treatment of planning and management for this area. Chapter 16 (Items 313–325), divided into three sections, deals with statistical analysis. The first section on models (Items 313–315) considers the use of the General Linear Model (GLM) in the analysis of survey data, followed by a discussion of the latent-class model as preferential to the GLM, and closing with a handbook treatment of the analysis of qualitative data. Section two (Items 316–320) on missing/incomplete data includes a review of the literature, means by which missing data can be compensated for, and three volumes on incomplete data, which encompass case studies, theory, bibliographies, and the proceedings of a symposium. The miscellaneous section (Items 321–325) includes a study on the continuity and change in the methods of data analysis, attrition in longitudinal research, replications, significance and confidence in findings, the analysis of complex sample data, and the analysis of attitude items and the selection of the best question from a group of questions.

Chapter 17 (Items 326–336) concerns results, their quality, accuracy, and secondary analysis. Section one on quality and variation (Items 326–329) examines the variation in the Democratic–Republican partisan gap in polls, reviews the literature on data quality, discusses the 1980 political poll result differences, and includes a literature review and discussions on hypotheses about and examples of survey disagreement. Section two on accuracy (Items 330–334) provides citations which evaluate the accuracy of polls, examine factors in poll interpretation, ask whether inaccuracy is item specific or respondent specific and also whether polls are accurate, and closes with a brief article on the new technologies available to pollsters as aids to improving accuracy. The secondary analysis and context section (Items 335–336) includes an article on the value of the Harris public opinion survey data for secondary analysis, and another item on the impact of belief systems on poll results.

Chapter 18 (Items 337–346) has three sections, and begins with comparative studies (Items 337–340) on three methods of polling, methodologies of telephone and face-to-face interviewing, effects (comparing the General Social Survey with the American National Election Study), and media opinion versus polled opinion on the abortion issue. The second section on ethnic/minority populations (Items 341–343) reviews significant involvement and functional relevance, polls and ethnic minorities, and the measurement of black public opinion. The additional studies section (Items 344–346) provides a redefinition of public focusing on the fact that organizations have opinions, discusses pseudo or phony polls, and reviews the work of researchers surveying deaf adults and others with disabilities.

Chapter 19 (Items 347–352) on cross-disciplinary research deals with cognitive psychology and survey research. The subjects covered include a presentation of one dozen postulates in social cognition; social information processing and survey methodology; cognitive aspects of survey methodology; cognitive psychology and the National Survey; suggested future developments and research priorities for survey research; and a cognitive perspective of attitude measurement.

Chapter 20 (Items 353–359) contains models and theories from a variety of areas and subjects within survey research. The final chapter begins with the Converse model of attitude stability, and continues with the silence effect, the spiral of silence theory, the information processing theory, a theory of public opinion, and concludes with an information processing approach to bipolar survey items.

Addendum and Appendixes

Many of the citations in the Addendum consist of books and journals that this author was unable to obtain. Others were received too late for annotating, but appeared to be of value. The most recent additions to the literature are listed here. Addendum citations are indexed in the Author Index and the Selective Key Word Index. Addendum items are arranged alphabetically by author name.

Appendix A provides the acronyms used in the work, along with the full form of each. Appendix B lists all journal titles found in the citations, and provides the item number(s) for each. Appendix C lists all the subject-relevant dissertations found, and includes the entry number. Appendix D lists all of the monograph series names, and references the entry number(s) for each. Appendix F annotates the primary indexing and abstracting resources consulted. Appendix G lists the names, addresses, and telephone numbers for organizations relevant to the topics covered. Appendix H provides a stop list of words not found in the Selective Key Word Index.

Indexes

The Author Index includes the names of all authors cited in the bibliographic portion of each entry including joint authors, editors, compilers, multiple authors, and corporate authors. The numbers following each entry refer to entry numbers in the text.

The Selective Key Word Index is designed to enable the user to search narrow words or phrases. All names used in the annotations appear as they were written in the original text. Enhancements, such as the addition of a first name, are occasionally supplied for clarification. Books and journals referred to in the annotations (those without item numbers) are indexed by author and title. Phrases are used extensively to place individual words in more meaningful contexts. Cross references ("see" and "see also") are not present. However, due to the nature of the indexing, a single annotated entry may have as many as twenty indexing points (depending upon the nature of the topic and the length of the annotation). Some words and phrases occurred too frequently to be useful as indexing terms, and therefore were added to the stop list (Appendix H).

Sources of Future Information

Appendix G (pages 261–262), as noted above, lists the pertinent professional organizations, councils, and academies that should be contacted to learn about future conferences; the reader should also check notices in the journals listed below.

Appendix B (pages 241–245) lists all the journal sources used in this book. Key titles that would be useful for update purposes include the *American Journal of Political Science, Annals of the American Academy of Political and Social Science, Educational and Psychological Measurement, Journal of Marketing Research, Journal of the American Statistical Association, National Journal, Political Behavior, Public Opinion, Public Opinion Quarterly, Science,* and *Sociological Methods & Research.*

Clearly the single most useful periodical is *Public Opinion Quarterly,* entries from which represent a significant portion of the text of this bibliography. The book review section of this journal is one source for forthcoming publications, as are all of the volumes listed in Appendix E (pages 253–254). For researchers seeking to keep abreast of forthcoming works with the minimum number of reference tools, but at the same time achieving the highest possible success ratio, the following three sources are recommended: *Public Affairs Information Service, Social Sciences Citation Index,* and the *Subject Guide to Forthcoming Books.*

In conclusion, the reason for pursuing this project was to make the methodology and instructional literature in polling and survey research readily accessible in a single volume. The special attention to thorough indexing permits the volume to be used for ready reference, by both professional and nonprofessional. The focus in this volume has been on the decade of the eighties as a starting point in establishing bibliographic control. As Dr. Sudman indicates in the Foreword, the first update to this volume may well "be accessed online by computer." I look forward to that possibility as a full-text database approach would provide many advantages to the user. For this author, one of the fascinations in working with this literature has been the realization of the degree to which polls and surveys have come to influence the fabric of our daily lives—and no longer just in the non-communist world (at least one Moscow newspaper editor has recently conducted a poll). It is hoped that through compiling and presenting this literature that the sources of answers to questions will be more readily accessible than before, and that assistance will have been rendered that might otherwise not have been possible or at the very least would have been substantially more difficult to locate.

Graham R. Walden
Information Services Department
The Ohio State University Libraries

Acknowledgments

Among the many components needed to complete an in-depth annotated bibliography, time and financial resources are essential. Research time, in part, was provided by The Ohio State University Libraries through a Special Research Assignment. Partial financial assistance was awarded through a grant from the Advisory Committee on Research of The Ohio State University Libraries. The author wishes to thank Dr. William J. Studer, Director of Libraries, for approving these research opportunities.

Assistance toward the completion of this volume has come from many individuals. The staff of The Ohio State University Interlibrary Loan Department was helpful, as well as my fellow reference librarians in the Information Services Department. In particular, I wish to acknowledge two ISD members, Associate Professor Marjorie Murfin and Associate Professor Carol Ann Winchell. Both are experienced authors of annotated bibliographies. Their knowledge, expertise, and helpful suggestions have served to guide this author through the many challenges encountered during the preparation of this volume. Of course, all errors, oversights, and mistakes are those of the author, and his to learn from for the benefit of future research publications.

public opinion polls and
survey research

1. Reference Sources

1.1 BIBLIOGRAPHIES

1.   Berdie, Douglas R., John F. Anderson, and Marsha A. Niebuhr.
      Questionnaires: Design and Use. 2d ed. Metuchen, NJ: Scarecrow
      Press, 1986. 330p.
The purposes of this volume are to serve as a practical learning tool to
teach the design and use of the questionnaire and to stimulate questions
in the readers' minds so that appropriate preparations can be made to
accommodate the issues raised. The text is sensitive to the belief that
many questions on questionnaires are dependent upon "study-specific"
variables. The authors suggest that much of the criticism levied against
questionnaires is a product of poor research design or poorly constructed
instruments. The first edition of the book was published in 1974. In the
same year, the authors opened the survey research firm of Anderson,
Niebuhr & Associates, producing reliable and valid data, with response
rates in excess of 90 percent. It is suggested that adherence to the principles outlined in the first edition is responsible for their success. The
contents have been divided into outline format with subheadings used
throughout, enabling quick reference from either the table of contents or
the general index. Chapters cover the issues of interview or mail format;
design, including a checklist; and ways to stimulate responses. The last
chapter analyzes the results. A bibliography of 494 entries follows; it
predominately covers the period from the 1970s and includes short
annotations (on average about twenty-eight words). About 10 percent of
the material covers book literature, and approximately 40 percent covers
articles from *Public Opinion Quarterly*. The other half of the bibliography represents a diverse range of periodical titles. There are four appendixes to the book, followed by an index to the annotated bibliography.

2.   Sharma, Prakash C. *Public Opinion Polls: A Selected Research Bibliography*. Exchange Bibliography, edited by Mary Vance, no. 757. Monticello, IL: Council of Planning Librarians, 1975. 11p.

The bibliography, composed of 156 unannotated entries, is divided into two parts: the first covers books and monographs, the second considers articles and periodicals. In the preface, Dr. Sharma, a member of the Department of Sociology at the University of Alabama during the preparation of the publication, advises that the bibliography covers works "published chiefly during 1950–1965." An analysis of the bibliography reveals that 54 items, or about 33 percent, are from the 1960s, 28 items, or about 18 percent, are from the 1950s, with almost half of the total entries from earlier decades. There are no entries from the 1970s. There are 63 book titles considered (although two entries should have been filed with the articles and periodicals), and 93 articles and periodicals. About 10 percent of the works cited are non-United States—with the actual percentage possibly higher. The bibliography has a number of bibliographic omissions: 57 percent, or 35, of the book titles do not show a place of publication; 23 percent, or 14, of the book titles do not indicate a publisher; and 33 percent of the periodical entries do not indicate pagination. *Public Opinion Quarterly* is the most frequently cited journal, occurring 28 times, or about 30 percent of the periodicals section of the bibliography. Five other journal titles occurred three or more times: *Journalism Quarterly, American Sociological Review, Journal of the American Statistical Association, American Political Science Review*, and *American Journal of Sociology*. (This item is included because it may be the only pre-1980 bibliography available on the subject.)

3.   Vance, Mary A. *Public Opinion Polls: A Bibliography*. Public Administration Series, Bibliography no. P-710. Monticello, IL: Vance Bibliographies, 1981. 6p.

There are 73 items listed in this unannotated bibliography of which 27 are serial title entries. Several reprints are included, with the original year of publication being as follows: 2 from the 1930s; 3 from the 1940s; 2 from the 1950s; and 1 from 1962. The breakdown by year of publication clearly shows that most of the works represented are from the mid- to late-1970s. In detail, the volume includes works in the following categories: 1 from 1937; 2 from 1949; 6 from the 1960s; 17 from 1970 to 1974; 40 from 1975 to 1979; 5 from 1980; and 2 are undated. Although the place of publication is not included, it is evident from the nature of a number of entries that non-United States works have also been included—this encompasses both serial and monographic titles. Of total number of citations listed, 26 include the purchase price as of 1981, suggesting that one of the intended purposes of this bibliography was to be a collection development aid to librarians and perhaps a teachers' selection tool for classroom texts.

4.   White, Anthony G. *Survey and Questionnaire Design: A Bibliography.* Public Administration Series, Bibliography, P 2021. Monticello, IL: Vance Bibliographies, 1986. 8p.

There are 81 unannotated items in this bibliography. The work is divided into two parts, with the first consisting of items relating to questionnaire design, followed by the survey design items (beginning on page 5). The bibliography is comprised of 22 items from the 1970s (about 25 percent) and 59 items from the 1980s (about 75 percent). In detail, 10 of the questionnaire items are from the 1970s and 12 survey items are from the same period. The 1980s literature is comprised of 31 in the questionnaire section and 28 covering survey design. Overall, 41 items are on questionnaire design, with the remaining 40 covering survey design. The bibliography contains 30 book titles and 51 items from journals. *Public Opinion Quarterly* appears 22 times. There are 24 other journal titles included, none appearing more than two times. There is only one foreign journal title included. This bibliography is designed to update earlier Vance bibliographies, such as those found in Item Nos. 2 and 3 in this annotated bibliography.

1.2 DIRECTORIES

5.   Barry, John M., with Sidebar by Burns W. Roper. "The Roper Center: The World's Largest Archive of Survey Data." *RSR Reference Services Review* 16, nos. 1 and 2 (1988): 41–50.

Barry is the manager of User Services Development at the Roper Center for Public Opinion Research in Storrs, Connecticut. The article in *RSR* provides an overview of the Center, beginning with a historical perspective, followed by a discussion of the holdings, the user services provided, and the online database called POLL. The balance of the article reviews the costs and mechanisms by which people can gain access to the resources, along with a summary of future plans. Burns W.

Roper provides a "Sidebar" on the historical value of poll data. Roper is chairman of the Roper Organization (New York) and the Roper Center. A list labelled "Sidebar 2" provides the names of forty-seven organizations that contribute data to the Roper Center. The list includes references to all the polling organizations known to the general public, along with the significant networks, newspapers, and marketing firms. The Center's archive of public opinion data contains nearly eleven thousand separate studies conducted in more than seventy-five countries by major survey organizations. No references are included.

6.   *Surveys, Polls, Censuses & Forecasts Directory: A Guide to Sources of Statistical Studies in the Area of Business, Social Science, Education, Science and Technology.* Detroit, MI: Gale Research Company, nos. 1–3, 1983. Issue no. 1 (1–92); Issue no. 2 (93–182); Issue no. 3 (183–265); Cumulative Issue (1–284).

Intended to be an ongoing periodical format with three issues per year and a bound cumulative volume at the end of the year, the title ceased after one year. [An unfavorable review in *Choice* (April, 1984, page 118) may not have helped to secure the continuance of the title.] Each issue provided an alphabetical listing by title. Individual entries included the name, address, and telephone number of the sponsoring agency, frequency and (where appropriate) the year started, a brief description, geographic coverage, and also the availability of the data. Indexing access is provided through sponsoring agency name and a modest subject index. Each of the three issues contained about four hundred entries.

7.   Walden, Graham R. "Public Opinion Polls: A Guide to Accessing the Literature." *RSR Reference Services Review* 16, no. 4 (1988): 65–74.

The article provides a guide to the major sources of published polls, including brief annotated bibliographic information to the works available from the Gallup organization, Louis Harris and Associates, the National Opinion Research Center (NORC), *Public Opinion*, Roper Reports, and other published polls. Short descriptive paragraphs providing company and biographical information accompany each section. One dozen polling indexes and abstracts are described, including the scope of the coverage through a listing of the relevant polling journals indexed. The primary access term(s) used in each resource is given. Online availability is specified where appropriate. An annotated bibliography of fifteen sources from the 1980s is included. The introduction qualified the inclusion of poll results in the article to those that are regularly available at moderate library subscription rates, and that the results are those that have been widely disseminated by the public opinion polling organization. As a mechanism to give scale to the size of polling in the United States, the author cites 1986 data which shows that the top forty-four companies had revenues of more than $1.5 billion. There are twenty-seven references included.

2. Instructional Materials

2.1 EXPLANATORY

8.   Asher, Herbert B. *Polling and the Public: What Every Citizen Should Know*. Washington, DC: CQ Press, a Division of Congressional Quarterly, 1988. 168p.

The basis for this work is that Asher believes polls are not well understood by the general public, and that a reference tool is needed for consumers of public opinion polls to help in evaluating poll methods and merits. The intended audience is not narrowly defined. There are nine chapters, the first of which introduces poll types, their significance, and how citizens view polling. Successive chapters cover nonattitudes, the wording and context of questions, sampling techniques, and interviewing procedures. These chapters review the methodological elements of opinion research with the use of contemporary examples and a number of cartoons. The following chapters deal with the arena of polling with which the general public is most familiar: news reporting of polls and election-time use of polls. Asher proceeds to discuss the analysis and interpretation of polls. The final chapter considers the role of polls in a democratic society and provides a summary of how to evaluate polls. The volume includes 164 references and four pages of subject indexing.

9.   Bogart, Leo. *Silent Politics: Polls and the Awareness of Public Opinion*. New York: Wiley-Interscience, 1972. 250p. Reprint. *Polls and the Awareness of Public Opinion*. Communications Series. New Brunswick, NJ: Transaction Books, 1985. 264p.

The interrelationships of polls and politics are discussed with special emphasis placed on the 1968 presidential campaign. Change and movement of opinion are covered, as are ambiguous and unheard opinions. Additional chapters examine opinions in revolutions and the responsibilities which opinion holding carries. The opening chapter is titled "Polls and Politics" and covers topics such as: "Should Polls Make Policy"; "Polling and the Concept of Opinion"; "Reporting the Polls"; "On Predicting Elections"; and "Polls and the Campaign of 1968." The emphasis of the volume is on public opinion—movement, changes, ambiguities, and associated responsibilities. The notes and addenda sections number over forty pages and include lengthy explanations to the textual matter.

10.   Bradburn, Norman M., and Seymour Sudman. *Polls & Surveys: Understanding What They Tell Us.* A Joint Publication in the Jossey-Bass Social and Behavioral Science Series and the Jossey-Bass Public Administration Series. San Francisco, CA: Jossey-Bass, 1988. 249p.

The work is intended as a comprehensive overview for nonspecialists. Newcomers to public opinion measurement and students of political science, sociology, business, and communications studying public opinion or market research are the intended audience. The chapter titles in order of appearance are: "Polling and the Public: Purposes and Process"; "Growth of Public Opinion Polling"; "Proper and Improper Uses of Surveys"; "The Organizations That Do the Polling"; "How Information Is Collected"; "How Respondents Are Selected"; "Asking the Question: How Wording Affects Response"; "What Do the Answers Mean?"; "Understanding Sources of Error"; "Should Polls Be Banned?"; and "Effects of Polls on Elections, Governments, Business and Media." The book assists in the recognition of which polls and surveys (terms which the authors use synonymously) may be valuable and which should be disregarded. Among professionals, journalists, market researchers, and advertisers, along with sociologists and political scientists, are the most likely beneficiaries of the explanations given. Bradburn and Sudman have provided answers throughout the volume to those questions which respondents ask most frequently when answering surveys. The volume closes with a five-page glossary of terms, six pages of references, and a six-page subject index.

11.   Britton, Gary L. "A History of Some Recent Applications of Survey Sampling for Human Populations." Ph.D. diss., University of Northern Colorado, 1983. 202p.

The purpose of this dissertation is to help "instructors and users of survey sampling who are not experts in the field" to understand the procedures used in public opinion polls. Theory development and applications of selected major aspects of survey sampling are covered. Quoting Britton, "each of the survey sampling procedures discussed is illustrated by detailed reference to specific studies which have been conducted using that procedure and reported elsewhere." The theorems proved by W.C. Madow and L.H. Madow in 1944 are cited. These theorems show under which conditions systematic sampling gives a better estimate than simple random sampling. Random digit dialing (RDD) and modifications theorems are discussed, along with studies demonstrating the effectiveness of the telephone in survey research. Late shifts in voter preference in presidential elections are reviewed with attention directed toward the elections of 1936, 1948, and 1980. Randomized response (RR) for sensitive issue surveys, as proposed by Stanley L. Warner, is explained, and further developments of this approach are examined. It should be noted that Britton was a student in the mathematics department and that the statistical discussion provided is far above the level of the average reader. There is a bibliography of 170 items.

12.   Butts, David P. "The Survey—A Research Strategy Rediscovered." *Journal of Research in Science Teaching* 20, no. 3 (March 1983): 187–93.

A review of the basic characteristics of surveys is presented, along with some associated issues. The value of survey research in science education is highlighted, especially four specific areas in which surveys could be used to generate new knowledge in science education. Four different areas of measurement errors are outlined in the final section which reviews some of the challenges in survey research. Nineteen references are provided; four are from the 1980s.

13.   Dillman, Don A. "Mail and Other Self-Administered Questionnaires." Chap. 10 in *Handbook of Survey Research*, edited by Peter H. Rossi, James D. Wright, and Andy B. Anderson, 359–77. Quantitative Studies in Social Relations, consulting editor Peter H. Rossi. New York: Academic Press, 1983.

Two main benefits of mail and other self-administered questionnaires cited by Dillman are the lower survey costs and the gathering of data from populations that might otherwise not be surveyed. The challenges of self-administered approaches are that they have to be visually appealing and generate sufficient interest in the reader to encourage the survey respondent to keep working through the survey and complete it satisfactorily. Dillman cites careful question order, text that explains the value of survey completion, and the avoidance of dull and wordy questions as some of the keys to better results. The Shortcomings of self-administered questionnaires are that there is not an interviewer present to assist in the motivation to complete the task, nor is there assistance with possible misreading or misinterpretation by the respondents. Low response rates and difficulties in generating appropriate samples are given as explanations as to why mail surveys are often considered the least desirable choice given the alternatives of face-to-face or telephone interviews. Dillman considers the Total Design Method (TDM), shortcomings of mail surveys, and expenses involved in TDM. A number of approaches of using the self-administered questionnaire are reviewed. Eighteen references conclude the chapter, with over 75 percent of the items from the 1970s.

14.   Ferber, Robert, Paul Sheatsley, Anthony Turner, and Joseph Waksberg. *What Is a Survey?* Subcommittee of the Section on Survey Research Methods. Washington, DC: American Statistical Association, [1980]. 25p.

The purpose of this publication is to explain survey research without using technical language so that nonstatisticians can understand the survey process. Most of the attention of the publication is devoted to the design of surveys and the collection of survey data. The possible uses of the "brochure" include background reading for survey research clients; for nonresearchers as a tool for extending understanding; for use in introductory social science courses; and for use abroad as an information tool for government officials. Sections in the publication cover characteristics of surveys, with discussions covering the need for surveys, who conducts them, the various types of surveys, and the issue of confidentiality. Survey design, sampling, and how surveys are conducted are discussed. Some common pitfalls are outlined, along with approaches for determining the quality of a survey as well as sources of errors. The subject of the survey budget concludes the brief review, with sources of further information provided. No references are included.

15.   Field, Mervin D. "How to Read the Polls." *Taxing & Spending* 3 (Winter 1980): 83–90.

Addressed here are the classic questions asked about polls. Field discusses the variety of polls, their functions, the sponsorship and purpose of polls, methodological failures, the prediction capabilities of polls, media sponsorship of polls, shortcomings, and contributing to the broadening of participation in political decisions. In reviewing media-sponsored polls, Field comments that for each media-sponsored poll there are an estimated ten unpublished "private" polls. Citing the fact that a poll is only a "snapshot taken at a particular point in time," he observes that the predictive value is very "chancey." Public opinion can change quickly and dramatically. Reviewed are the "politics by poll" phenomena where candidates try to manipulate the timing and place of a poll to garner the best possible showing. Critical commentary is made of the news media for limiting qualifying statements about poll results to the now standard sampling error plus/minus statement. It is suggested that inclusion or omission of a value-laden word or phrase can generate as much as a 20-percent change in the response data. The last topic is that of the combined poll-taker and campaign strategist. Field believes that this is likely to lead to less objective survey research. No references are included.

16.   Klapper, Joseph T. *How to Judge a Poll: An Amiable Discourse Designed to Enable the Reader to Look a Poll Firmly in the Eye.* [New York]: Office of Social Research, Economics and Research, CBS, 1980. 64p.

The Klapper "paper" seeks to assist the reader to evaluate published poll results as well as to answer frequently asked questions about polls. The emphasis is directed toward preelection polls. The author cites the lists of information readers need to make evaluations of polls, and reproduces three such lists from the American Association for Public Opinion Research (AAPOR), the National Council on Public Polls (NCPP), and the Council of American Survey Research Organizations (CASRO). The publication examines each of the areas within these lists. Discussed are poll sponsors, timing of data collection, the population sampled, samples, subsamples, sampling errors, data-gathering modes, issues concerning the questions, percentages, and the issue of how to treat "undecideds." A series of six questions and answers follows. Three appendixes include a chart of sampling tolerances, the lists described above, and the association memberships in NCPP and CASRO as of 15 June 1980. A seventeen-entry list of references is provided.

2.2 GUIDES

17.   Fink, Arlene, and Jacqueline Kosecoff. *How to Conduct Surveys: A Step-by-Step Guide*. Beverly Hills, CA: Sage Publications, 1985. 119p.

The "how-to" approach employed here is designed to reach all who need to conduct a survey, no matter the level of skill or technical knowledge present at the outset. The volume is divided into several chapters beginning with an overview chapter, followed by a discussion of questions, scales, and the appearance of the survey form. Issues of survey length, question order, and confidentiality follow. Sampling, survey design, and data analysis are successive chapter topics, with a concluding chapter on the presentation of survey results. An appendix includes four different statistical tables. Twenty-two bibliographic references are provided at the end of the volume, plus two pages of subject indexing.

18.   Lavrakas, Paul J. *Telephone Survey Methods: Sampling, Selection, and Supervision*. Applied Social Research Methods Series, vol. 7. Beverly Hills, CA: Sage Publications, 1987. 157p.

Lavrakas has written a "how-to" book whose approach is "applied" from beginning to end, providing both mundane and specific details which the author believes are necessary when planning and implementing a telephone survey in which quality data is to be the outcome. Developing questionnaires is not discussed here. Rather, the author prefers to focus on the administering of the questionnaire by the interviewer. A local area (instead of regional or national) telephone survey approach is used. Computer-assisted telephone interviewing (CATI) is also left to others, with Lavrakas discussing pen-and-paper possibilities. Chapters cover generating sample pools, processing the sample pools, and selecting respondents. The last two chapters examine structuring the interviewers' work and structuring supervisory work—both from the supervisory perspective. Lavrakas provides a historical note, reminding readers that prior to the 1960s the number of homes with telephones did not allow for appropriate telephone sampling methods. The work has a three-page glossary, three appendixes, and a two-page bibliography.

19.   Mitofsky, Warren, and Martin Plissner. "A Reporter's Guide to Published Polls." *Public Opinion* 3, no. 3 (June/July 1980): 16–19.

The article reviews the rather questionable record of primary race poll results from the 1980 presidential campaign. Cited are the many possible causes for erroneous results including samples composed of those who refuse to be interviewed, interviewers who misread questions, and computational errors by those recording data. These causes are given as only some of the hidden potential side steps occurring in polling. More emphasis is placed on the larger problems of subsample analysis and the practice of the media to distort or overstate inappropriately a poll result which would be more sensibly dismissed based on the error margin associated with subsample data. A table titled "How to Estimate Sampling Error" is reprinted in page 19. Another issue in political polling is whether or not the sample interviewed will actually vote and are the interviewees properly registered to enable voting. Gallup, Harris, and Roper each use different language to describe their samples, respectively—registered voters "most of the time," "likely voters," and "certain" registered voters. This practice may create confusion when it comes to analyzing the data and when attempting to report on the findings. It is suggested by the authors that poll conclusions are not always consistent with their results. No references are included.

20.   Wilhoit, G. Cleveland, and David H. Weaver. *Newsroom Guide to Polls & Surveys*. Washington, DC: American Newspaper Publishers Association, 1980. 82p.

This book was commissioned by the News Research Committee of the American Newspaper Publishers Association in response to what the committee perceived to be a lower level of scrutiny by reporters and editors of poll and survey data, the view being that material was being published more easily simply because it was in the form of a poll or survey. A six-part volume, the material is designed to be a quick reference for the busy reporter. Considered are evaluating survey questionnaires, interviewing, sampling, results, and the reporting of survey data. Most of the last part, summing up, provides actual questions for reporters to ask about polls and surveys. The guide provides a means for the nonexpert to grasp the important elements of a poll or survey which should be questioned, examined, and subjected to careful evaluation before being dispatched for printing or broadcasting. There is a three-page subject index. No references are included.

2.3 HANDBOOKS

21.   Alreck, Pamela L., and Robert B. Settle. *The Survey Research Handbook*. Homewood, IL: Richard D. Irwin, 1985. 429p.

The authors explain in the preface that the purpose of the volume is to provide practical and technical information rather than approaching the subject from a conceptual and theoretical standpoint. Further, the writers chose to avoid jargon and instead have written, wherever possible, using ordinary language. Divided into four main parts, the book considers: survey planning and design, survey instrumentation, data collection and processing, and analysis and reporting. Several interesting features of the book include the checklists, guidelists, examples, and figures. There are seventeen checklists scattered throughout the text. The first checklist contains eight points to consider when choosing between an interview or mail approach. There are over eighty guidelists which provide summaries and specific instructions, such as using the fixed sum scale as outlined in chapter 5. There is a twenty-page glossary with approximately 250 entries at the end of the volume. No references are included.

22.   Lake, Celinda C., with Pat Callbeck Harper. *Public Opinion Polling: A Handbook for Public Interest and Citizen Advocacy Groups*. Washington, DC: Island Press, 1987. 162p.

As the title states, this volume is designed to enable the reader to plan, administer, and analyze public opinion polls. It also contains guidelines on how to interpret public opinion polls conducted elsewhere. Although this "how-to" handbook is focused for use by public interest and citizen advocacy groups, it could certainly be used by a much wider audience. Chapters cover questionnaire wording and construction; interviewing; the preparation for, and management of, interviews; sampling; methods and options available for processing poll data; analysis; and a final chapter on shortcuts and pitfalls. There are seven appendixes, including one on POLLSTART, a software package. Other appendixes include a glossary of seventy-six polling terms and a case study with a checklist of steps. Twenty-four briefly annotated citations appear in a bibliography of which about one-third are from the 1980s. A four-page index completes the volume.

23.   Rossi, Peter H., James D. Wright, and Andy B. Anderson, eds.
       Handbook of Survey Research. Quantitative Studies in Social
       Relations, consulting editor Peter H. Rossi. New York: Academic
       Press, 1983. 755p.

The editors conceived this work to fill a perceived gap in the literature,
namely to provide a single volume which could serve as a graduate-level
textbook as well as an advanced handbook covering the major issues in
survey design and analysis. The *Handbook* is designed to be a central
reference source serving as a resource to the critical literature in the
many areas covered. Each of the sixteen chapters has accompanying
references, varying from fewer than ten references to over two hundred.
Each chapter has been separately considered and can be found under the
following item numbers in this annotated bibliography.

Contents:

Chapter   1:   Sample Surveys: History, Current Practice, and Future
                 Prospects (Rossi, Wright, and Anderson—Item No. 43).
Chapter   2:   Sampling Theory (Frankel—Item No. 234).
Chapter   3:   Measurement (Bohrnstedt—Item No. 158).
Chapter   4:   Management of Survey Organizations (Prewitt—Item
                 No. 145).
Chapter   5:   Applied Sampling (Sudman—Item No. 215).
Chapter   6:   Questionnaire Construction and Item Writing (Sheats-
                 ley—Item No. 24).
Chapter   7:   Measurement: Theory and Techniques (Anderson,
                 Basilevsky, and Hum—Item No. 155).
Chapter   8:   Response Effects (Bradburn—Item No. 280).
Chapter   9:   Data Collection: Planning and Management (Wein-
                 berg—Item No. 312).
Chapter   10:   Mail and Other Self-Administered Questionnaires
                 (Dillman—Item No. 13).
Chapter   11:   Computers in Survey Research (Karweit and Meyers—
                 Item No. 153).
Chapter   12:   Missing Data: A Review of the Literature (Anderson,
                 Basilevsky, and Hum—Item No. 316).
Chapter   13:   Applications of the General Linear Model to Survey
                 Data (Berk—Item No. 313).
Chapter   14:   Analyzing Qualitative Data (Taylor—Item No. 315).
Chapter   15:   Causal Modeling and Survey Research (Stolzenberg and
                 Land—Item No. 163).

Chapter 16:   Surveys as Social Indicators: Problems in Monitoring
Trends (Martin—Item No. 161).

24.   Sheatsley, Paul B. "Questionnaire Construction and Item
Writing." Chap. 6 in *Handbook of Survey Research*, edited by
Peter H. Rossi, James D. Wright, and Andy B. Anderson, 195–
230. Quantitative Studies in Social Relations, consulting editor
Peter H. Rossi. New York: Academic Press, 1983.

As stated in the summary, "there are no simple, rigorous rules for questionnaire design and question writing." Sheatsley cites the need for flexi-
bility in dealing with the wide variety of survey purposes. The chapter
covers the general principles of the decisions and choices researchers
face when writing questionnaires. The author indicates at least three
elements which are helpful: (1) intellectual effort; (2) trial and error; and
(3) the helpful hand of experience. The subsections of the chapter
include discussions of standardized questionnaires; how questionnaires
can be administered; sample types; consideration of the qualities of a
"good questionnaire"; content decisions; writing the question, including
types, response options, principles, and some common errors; question
order and format; pretesting; responding to knowledge gained during
pretesting; options for database management formats. The foregoing are
in the context of personal interviews. A brief discussion follows which
advises how these approaches can be used in telephone interviews or
self-administered questionnaires. Sheatsley was associated with the
National Opinion Research Center (NORC) in 1983. Eight references
conclude the chapter, with the earliest reference from 1946 and the most
recent item from 1974.

25.   Smith, Robert B., ed. *A Handbook of Social Science Methods.*
Vol. 3, *Quantitative Methods: Focused Survey Research and
Causal Modeling.* New York: Praeger Publishers, 1985. 536p.

The volume is designed to be both a textbook for undergraduate and
graduate courses on empirical inquiry and a reference tool for professionals. The volume has an introduction by Robert B. Smith which
"bridges qualitative and quantitative methods" and is titled "Linking
Quality and Quantity" (pp. 1-51). The book is divided into two parts:
Part 1 "Focused Survey Research" (pp. 53-286), and Part 2 "Causal
Modeling" (pp. 287-463). The five chapters in Part 1 include: Chapter 1:
"Aspects of the Perspective and Method," by Robert B. Smith (pp. 59-
96). This chapter discusses two process models of voting, the politics of
professors, and Lazarsfeld's research which has been advanced by Lipset

and others. Lazarsfeld's elaboration procedure is also addressed. Chapter 2: "Strategies in Comparative Survey Research," by Herbert H. Hyman (pp. 97-153). Comparative survey research is discussed in the context of political research. Comparative surveys are described as having two key functions: to be descriptive and to provide explanations. Chapter 3: "The Survey Research Process," by David Nasatir (pp. 154-92). Solutions to challenges in design, data gathering, and analysis are discussed. Chapter 4: "Concepts, Indices & Contexts," by David Caplovitz (pp. 193-240). Aspects of Lazarsfeld's measures of individual and group variables are considered. Chapter 5: "The Logic of Survey Analysis," by Charles Y. Glock (pp. 241-86). Procedural explanations for the exploratory analysis by close inspection of cross-sectional surveys are given. Part 2 contains chapters 6 through 10. These include: Chapter 6: "A User's Guide to Log-Linear Models," by Peter J. Burke and David Knoke (pp. 297-335). Chapter 7: "Statistical Inference with Proportions," by James A. Davis (pp. 336-66). Chapter 8: "D Systems and Effect Parameters: Some Complementarities," by Peter V. Marsden (pp. 367-89). Chapter 9: "A Path Analysis Primer," by David Knoke (pp. 390-407). Chapter 10: "A General Structural Equation Modeling Framework for the Social & Behavioral Sciences," by Peter F. Cuttance (pp. 408-63). Each chapter throughout the volume includes references. The "Epilogue" is called "An Appreciation of Paul Felix Lazarsfeld," by Seymour Martin Lipset (pp. 469-84). Biographical notes on the editor and contributors follow, as well as assignment-type problems associated with each chapter. A twelve-page index concludes the volume.

2.4 TEXTBOOKS

26. Babbie, Earl R. "Survey Research." Chap. 6 in *Social Research for Consumers*, 135–64. Belmont, CA: Wadsworth Publishing Company, 1982.

This volume is a textbook designed for students of social science research methods, specifically for the consumer of social research. There are a number of chapters that are of interest—those that cover research design, measurement, sampling, and analysis of data. Attention is drawn specifically to chapter 6 on survey research, which covers the types of surveys available, how to construct and administer questionnaires, secondary analysis, and data archives. Key chapter words are listed, the main points are outlined, review questions are supplied, and six items are suggested for further reading. A cumulative bibliography is included as well as an eight-page index.

27.   Babbie, Earl R. "Survey Research." Chap. 9 in *The Practice of Social Research*, 202–37. 4th ed. Belmont, CA: Wadsworth Publishing Company, 1986.

The twofold uses of the volume are to prepare the reader to conduct social research and to become a "responsible consumer" of social scientific research. The book has 577 pages and covers the full range of issues in social research. Chapter 9 focuses on survey research and covers these areas: "Topics Appropriate to Survey Research"; "Questionnaire Construction: Self-Administered Questionnaires"; "Interview Surveys"; "Comparison of Two Survey Methods"; "Strengths and Weaknesses of Survey Research"; and "Secondary Analysis." The volume is for undergraduate students, and, perhaps, as an introductory graduate textbook. The chapter closes with a review of the main points, review questions and exercises, and a list of seven items for further reading (these are briefly annotated).

28.   Backstrom, Charles H., and Gerald D. Hursh-César. *Survey Research*. 2d ed. New York: John Wiley & Sons, 1981. 436p.

This textbook has a table of contents covering over eight pages, with separate lists for figures, tables, and checklists, and a twenty-three-page index. There are six chapters, with the following titles: "Planning Surveys"; "Drawing Samples"; "Writing Questions"; "Designing Questionnaires"; "Conducting Interviews"; and "Processing Data." There are eighty-five diagrams, tables, and charts designed to assist the reader. The practice of using checklists occurs thirty-six times. These lists provide the novice with a source for ready reference and may suggest opportunities for further research for those already familiar with the process. The book uses a "Model Survey" approach to discuss the process. This survey is a "one-time, in-person, at-the-door, general population opinion poll." Other modes of research including telephone, mail, panel studies, and intercept surveys are also described in each chapter. The book has been updated to incorporate the extensive use of computers in today's survey research. Each chapter has from five to seven sections, and there is a list of suggested further readings at the end of each chapter.

29.   Erdos, Paul L., with the assistance of Arthur J. Morgan. *Professional Mail Surveys*. Rev. ed. Malabar, FL: Robert E. Krieger Publishing Company, 1983. 286p.

The purpose of the Erdos book, an update of the original edition of 1970, is to enable readers to conduct their own surveys, to be able to evaluate the surveys of others, and to become generally acquainted with established procedures employed in mail surveys. The various types of mail surveys are reviewed in one of the early chapters. Erdos notes that the techniques discussed in much of the volume are from his experience with market research surveys. There are twenty-seven chapters which cover the pertinent elements of survey research as applicable to mail surveys. Erdos covers the range of knowledge in statistics, sampling, and electronic data processing as the information relates to mail surveys only. Topics covered include: survey design, cost estimating, mailing procedures, editing and coding, and evaluating mail surveys. As indicated, many other chapters address each area of concern that would be met by the individual seeking to begin mail surveying. A glossary with over ten pages of terms is included, along with a page which lists books on related subjects (this would appear to be unchanged from the original edition). The eight-plus-page index is detailed, permitting the reader to refer to a single page or, at most, to a small number of pages for each detailed subject selected.

30.   Fowler, Floyd J., Jr. *Survey Research Methods*. Applied Social Research Methods Series, vol. 1. Beverly Hills, CA: Sage Publications, 1984. 159p.

This book deals with standards and practical procedures for surveys. The text is designed for those who wish to collect, analyze, or read survey data and become aware of how aspects of each stage in the process of survey research can affect its precision, accuracy, and credibility. The chapters following the introduction are: "Sampling"; "Nonresponse"; "Implementing a Sample Design"; "Methods of Data Collection"; "Designing Questions to Be Good Measures"; "Design of a Questionnaire"; "Survey Interviewing"; "Preparing Survey Data for Analysis"; "Ethical Issues in Survey Research"; "Providing Information About Survey Methods"; and "Survey Error in Perspective." Fowler has provided an overview covering the errors which can arise in survey research, along with a discussion of major methodological issues in data collection. It is both a textbook and reference volume with some sixty references at the end. A one-page index completes the volume.

31.   Frey, James H. *Survey Research by Telephone*. Sage Library of Social Research, vol. 150. Beverly Hills, CA: Sage Publications, 1983. 208p.

The work is intended for those survey researchers who may be currently operating small- to medium-scale survey research facilities. The introductory chapter discusses the telephone in terms of its impact on our social life, as well as the economic implications of the technology. Face-to-face, mail, and telephone surveys are compared in the next chapter, which includes a table rating the advantage/disadvantage scale of the three approaches in response to twenty-two factors, e.g., cost, item non-response, ability to clarify, etc. Other chapters are devoted to the topics of sampling, questionnaire design, and administration. Some of the positive elements of telephone surveys cited include reduced cost, acceptable data quality, the ease with which the survey can be administered, and the smaller amount of time needed to collect the data. Two appendixes reproduce the National Council on Public Polls (NCPP) Principles of Disclosure and the American Association for Public Opinion Research (AAPOR) Code of Professional Ethics and Practices. Approximately 50 percent of the references are drawn from the 1970s, 25 percent from the 1980s, 15 percent from the 1960s, and the remaining 10 percent from the 1940s and 1950s.

32.   Guy, Rebecca F., Charles E. Edgley, Ibtihaj Arafat, and Donald E. Allen. "The Survey." Chap. 9 in *Social Research Methods: Puzzles and Solutions*, 219–52. Boston, MA: Allyn and Bacon, 1987.

Numerous chapters in this textbook are of interest to the survey researcher (such as chapter 7 covering sampling). The focal point of interest for this annotated bibliography is chapter 9 dealing with surveys (located in section 2 titled "Measurement, Data Collection, and Analysis," pages 135 to 364). The authors cover self-administered questionnaires, mailed questionnaires, face-to-face interviews, and telephone interviews. Also defined and discussed are surveys, public opinion polls, and market surveys. A survey design plan is outlined, along with suggestions and guides for each survey format described. The textbook includes a ten-page glossary, eight pages of references, and six pages of indexing.

33.   Hennessy, Bernard C. "Survey Research: What It Is and How to Do It." Chap. 5 in *Public Opinion*, 65–88. 5th ed. Monterey, CA: Brooks/Cole Publishing Company, 1985.
This 366-page textbook is designed for college and university use. The book deals with public opinion in a variety of ways through twenty chapters of text. Of particular relevance to this annotated bibliography is chapter 5, composed of twenty-three pages and thirteen sections. Hennessy covers the field of survey research with a broad overview, beginning with a historical sketch and concluding with the methods by which data is processed and analyzed. Other sections in the chapter cover techniques used in surveys, sample size, sample selection, pretesting, and fieldwork. Additional chapters in the volume consider the context in which opinion comes to exist (be it through television, radio, or the print media) and provide an understanding of context, scope, and meaning. The textbook was first published in 1965 with, on average, a new edition every five years. There are footnotes at the end of each chapter.

34.   Jones, Russell A. "Survey Research." Chap. 6 in *Research Methods in the Social and Behavioral Sciences*, 171–209. Sunderland, MD: Sinauer Associates, 1985.
The volume is designed as a textbook to teach research methods to students in a variety of disciplines within the broad spectrum of social sciences. Many chapters in this book contain useful presentations in areas related to survey research. Confining this annotation to the narrower picture, chapter 6 discusses the variety of survey types, covers explanatory analysis, and presents sampling issues and solutions. Jones reminds the reader that more than any other research method, survey research relies on self-reported characteristics, and he proceeds to highlight special considerations that must be taken into account—among other items, dealing with the challenge of the "extremely unreliable" nature of human memory. Cartoons, tables, and figures are used throughout the text. Five annotated items are provided for recommended reading at the end of chapter 6. The book contains a twenty-page glossary, a seventeen-page bibliography, and name and subject indexes.

35.   Nieburg, Harold L. *Public Opinion, Tracking and Targeting*. New York: Praeger Publishers, 1984. 287p.
In the introduction Nieburg defines tracking as "the ability to study with great rapidity the reactions and changes of sentiment of the public on a day-to-day basis." Targeting refers to "the ability to define the differentiated segments of that public and to communicate selectively

with each segment as deemed appropriate." Nieburg views the work as a synthesis of public opinion study. The book is designed to be used as a college textbook, especially with courses in which up to 50 percent of the classroom time is devoted to a workshop format with students actually designing and implementing survey research projects. Early chapters differentiate between straw polls and scientific polls, with subsequent chapters covering all the major areas of survey research, such as: audiences, interviewing, questioning, sampling, statistics, and the search for polling standards. Fourteen graphs and tables appear in the volume, as well as endnotes with each chapter.

36.   Sanders, William B., and Thomas K. Pinhey. "Survey Research Methods." Chap. 7 in *The Conduct of Social Research*, 126–60. New York: Holt, Rinehart and Winston, 1983.

Designed as a textbook, this volume covers the range of areas of interest to the "conduct of social research." Chapter 7 focuses on the methods of survey research and addresses the topics of questionnaire construction, matrix questions, inventory formats, question order, wording and item construction, and the different kinds of instructions necessary for self-administered questionnaires and those conducted by interviewers. Group, mail, interview, and telephone surveys receive discussion. The authors use examples throughout the chapter to illustrate aspects under consideration. There are four tables within the chapter, followed by a summary section and a nineteen-entry glossary. Twenty-two endnotes close the chapter (there is no cumulative bibliography at the end of the book). The volume has a twelve-page index.

37.   Sheskin, Ira M. *Survey Research for Geographers*. Resource Publications in Geography Series, edited by C. Gregory Knight. Washington, DC: Association of American Geographers, 1985. 112p.

Series editor Knight suggests in his foreword that this volume is perhaps the most comprehensive reference, within the profession of geography, in providing principles which can guide the practitioner in the development of survey research projects. The introductory chapter reviews survey research history, survey research in geography, ethical considerations, the overall survey process, and provides examples of surveys. Survey types are considered next. Sampling options are described with probability and nonprobability designs outlined. Question types, construction, format, and design follow with sample questions provided. Survey personnel recruitment, coding, ethics, budgeting and survey timing are all aspects of survey logistics which are briefly discussed. The execution and analysis of data are the subjects of the last chapter which includes remarks on the reporting of the survey results. The volume includes twenty-four figures and three tables, as well as an appendix which is an annotated bibliography of nine recommended survey research textbooks. Literature of the 1980s is represented in 83 of the 191 references.

3. History

38. Converse, Jean M. *Survey Research in the United States: Roots and Emergence 1890–1960*. Berkeley, CA: University of California Press, 1987. 564p.

Divided into three parts, this volume explores the first seventy-year span of survey research in America. Part 1, titled "The Ancestors: 1890–1940," covers the social survey, attitude measurement in psychology, sociology, market research, and opinion polling. Part 2 deals with "The Prewar and Wartime Generation: 1935–1945." The prewar chapter covers academic entrepreneurs and survey and poll data. The chapters dealing with the war years discuss policy research and science. Part 3 examines the "Migrations to the Universities: 1940–1960." Three environments are covered in considerable depth: the Bureau of Applied Social Research; the National Opinion Research Center (NORC); and the Survey Research Center (SRC) at the University of Michigan, with which Converse has been affiliated for more than ten years in research and writing roles. The author used extensive personal interviews throughout her work. The volume can be read as a work of history as well as serving as a highly indexed tool for reference purposes. There are 126 pages of notes and seventeen pages of indexing.

39. Frankel, Martin R., and Lester R. Frankel. "Fifty Years of Survey Sampling in the United States." *Public Opinion Quarterly* 51, no. 4, pt. 2 (Winter 1987): S127–S138.

Survey sampling was first introduced in Europe at the turn of the century and has been used in the United States for about fifty years. The article traces the development of sampling through five decades, beginning with the first phase in the mid-1930s. The authors describe this period as one of the development of basic methods and applications. The late 1960s and early 1970s saw the beginning of phase two, or the period of innovations and new techniques as the authors view it. In phase two the authors discuss network or multiplicity sampling, estimation of sampling errors for complex statistics and complex samples, probability sample surveys by telephone, coping with decreasing response rates, evaluation and control of total survey error, and, finally, pseudosample surveys. There are thirty-five references provided.

40.   Jensen, Richard, with Sidebar by Richard Link. "Polls and Politics: Democracy by the Numbers." *Public Opinion* 3, no. 1A (February/March 1980): 53–59.

The article provides a brief sketch of the history of public opinion polls, beginning with an overview of straw polls (with attention to the experience of the *Literary Digest*). Jensen cites Henry Link as the originator of the first modern poll with the "Psychological Barometer" for the Psychological Corporation in 1932. Gallup, Crossley and Roper are described as having "simultaneously launched the modern attitudinal polls in 1935." Jensen suggests that "the ideal of statistical democracy" died on 2 November 1948, the year when all the major pollsters and commentators forecast a victory for John Dewey. A "Sidebar" by Richard Link is titled "The Literary Digest Poll: Appearances Can Be Deceiving" and appears on page 55. Basically, Link makes the point that the *Literary Digest* failed to adjust the data. Two adjustment methods described are those by swings and ratio. No references are included.

41.   Martin, L. John. "The Genealogy of Public Opinion Polling." In *Polling and the Democratic Consensus*, edited by L. John Martin, 12–23. *Annals of the American Academy of Political and Social Science*, edited by Richard D. Lambert, vol. 472. Beverly Hills, CA: Sage Publications, 1984.

Martin defines public opinion through a historical perspective beginning with Plato. Similarly, Martin traces the earliest social surveys, moving to Charles Booth and his seventeen-volume set (on London during the last two decades of the nineteenth century) and into the 1980s. A short history of the questionnaire follows, starting with Sir John Sinclair of Scotland in the 1780s, and progressing to the first polls on record, i.e., those conducted on the presidential elections of 1824 by the *Harrisburg Pennsylvanian* and the *Raleigh Star* in North Carolina. The first attitudinal polls on record were done by Adolf Levenstein, a German labor leader. Sampling is the next topic covered. A.L. Bowley, a British statistician and economist, forced by inadequate funds, was channeled toward using the representative sample method—a method used in Reading, England to study working-class conditions in the city. Continuing with various enhancements to the idea, Martin discusses the major minds in mathematics and statistics whose contributions have made modern day polling possible. Sociologist Paul Felix Lazarsfeld, a Viennese immigrant to the United States, receives attention in the final section of the chapter. The author has included twenty-nine footnotes.

42. Presser, Stanley. "The Use of Survey Data in Basic Research in the Social Sciences." Chap. 3 in *Surveying Subjective Phenomena*, edited by Charles F. Turner, and Elizabeth Martin, vol. 2, pt. 1, 93–114. Panel on Survey Measurement of Subjective Phenomena, Committee on National Statistics, Commission on Behavioral and Social Sciences and Education, National Research Council. New York: Russell Sage Foundation, 1984.

The role of the survey in basic social science research has become increasingly more central in the view of the author. A possible criticism might be that surveys have concentrated on the effort to study attitudes to the considerable exclusion of objective phenomena which may not be subject to the same degree of accurate measurement by the survey approach. Another challenge that Presser discusses is the modest level of focus on the manner in which survey data is produced. Presser suggests that the separation of tasks into data analyst and data collector may be responsible to some degree. Turning to the quantitative use of surveys, Presser reports that some fields may already have seen peak survey use, e.g., as in the area of sociology. Overall, three decades are examined starting with the 1950s and tracing the growth of surveys, their uses, and evaluating the way in which they have been utilized. Five tables provide various breakdowns by percentages, which compare the factors tabulated across the three decades prior to 1980.

43. Rossi, Peter H., James D. Wright, and Andy B. Anderson. "Sample Surveys: History, Current Practice, and Future Prospects." Chap. 1 in *Handbook of Survey Research*, edited by Peter H. Rossi, James D. Wright, and Andy B. Anderson, 1–20. Quantitative Studies in Social Relations, consulting editor Peter H. Rossi. New York: Academic Press, 1983.

The three editors of the *Handbook*, all members of the Social and Demographic Research Institute and associated with the Department of Sociology at the University of Massachusetts, present chapter 1 as an introduction to the various elements of the following fourteen chapters. A seven-page essay highlights the major historical events in sample surveys, concentrating on events from the 1930s through the end of the

1970s. A five-page section covers survey research in the early 1980s. The National Research Council [NRC], in a 1981 survey, found that the survey research industry contacts thirty-two million households each year and conducts one hundred million interviews. It is suggested by the chapter authors that the total gross revenues for the industry is between $2.5 and $5 billion [as of the date of the preparation of the *Handbook* manuscript]. The various "sections" of the survey industry are identified and discussed. These include the academic, private, mass media, and ad hoc and in-house sectors. Current developments and issues introduced include the rising costs of surveys at the same juncture as the level of federal support is decreasing. Also mentioned are the topics of measurement and analysis of survey data. The last area of chapter 1 is an overview of the *Handbook*'s primary elements as well as an explanation of the guidelines that were given to contributors. There are twenty-five references provided.

44.   Squire, Peverill. "Why the 1936 *Literary Digest* Poll Failed." *Public Opinion Quarterly* 52, no. 1 (Spring 1988): 125–33.
The 1937 Gallup survey asked respondents about their participation in the 1936 *Literary Digest* poll. Using the data, Squire concludes that both the sample and the response to the *Literary Digest* were biased and together produced a seriously mistaken estimate of the vote. Squire suggests that if all those who were polled had responded, then the *Literary Digest* would have correctly predicted Franklin D. Roosevelt the winner. The study shows that "those who reported receiving straw vote ballots were supportive of the president" [Franklin D. Roosevelt]. On the other hand, a small majority of those who maintained that they returned their ballots were in support of Alf Landon. The relevance of the study, according to the author, is the continued existence today of nonrandom sample surveys, such as those asking who "won" a presidential debate. The flaws and dubious results of such surveys are mentioned. The author is particularly concerned about nonresponse bias and the absence of the reporting of response rates by many surveys. Squire explains the circumstances which surrounded the *Literary Digest*'s polling activities, and how the results of the 1936 poll led to the eventual demise of the magazine in 1938. The author reviews the record of explanations of what went wrong. Three tables are used to aid in the analysis of the data. There are twenty-seven references, seven from the 1980s.

45. Sudman, Seymour, and Norman M. Bradburn. "The Organizational Growth of Public Opinion Research in the United States." *Public Opinion Quarterly* 51, no. 4, pt. 2 (Winter 1987): S67–S78. The article was written for the anniversary issue of *Public Opinion Quarterly*. The years covered are the first fifty years of the journal, namely 1937–1987. Gallup, Roper, and Crossley had already established their polling organizations by 1937. These companies grew in the post-World War I commercial market research environment. The historical view is treated chronologically with many subheadings, including: "1937–1946: The Proliferation of Survey Organizations"; "The Founding of AAPOR"; "The Survey Research Center of the University of Michigan"; "Postwar Expansion"; "The Political Use of Polls"; "Developments Overseas"; "The Polls Today"; and "Continuing Problems of Survey Organizations." The authors refer the reader to Jean Converse's 1987 book *Survey Research in the United States: Roots and Emergence 1890–1960* (Item No. 38), which had not appeared at the time of this Sudman and Bradburn article, for an in-depth history of the early years of survey research in the United States. The rate of growth of organizations has decreased in the United States but continues to expand in developing countries. Some concern was expressed that there may come a time when the collection of data could be subject to some controls to deal with issues of privacy and possible excess polling. Six references are cited, half from the 1980s.

46. U.S. Congress. House. Committee on House Administration, Subcommittee on Library and Memorials. *Public Opinion Polls. To Provide for the Disclosure of Certain Information Relating to Certain Public Opinion Polls: Hearings on H.R. 5003.* 93d Cong., 1st sess., 1972. Washington, DC: U.S. Government Printing Office, 1973. 260p.

These hearings concern the "Truth-in-Polling-Act" which would require those conducting public opinion polls involving federal office or which deal with any political issue "the results of which are intended to be and are disseminated to the public through the mail or through interstate commerce" to file certain information with the Librarian of the Library of Congress within seventy-two hours after the results are made available. Eight points of information cover: name of the poll requester; method used in sample; sample size; dates of poll; questions asked; methodology used; number contacted and responded, number contacted but with no response, and number not contacted; and finally, the results of the poll. The information is to be publicly available. Punishment for failure to comply is established with a maximum of $1000 fine or thirty days, or both. Twenty individuals appeared before the subcommittee, many reading prepared statements before being questioned. An additional seven individuals had prepared statements submitted for the record. Representatives from national polling organizations, academic researchers, media units, and market researchers presented extensive testimony over the four days of the hearings (19, 20, 21 September, and 5 October 1972). No references are included.

4. Overview

47.　　Brower, Brock. "The Pernicious Power of the Polls: How Pollsters and Marketing Gurus Are Measuring Your Choices—and Shaping Them." *Money* 17, no. 3 (March 1988): 144–63.

The article highlights major polling pitfalls, discusses new developments, and keeps *Money* magazine readers up-to-date, while at the same time providing pointers in areas where Brower observes abuse. A number of graphic displays appear throughout the article. Each focuses on what Brower refers to as polling "hazards"—the dubious assumption, the bogus poll, the "bum" sample, the loaded question, and divide and conquer. The author describes public opinion polls as "all-purpose, universal, substitute voting machine[s]," and sees a loop between polls and television, with the networks running polls and then reporting the results "at the top of the evening news." According to Walker Research Inc. of Indianapolis, about one-third of all adults in the United States are polled each year. Of these, 24 percent are polled once, 28 percent twice, 16 percent three times, and 32 percent four or more times. *USA Today* is cited as the first all-poll newspaper, one in which bar graphs and other representations of data help set the news agenda. Brower is particularly critical of 900 numbers used by television networks in their so-called polls. The author comments on the increasing refusal rate for poll participation—now more than 20 percent. The issue of the right to privacy is raised in connection with requests for sensitive information. No references are included.

48.　　Cantril, Albert Hadley, ed. *Polling on the Issues: A Report from the Kettering Foundation*. Cabin John, MD: Seven Locks Press, 1980. 210p.

This volume represents the proceedings of a 1979 conference to which one hundred guests from the following three areas were invited: pollsters, journalists, and decision makers. At least twenty contributors are named with the fourteen papers presented. The book is divided into four sections: "Polling: Journalism or Social Science?"; "Issues into Percentages"; "The Impact of the Polls on the Policy Environment"; and "Polling: A Political Institution." The contributors include Patrick H. Caddell, George Gallup, Peter Hart, Burns W. Roper, and many other leading figures from the polling industry. The last section of the volume provides a list of the membership of the National Council on Public Polls (NCPP), along with the Principles of Disclosure. The book gives the responses each panel made to a question posed within each of the four areas considered. Each panelist's remarks are shown along with the interchanges which occurred during the floor discussion of the topic. There were from three to seven panelists per major question. The conference was sponsored by both the Kettering Foundation and the NCPP. References, endnotes, and a six-page index are included.

49.   Fienberg, Stephen E., and Judith M. Tanur. "Large-Scale Social Surveys: Problems, and Prospects." *Behavioral Science* 28, no. 2 (April 1983): 135–53.

A brief history of large-scale social surveys, starting in the 1930s, begins the article. Special features of large-scale surveys are discussed next. The main focus of the article is on the many challenges posed with this category of survey. Topics covered include: aggregate estimation and the measurement of sampling error; treatment of missing data; sources of nonsampling error; mode of interviewing; rotation group bias; and statistical analysis. The authors point out that large-scale surveys are significant sources for the administration of government and that they are major sources for basic and applied research. The size of these projects practically requires some degree of government financing. Interviewing for large-scale social surveys is now almost continuous, with notation group structures and multistage area probability sampling a necessity. A discussion of the controversy over design-based versus model-based statistical inference is included. Seventy-seven references complete the article, with about one-third from the 1980s.

50.   Jaroslovsky, Rich. "What's on Your Mind, America?: We Allow Pollsters to Probe Our Every Attitude, Opinion and Action. But Our Answers May Not Reveal What We Really Mean." *Psychology Today* 22, no. 7/8 (July/August 1988): 54–59.

The author covers the much written about polling challenges of question wording, wording and context, and fatigue that can set in among respondents asked to answer questions by telephone with interviews exceeding twenty minutes. The author reviews some of the difficulties of getting even factual information correctly, let along the more challenging achievement of correctly evaluating attitudinal positions. When the article was written Jaroslovsky was political editor and a columnist in the *Wall Street Journal*'s Washington bureau. No references are included.

51. Margolis, Michael. "Public Opinion, Polling, and Political Behavior." In *Polling and the Democratic Consensus*, edited by L. John Martin, 61–71. *Annals of the American Academy of Political and Social Science*, edited by Richard D. Lambert, vol. 472. Beverly Hills, CA: Sage Publications, 1984.

Three major questions are raised in this article: (1) Are those we question in public opinion polls sufficiently knowledgeable to consider the complex questions and challenges which face modern governments? (2) Will respondents tell their true view or will it be the view they think is socially acceptable? and (3) Are governmental representatives of the people bound by the expressed opinion of the public? Margolis argues that these questions are ignored. Prior to scientific polling, Margolis suggests that connections between actual outcomes of public opinion and the formulation of public policy were the subject of considerable attention. In the section dealing with the limits of polling, he states that polling may not be a valid measure when comparing public opinion with public policy outcomes. He states, "polling data are simply surrogates for direct observations of behavior." Margolis is particularly concerned with the discrepancies between expressed opinion and actual behavior. He views the neglect of pre-World War II literature as partly to blame for the oversight by researchers who fail to explore the linkage or lack of linkage between words and actions. The issue of poll context is stressed as well as the need to view subsequent political behavior before a proper understanding of poll data can be reached. The paper has thirty-nine footnotes.

52. Martin, L. John, ed. *Polling and the Democratic Consensus. Annals of the American Academy of Political and Social Science*, edited by Richard D. Lambert, vol. 472. Beverly Hills, CA: Sage Publications, 1984. 208p.

In the preface Martin comments on the degree to which polling has come to be used today: politicians decide whether to run for office or remove themselves from further consideration; U.S. presidents resign or ask top aides to leave the government; and continuance of many services, both private and public, is predicated on the findings of polls. Martin states that there are over two thousand research organizations engaged in public opinion polling, with more than $4 billion spent each year trying to get people's reactions on everything from A to Z. The book has thirteen essays which discuss polls in four basic areas. The first section, titled "Public Opinion Polling," deals with the genealogy of public opinion polling; accuracy, belief systems and poll results; ideological trends; and how the results of polls are used in relation to the actual behavior of respondents. Other sections deal with polls and politicians, the media, and the public. There is a three-page index and a thirty-eight page book review section of materials unrelated to the papers edited by Martin. Each chapter has been separately considered, and can be found under the following item numbers in this annotated bibliography.

Contents:

The Genealogy of Public Opinion Polling (Martin—Item No. 41).

Are Polls Accurate? (Roper – Item No. 333).

The Context of Public Opinion: How Our Belief Systems Can Affect Poll Results (Milbrath—Item No. 336).

Ideological Trends in American Public Opinion (Robinson and Fleishman—Item No. 88).

Public Opinion, Polling, and Political Behavior (Margolis—Item No. 51).

Presidential Decision Making and Opinion Polls (Beal and Hinckley—Item No. 72).

Polling and the Presidential Election (Levy—Item No. 84).

The Use of Polls in Congressional, State, and Local Elections (Conway—Item No. 74).

Polling as a News-Gathering Tool (Ismach—Item No. 109).

The Impact of Polling on the Mass Media (Atkin and Gaudino—Item No. 101).

The Impact of Polls on Public Opinion (Lang and Lang—Item No. 66).

Polling the Attentive Public (Adler—Item No. 210).

The Polls and Ethnic Minorities (Hill—Item No. 342).

53.   Neuman, W. Russell. *The Paradox of Mass Politics: Knowledge and Opinion in the American Electorate.* Cambridge, MA: Harvard University Press, 1986. 241p.

The "paradox" Neuman discusses is the one between low public knowledge or awareness versus the studies of decision making in Washington which indicate "that an articulate voice of attentive public opinion is being heard." The book deals with voting, elections, and public opinion in the United States. Specifically, topics such as political participation, political socialization, and the role of the mass media are considered. Discussion of survey research is brief. Neuman divides thinking about survey research data into three schools (this appears on page 182). He believes that the first school, those that rely heavily on survey use, fails to grant sufficient attention to the weaknesses of the methodology. The second school consists of those who do not use survey research. These individuals doubt the ability of surveys to measure beliefs and opinions. Case studies, participant observation, and depth interviews are preferred by this group. The third school uses surveys but feels uncomfortable about it. They believe that refinements and careful qualifications about data can yield useful and important results. There are fourteen pages of references and a four-page index.

54. Schuman, Howard. "Artifacts Are in the Mind of the Beholder." *American Sociologist* 17, no. 1 (February 1982): 21–28.
The article was read as a paper at the thematic session on "Fact or Artifact? Are Surveys Worth Anything?" at the annual meeting of the American Sociological Association held in New York City on 27 August 1980. The thrust of the research is that while artifacts can be introduced at various points in the many steps of conducting surveys, they also create opportunities for greater understanding of both the responses and the respondents. Schuman concentrates on the challenges presented by language, interviewing, and sampling. The issue of whether a survey should be conducted at all is reviewed. (The author avoids "employing the opposition of polls and surveys, because that distinction probably is more etymological and status-related than conceptual.") Schuman differentiates between scientific surveys and simple surveys by stating that the former treats survey research as a "search for meaning" while the latter views the responses literally. Other topics discussed include: "question constraint"; the effect of question context; the low relation between survey answers and relevant behavior outside the survey; the declining percentage of potential respondents interviewed; and the usefulness of artifacts when the survey method is treated as a means to search for the meaning of human action. There are eighteen references provided (one from the 1980s).

55.   Schuman, Howard. "Survey Research and the Fundamental
Attribution Errror." *Personality and Social Psychology Bulletin* 9,
no. 1 (March 1983): 103–4.

The "fundamental attribution error" described by L. Ross (*Advances in
Experimental Social Psychology*, vol. 10, 1977) as the tendency "to
overestimate the importance of personal and dispositional factors relative
to environmental influences" is applied by Schuman to survey research.
Schuman maintains that the environment is "usually a more important
source of behavior than we expect." In survey research the impact of this
error is to view "marginals" as being representative of the views of the
general population. The impact of the "no opinion" option is cited as an
example of how significantly results can be changed, and also how
marginals can be altered by changing the sex or race of the interviewers.
Schuman observes that survey researchers need to be sensitive to
"situational pressures—especially the social pressures." Seven references
accompany the article, one from the 1980s.

56.   Shapiro, Leopold J. "The Opinion Poll." Ph.D. diss., The
University of Chicago, 1956. 202p.

The study considers the manner by which opinion polls are initiated,
planned, and conducted. Shapiro provides a definition of polling which is
still useful more than thirty years later. He writes that "an opinion poll is
any effort to gain information about a phenomenon by collecting opinion
about that phenomenon by polling persons in an interview situation."
Some of the questions the research seeks to answer are: (1) "What
societal processes give rise to the opinion poll?" (2) "What needs does it
serve?" (3) "How does it fit into our society?" (4) "How are the topics of
opinion polls determined?" (5) "What gives continuity to opinion polling
activity?" (6) "How does the opinion poll secure needed resources from
society?" and (7) "Who pays and why?" The research method used was
that of participant-observation. A lengthy analysis of the data follows the
descriptions of three environments—commercial, government, and
nonprofit. The dissertation closes by relating this study to sociological
theory. A bibliography is not present; however, there are a few footnotes,
although these are not numbered consecutively—being numbered for
each page at a time.

5. Impact, Influence, and Perceptions

57.　Alpern, David M. "The Impact of the Polls." *Newsweek* 104, no. 21, Special Issue (November/December 1984): 8.

This article discusses the perceived impact of polling in the 1984 presidential election. Significant points raised include the serious disparity in pollsters' predicted outcome of the election. Many believe that these differences damage the image of polling. Some politicians feel that public opinion surveys "tend to reinforce and expand the sentiments they reflect." Additionally, polls which are conducted early in the presidential season showing poor numbers for lesser-known candidates can hurt the fund-raising efforts of those individuals. Burns W. Roper cites methodological problems which need to be addressed. Question framing and positioning, as well as the way in which samples are weighted to create demographic balance, are some of the areas where attention may need to be directed. No references are included.

58.　Bogart, Leo. "Polls and Public Opinion." *Society: Social Science and Modern Society* 23, no. 1 (November/December 1985): 16–25.

The article presented here was adapted from the introduction to Bogart's 1985 book, *Polls and the Awareness of Public Opinion* (Item No. 9), a reprint of his *Silent Politics: Polls and the Awareness of Public Opinion*, 1972. The role that polls play in shaping the news and in election campaigns is discussed. The impact of political campaign debates and consultants is outlined, along with the issue of how polls are used in public relations efforts. The manner in which polls are reported and the use of polls in election night projections are reviewed. Bogart discusses the new technologies which are changing the way in which polling is conducted. The role of computers is briefly addressed, with some of the potentially onerous aspects thereof suggested, e.g., equipment which can be operated by a minimum wage employee and can be used to "conduct polls on a daily or weekly basis to learn the opinions or reactions of the public to news events or current public issues." Bogart is quoting the sponsors of a device called Instapoll which was "used by over one hundred television stations within a year after it was placed on the market." A list of seven items for further reading is provided.

59.   Brams, Steven J. "Strategic Information and Voting Behavior." *Society: Social Science and Modern Society* 19, no. 6 (September/October 1982): 4–11.
According to Brams, there are very few theoretical models to explain how voter reactions to the strategic information that polls provide affect individual voting decisions and how elections may be impacted. Brams perceives polls to have been "vehemently attacked" since they began in the 1930s. He believes that the largest controversy has been over projections on election day with the issues of voter turnout and decision making in states where the polls are still open. The author sees polls as introducing information to voters about the candidates' standings which enables the voter to "react strategically." Toward the goal of model design of voter behavior, Brams introduces the Condorcet Criterion and applies it to plurality voting, approval voting, runoff systems, and comparative pathologies. In 1785 the Marquis de Condorcet proposed a means of determining the winner in a multi-candidate race. Quoting Brams, Condorcet's proposal was that "if there is one candidate who can defeat each of the other candidates in separate pairwise contests, define him to be the social choice." Brams calls such a person the "Condorcet candidate" and compares "voting systems in terms of their ability to elect this candidate before and after the introduction of poll information." No references are included.

60.   Brudney, Jeffrey L. "An Elite View of the Polls." *Public Opinion Quarterly* 46, no. 4 (Winter 1982): 503–9.
The elite considered here is a sample of the delegates elected to the 1980 state conventions of the Oklahoma Democratic and Republican parties. The attitudes explored fall into two areas, namely the trust in the results of election polls and the perception of the poll's impact on voters. Brudney worked with two hypotheses: (1) "Confidence in poll results and perception of their impact on voters increase with the level of political activism"; and (2) "Elite trust in polls and belief in their effects varies with the focus of political involvement—delegates involved primarily in national politics will exhibit greatest trust and perception of impact, followed by those active in state politics, and finally by those

working at the local level." The findings were that the rate of significant trust in election poll results was low—13 percent overall (with a range from 11 to 32 percent for selected groups). The belief that polls affect voter behavior was held by 45 percent of the delegates. The author cites these data to possibly explain why funds and support move away from candidates doing poorly in the polls. This would suggest that the band-wagon effect occurs not among voters but rather among political elites. There are ten references; seven are from the 1980s.

61.   Ceci, Stephen J., and Edward L. Kain. "Jumping on the Bandwagon with the Underdog: The Impact of Attitude Polls on Polling Behavior." *Public Opinion Quarterly* 46, no. 2 (Summer 1982): 228–42.

The purpose of the research conducted by Ceci and Kain is to determine what impact the information from public opinion polls has on the behavior of individuals in subsequent attitude surveys. The authors were particularly concerned with the strength and direction of candidate preference and whether or not a candidate will be supported who is currently shown to be leading in national polls. The analysis of the study data suggests that not all fluctuations in voter preference necessarily reflect real movement in the perceptions voters have about a candidate's personality or position, but may in fact represent "oppositional reactivity." This oppositional reactivity can be caused by the knowledge of a candidate's dominance which may then cause subjects to "react oppositionally toward the dominant candidate without actually becoming more favorable toward the underdog." During the study, the only intervening information received by the study participants concerning the status of the candidate was in national opinion polls. The authors state that the poll information significantly modified voter preferences in a very short period of time. The text includes several figures and tables. Fourteen references are present with four from the 1980s.

62.   Ginsberg, Benjamin. "Polling and the Transformation of Public Opinion." Chap. 3 in *The Captive Public: How Mass Opinion Promotes State Power*, 58–85. New York: Basic Books, 1986.

According to the author, polling has aided in the governance of opinion—a reversal of what once was believed, i.e., that polling provided for "government by opinion." Section titles within the chapter include: "Publicizing Opinion"; "From Volunteerism to Subsidy"; "From Behavior to Attitude"; "From Group to Individual"; "From Assertion to Response"; and "Making Opinion Safer for Government." Ginsberg states that "polling has rendered public opinion less dangerous, less disruptive, more permissive, and perhaps, more amenable to governmental control." This, then, is the transformation—the conversion of opinion from a "politically potent, often disruptive force into more docile, plebiscitary phenomenon." An earlier version of this material was presented at a meeting of the American Political Science Association (APSA). There are fifty-one endnotes—these are cumulated for all chapters at the end of the book.

63.   Koch, Nadine Sue. "Perceptions of Public Opinion Polls." Ph.D. diss., The Ohio State University, 1985. 239p.

Focus group sessions involving sixty residents of Columbus, Ohio were used to examine the relationship between individuals and public opinion polls. Koch suggests that the perspective that the individual has with respect to polls is very important. The dissertation studies how individuals understand, perceive, and use poll data. A series of issue questions is posed by Koch which cover the spectrum from whether a distinction is made between scientific and nonscientific polls to whether the individual believes that polls affect opinions and later behavior. Chapter topics include a detailed description of the methodology used by Koch in this study, the findings of the study, and a discussion of political polls. Of interest is summary finding number seven, which states that "Comparisons of source preference suggested that, for many, expert opinion was preferred over mass opinion. Poll information fared rather poorly when compared to other sources of information that one might choose to support one's argument." The author also found that television networks were perceived as "self-serving in their poll activities." The belief expressed was that early projections in political campaigns were designed to increase television ratings. There is an eight-page bibliography.

64.   Kohut, Andrew. "Rating the Polls: The Views of Media Elites and the General Public." *Public Opinion Quarterly* 50, no. 1 (Spring 1986): 1–9.

The 1984 presidential election created an atmosphere of uncertainty and doubt concerning the precision of polls. Significant variation in poll results made some skeptical about the "scientific" nature of polling. The Gallup Organization, on behalf of the 1985 annual conference of the American Association for Public Opinion Research (AAPOR), conducted two surveys: one of the press and another survey of the general public. There were 246 questionnaires administered to members of the news media, and, separately, 1,120 adults were asked a series of questions first asked in 1944. The original questionnaire was conducted by Hadley Cantril's Princeton office of Public Opinion Research. Overall, the postelection image of polls as determined in both surveys was generally positive; in fact, the results from the general public were not very different from those found forty years earlier. Among the press, those who voted for Democratic presidential candidate Walter Mondale were far more inclined to view polls as interfering with the process than those who voted for the Republican candidate Ronald Reagan. Generally, the press seldom selected the most positive category when describing opinion polls. Andrew Kohut is president of the Gallup Organization. There are nine tables which graphically demonstrate the percentage votes in the major issue question. Six references are provided, four from the 1980s.

65. Koschnick, Wolfgang J. "Bandwagons and Underdogs." *Society: Social Science and Modern Society* 19, no. 6 (September/October 1982): 12–14.
Empirical investigations conducted by many researchers have produced "irrefutable evidence" that no statistically significant influence on voting behavior is exerted by public poll data. Even though the percentage may not be statistically significant, plus or minus three percentage points may be more than one million voters—a number that can account for wins or losses. The data suggests that although published polls do not affect the way people vote, it is possible that they "influence the propensity" to actually vote (rather than abstain). Koschnick suggests that the public can be mislead by private polls which are intentionally leaked with the aim of reinforcing a particular viewpoint. He sees polls as a "legitimate extension of the right to know" in democratic societies. The author discusses cases of banning or restricting opinion polling—citing the South African example where opinion polls are banned from the time candidates are nominated, even though partisan propaganda is permitted. Koschnick suggests that if voters use poll data as a basis for tactical voting, it is possible that election outcomes could be increasingly different from those suggested by opinion polls—a result which would doubtless lead to further questions of the validity of public opinion polls. No references are included.

66.   Lang, Kurt, and Gladys Engel Lang. "The Impact of Polls on Public Opinion." In *Polling and the Democratic Consensus*, edited by L. John Martin, 129–42. *Annals of the American Academy of Political and Social Science*, edited by Richard D. Lambert, vol. 472. Beverly Hills, CA: Sage Publications, 1984.

The Langs examine the ways and degrees by which public opinion polling does in fact play a role in the very opinion it is seeking to measure. They suggest three main areas of impact. First, just being interviewed may stimulate interest, cause or create a desire for information, and possibly even increase voting behavior. Second, the authors give less credence to the so-called bandwagon effect, observing that voters react with greater variety than previously thought and may employ such approaches as tactical voting. [Jay M. Shafritz defines tactical voting as "Voting not for one's preferred choice but for a candidate that is more likely to win." The quotation is from the *Dorsey Dictionary of American Government and Politics* (1988, p. 581)]. The third area, perhaps the one of deepest concern to democratic society, is the scenario in which polls shift or change the political climate causing minority positions to become increasingly unwilling to express their views, thereby reducing or eliminating those issues, and making the majority view appear greater and with little or no demonstrated opposition. The article is divided into four sections: "Effect of Polls on Respondents' Opinions"; "Direct Poll Effects"; "Tactical Voting"; and "Indirect Effects." There are sixteen footnotes.

67.   Marsh, Catherine. "Do Polls Affect What People Think?" Chap. 18 in *Surveying Subjective Phenomena*, edited by Charles F. Turner, and Elizabeth Martin, vol. 2, pt. 5, 565–91. Panel on Survey Measurement of Subjective Phenomena, Committee on National Statistics, Commission on Behavioral and Social Sciences and Education, National Research Council. New York: Russell Sage Foundation, 1984.

The issue of whether public opinion itself affects what people think is a question of long standing. The idea that public opinion polls might affect public opinion is explored by Marsh through a discussion of hypothetical models of "bandwagon" effects, followed by an examination of empirical, quasi-experimental, and nonexperimental evidence. Marsh observes that there is no experimental evidence that individuals switch their choices for candidates in line with the majority view, as described in a bandwagon hypothesis. The author believes that the research reviewed does not answer the question posed in the chapter title. The use of opinion polls by the news media in nonelection issues may have influence when understood in terms of agenda-setting rather than persuasion. Marsh suggests that issue polls can be used as part of the process to create a "climate of opinion." In a postscript the author writes about an experiment in which interviewees were told that the trend in recent polls had been in a particular direction—which led to a bandwagon effect. A table shows data from the research described in the postscript. There are five figures provided with the article along with references.

68. Roper, Burns W. "Evaluating Polls with Poll Data." *Public Opinion Quarterly* 50, no. 1 (Spring 1986): 10–16.
The Roper Organization conducted two surveys in 1985 designed to examine the public's attitude toward polls. While one survey involved a ten question interview, the other used a single question which asked for reactions to letters both critical and in praise of polls. National samples of adults were surveyed for the studies. In summary, the findings indicated that 41 percent had never previously been interviewed; 75 percent felt that opinion polls work for the public's interests; 58 percent felt "some influence" from polls; 46 percent felt that polls are "usually accurate"; 51 percent felt that pollsters are "usually honest"; 56 percent believed that a sample of 1,500 to 2,000 makes it "not possible with so few people" to "accurately reflect the views of the nation's population"; 80 percent believed that interviewers are "typical, representative people"; 53 percent maintained that "most" respondents tell the truth; and 51 percent expressed the view that being interviewed for a poll was "enjoyable and satisfactory." In response to a series of options as to what the most annoying aspects of polls are, 63 percent of those who found interviews annoying and unsatisfactory attributed the reason to the time requirements of the poll. The Roper Organization Chairman Burns W. Roper suggests shorter interviews and the avoidance of sales and/or unexpected follow-up calls. No references are included.

69. Schleifer, Stephen. "Trends in Attitudes Toward and Participation in Survey Research." *Public Opinion Quarterly* 50, no. 1 (Spring 1986): 17–26.
Since 1984, Walker Research, Inc. has conducted a biennial Industry Image Study. The survey determines the frequency of participation in polls and surveys, which is determined through a national telephone survey with a sample size of almost 500 people. The survey also examines participants' opinion of the interview experience and their feelings

concerning the research industry in general. Considered in this article are the findings of the 1984 survey. The overall results are "generally encouraging." Areas of perceived difficulties include interviewers who are poorly trained and supervised, interviews which are too lengthy and may also ask overly personal questions, and the issue of multiple participation (18 percent said they had been interviewed four or more times during the past year). Schleifer suggests that survey researchers should remember to evaluate their activities from the respondents' point of view. Survey data indicates that 75 percent of the survey participation was via the telephone, with mail surveys showing a significant decrease in 1984. Of those questioned, 17 percent indicated that they had been subject to false surveys in 1984 (i.e., someone trying to sell a product or service under the guise of a survey). The personality of the interviewer was cited by 47 percent of those who said the survey interview was a pleasant experience. On the matter of confidentiality of answers, only 54 percent believed that survey research firms maintain it. The appendix provides the question wording used in the Walker Research Survey. No references are included.

6. Discipline Oriented Studies

6.1 POLITICS

70.   Alpern, David M., with James Doyle. "Playing Hardball with Polls." *Newsweek* 97, no. 25 (22 June 1981): 37.

Reporters David M. Alpern and James Doyle contribute, in a brief fashion, to an understanding of puzzling poll results concerning Edward M. Kennedy of Massachusetts, Daniel Patrick Moynihan of New York, Lloyd Bentsen of Texas, and John Stennis of Mississippi. A year prior to the reelection of each of these Democratic Senators, it seems that the Republican campaign committee attempted to have it believed through the media that polls indicated that all four candidates were not as well supported by their constituents as was previously thought. Senator Bob Packwood, head of the GOP campaign committee, was forced to release the complete New York poll under the state's fair campaign practices code. Pollster Robert Teeter of Detroit, where Market Opinion Research, Inc. has frequently generated polls for Republicans, cites the need for greater public awareness of poll results. He maintains the public should accept only complete results, with the original questions accompanied by a statement of how the poll was conducted. No references are included.

71.   Altschuler, Bruce E. *Keeping a Finger on the Public Pulse: Private Polling and Presidential Elections*. Contributions in Political Science, no. 72. Westport, CT: Greenwood Press, 1982. 197p.

Chapter 1 is titled "Why Study Polls?" Cited are instances of favorable uses of polls, as well as less than useful approaches in polling. The last chapter, number 7, is titled "The Polls: Uses and Consequences." Here Altschuler describes how the seven basic uses of private polls, discussed in the first chapter, were applied during the five campaigns covered in chapters 2 through 6. Topics in chapter 7 include: "Deciding Whether to Run"; "Image"; "Issues"; "Key Subgroup Breakdowns"; "Resource Allocation"; "When to Leak"; and "Measuring Progress." The five campaigns studied are: 1968 Humphrey; 1968 McCarthy; 1968 Kennedy (Robert); 1972 McGovern; and 1976 Carter. Each chapter has accompanying notes; a cumulative bibliography appears at the end of the volume.

72.   Beal, Richard S., and Ronald H. Hinckley. "Presidential Decision Making and Opinion Polls." In *Polling and the Democratic Consensus*, edited by L. John Martin, 72–84. *Annals of the American Academy of Political and Social Science*, edited by Richard D. Lambert, vol. 472. Beverly Hills, CA: Sage Publications, 1984.

The main theme of this entry is that, contrary to the view of the general public and many pollsters, polls play a significant role in presidential decision making. Both authors have experience with the Republican presidency of Ronald Reagan. They cite the pollsters that each of the presidents have had since Roosevelt (Franklin Delano). The authors stress the importance of polls on the president and his key advisers. Various examples of how polls impact on policy choices and decisions on issues are provided. Major sources of polls are explained: the news media, the federal government, special interests, political action committees (PACs), corporations, and politicians. Four primary areas are discussed in which the role of polling is shown to have had great value. These issues include federalism, the gender gap, fairness, and unemployment. The role of foreign opinion polls is explored in brief. The experience of the Reagan years is the central focus of the section, describing an apparent increase in the number and use of such polls to augment Reagan's trips to Canada, France, and elsewhere. Beal and Hinckley seem to be suggesting that if it were not the case in the past, present and future presidents would continue to vigorously use pollsters and poll data long after the memory of the election is a faint glimmer. The authors include fifteen footnotes.

73.   Buchanan, William. "Election Predictions: An Empirical Assessment." *Public Opinion Quarterly* 50, no. 1 (Summer 1986): 222–27.

A review of 155 poll forecasts in sixty-eight elections since 1949 (which constitutes most of published national election forecasts) indicates that errors average nearly double what statistical theory would indicate. The author summarizes findings of the study into six points: (1) "the margin of error estimates based on probability theory seriously underestimate the empirical range of error"; (2) the degree to which winners' percentages are forecast correctly is, on average, underestimated by about one-half point and runners-up by one-fourth point; (3) the previous two "compensating underestimates" enable better predictions in the two-party distribution with the winner being correctly selected 85 percent of the time; (4) biases and random errors do not seem to have been reduced during the years studied; (5) the conservative vote tends to be underestimated; and (6) wrong predictions seem to have been made in a few elections when most of the polls have reached the same false conclusions. Buchanan observes that while polling methodology has improved, forecasting results have not. A table charts the error rates by decade, starting with the 1950s. There are six references provided, half from the 1980s.

74.   Conway, M. Margaret. "The Use of Polls in Congressional, State, and Local Elections." In *Polling and the Democratic Consensus*, edited by L. John Martin, 97–105. *Annals of the American Academy of Political and Social Science*, edited by Richard D. Lambert, vol. 472. Beverly Hills, CA: Sage Publications, 1984.

The author believes that considerable attention has been directed toward the use of polls in presidential campaigns, with state and local elections not enjoying similar review. Basically, the article has two parts: one examines the types of campaign surveys and the other describes the uses of surveys. The types discussed begin with the feasibility survey. Others include the benchmark survey, follow-up polls, panel surveys, tracking polls, focus groups, and postelection studies. Each type is defined along with an example of its possible use. The usefulness of a survey is dependent upon the following factors: the nature of the constituency; candidate and campaign characteristics, qualities of the campaign staff, and the nature of the political contest. Each use category is discussed in separate sections, again with examples to illustrate the concepts. Discussing local polls, Conway advises that in 1984 an average poll would have a sample size of four hundred and a cost of between $7,000 and

$12,000 for professionally contracted work. Professionally conducted surveys are most likely to be used by someone whose district has been radically redistricted, by challenges to incumbents, by those candidates with adequate funding, and by incumbents elected to their first term in Congress after the 1972 election. There are eight footnotes.

75.   Crespi, Irving. *Pre-Election Polling: Sources of Accuracy and Error.* New York: Russell Sage Foundation, 1988. 205p.

Citing a series of inaccurate poll results in the early 1980s at the presidential, senatorial, and mayoral levels, Crespi made a determination to look closely at the causes for these miscalls. The errors in preelection polling in the Reagan victories in 1980 and 1984 were of particular concern—with significant questioning of the nature of the "science" of polling. The purpose of the report is to evaluate the preelection practices of the 1980s. The study is "based on a review of the variety of methods used by numerous polls in a large number of different types of elections...." Crespi seeks to identify the sources of variability in the accuracy of polling. Preelection poll accuracy is defined as the "closeness in percentage points of voting preferences to election results." The research undertaken considers elections at the presidential, state, and local levels involving both general elections and primaries. Methodology is related to political context, and the words and thoughts of pollsters are analyzed in relationship to their contribution to poll accuracy. Crespi maintains that sizeable error found in preelection polls goes beyond sampling error. Two barriers to improving poll accuracy are inadequate following of professional standards by some media sponsors, and the preference by some pollsters and editors for judgmental interpretation over accurate measurement. The volume includes three pages of references.

76.   Davison, W. Phillips, and Leon Gordenker, eds. *Resolving Nationality Conflicts: The Role of Public Opinion Research.* New York: Praeger Publishers, 1980. 242p.

The Princeton University World War I Class of 1917 presented a new approach to the problem of violent conflicts concerning nationality issues. The presentation occurred January 1978 and involved a large array of contributors, including forty colleagues from the Class of 1917 and many others. One of the editors, W. Phillips Davison, was a former editor of the *Public Opinion Quarterly* and had also served as president of the American Association for Public Opinion Research (AAPOR) in 1972–1973. Several of the book's chapters have sections dealing with specific survey results in a particular conflict area, e.g., the community conflict within Belgium from 1830 to 1980 or the Arab minorities inside Israel. Chapter 10 by Davison deals more globally with the application of opinion research to conflict resolution. He considers the possibility of worldwide public opinion research, along with considerations of just what information is appropriate in the attempt to gauge popular attitudes. Clearly the view is that furthering the understandings of the entities between each other through the judicious application of survey research will speed the peace process. Gordenker wrote chapter 1 on self-determination, a key concept in this study. He is professor of politics at Princeton University and is also associated with the Center of International Studies. The volume was written under the auspices of the center. Seven of the ten chapters have endnotes; there is a twenty-one page cumulative bibliography at the end of the volume.

77. Day, Richard, and Kurt M. Becker. "Preelection Polling in the 1982 Illinois Gubernatorial Contest." *Public Opinion Quarterly* 48, no. 3 (Fall 1984): 606–14.

All preelection polls were inaccurate so far as the outcome of the 1982 Illinois gubernatorial election was concerned. The media and survey research critics had a field day. The authors sought to carefully examine the factors that may have caused so much miscueing. The finding is quite simple: although people said they preferred Republican incumbent Thompson, many voted a straight Democratic ticket once inside the voting booth. Not surprisingly, the authors cite the need for survey researchers to be sensitive to the possibility of straight ticket voting, as well as to particular issues that might induce the same behavior. Other factors which the article addresses as possible causes of error include: (1) last minute vote changing; (2) an unusually large Chicago voter turnout; (3) a change in the composition of those who came to vote (Democratic gain in all areas was noted); and (4) incorrectly reporting the "behavioral intentions" of the polled Chicago voters. The preelection poll used to examine the above factors was drawn from a sample of twelve hundred Illinois voters. There are seven tables that accompany the text, along with eleven references (seven from the 1980s).

78. Duquin, Lorene Hanley. "The Pluses and Minuses of Do-It-Yourself Polling." *Campaigns & Elections* 5 (Fall 1984): 18–25.

The thesis of this article is that when conducting a political campaign on the local level in an environment which is short on money but long on willingness to learn survey research methods, do-it-yourself polling is possible and could make a positive difference for a candidate. Several survey-analysis and telemarketing packages which are commercially available are mentioned. Duquin addresses the subject methodically by first defining a survey, and then by taking the reader through each of the steps of deciding whether a survey is appropriate, citing the dangers of do-it-yourself survey work, and helping in the decision-making process of evaluating whether it is worthwhile to attempt such a venture. The author then outlines the steps of the planning process: defining objectives, deciding how to gather the information, and selecting the sample. The questionnaire is discussed next, along with sample questions. A small extract from a sample attitude survey is also included. A section concerning the training of interviewers follows. The article closes with a discussion of how to analyze data and best use the results. Duquin informs the reader that the information gathered is valid only at the time the poll was taken. No references are included.

79.   Edwards, George C., III. "Understanding Public Opinion." Chap. 1 in *The Public Presidency: The Pursuit of Popular Support*, 8–37. New York: St. Martin's Press, 1983.

The uses of public opinion polls by U.S. presidents are discussed, along with the issue of whether presidents use polls to lead or to follow public opinion. Edwards divides the section into three parts covering—in his words—the limitations of polls, the uses of polls, and leadership versus followership. Limitations cited include: (1) poll questions usually do not measure the intensity of opinions held; (2) questions asked the public rarely tie-in with specific problems presidents face; (3) poll responses may be biased by the wording choice in the questions; (4) controversial issues are particularly vulnerable to "contamination" through the use of "loaded" symbols; and (5) polls, unless paid for by the president, are not conducted at his convenience. The author reviews some of the uses of polls made by presidents since Franklin D. Roosevelt, with the greatest attention reserved for President Carter and his pollster Patrick Caddell. In the last part of the section dealing with leadership versus followership, Edwards cites examples of each style. Roosevelt is described as having used polls to determine where the public stood relative to the position "he felt was best" for the country. The Reagan White House is described as having used polls in the "decision-making process and the selling of the presidency." The chapter includes endnotes.

80. Fenwick, Ian, Frederick Wiseman, John F. Becker, and James R. Heiman. "Classifying Undecided Voters in Pre-Election Polls." *Public Opinion Quarterly* 46, no. 3 (Fall 1982): 383–91.

The problem addressed by the authors concerns the number of respondents that are classified as undecided in telephone preelection surveys. Since the telephone does not provide a forum for a secret ballot, many people simply prefer not to reveal choices. The article suggests a model to overcome this difficulty. The technique involves examining the characteristics of decided voters to estimate "discriminant functions." These functions are then used to predict the voting patterns for those voters who are undecided. The data collection approach does not have a bearing on the use of the model. The setting for this discussion is the 1980 presidential election opinion polls. Employing a postelection survey to validate the discriminant analysis, the researchers found that the approach was correct for 61 percent of those who voted for one of the three major candidates. The follow-up survey involved a sample of fifty individuals, with forty-seven contacted. Four tables, one figure, and six pre-1980 references accompany the text.

81. Hagstrom, Jerry, and Robert Guskind. "Advice for Hire: Polling and Media Services for Senate and Gubernatorial Races Are Concentrated in about Two Dozen Republican and Democratic Firms." *National Journal* 18, no. 41 (11 October 1986): 2432–41.

A 1986 *National Journal* survey of 142 major candidates for U.S. Senate and governor indicated that there is a concentration of effort into about two dozen Republican and Democratic firms. Four Republican pollsters—Robert M. Teeter, Richard B. Wirthlin, V. Lance Tarrance, and Arthur J. Finkelstein—cover, between them, 44 of the 70 Republicans running for Senate or governor. Similarly, four Democratic firms operated by Peter D. Hart, Patrick H. Caddell, William R. Hamilton, and R. Harrison Hickman and Paul E. Maslin, have 34 of 70 Democratic candidates. About ten national firms dominate the media consulting business. These are identified by name, with the number of clients for each company specified. Two polling firms are discussed which began a practice previously avoided, i.e., the handling of both Republican and Democratic candidates. In 1986 there were ninety-nine firms providing polling and media services for statewide campaigns. It has become almost universal to use pollsters and media consultants in such races. A notable exception was New York Democratic Governor Mario M. Cuomo, who used campaign aides to produce his television advertisements. No references are included.

82.   Hawver, Carl Fullerton. *The Congressman's Conception of His Role: Based on a Study of the Use of Public Opinion Polls by Members of the United States House of Representatives.* Washington, DC: Hennage Lithograph Company, 1963. 295p.

This specially bound, commercially available work is actually a version of the author's 1963 dissertation completed at the American University. The original dissertation has 311 pages. The study was undertaken approximately halfway between the present time and the beginning of public opinion polling in the political arena. Hawver begins with a historical overview of the "attitude-opinion survey." This section is followed by a discussion of the use of public opinion surveys in political research. Analyzed are not only the uses to which congressmen employ polls, but also their attitudes toward polls. The attitudes range from the belief that polls provide useful sources of information to the view that polls are a waste of time. The data studied was gathered by means of a mailed questionnaire to every member of the U.S. House of Representatives. The 63 percent of the members who did not respond after the third mailing received personal interviews. Major issues of the survey included the anxiety factor, i.e., factors concerning reelection, redistricting, nearness of defeat, party affiliation, geographic and/or type of population served, and issues of personal characteristics of the congressman— age, sex, education, occupation, and so forth. References are provided.

83.   Katosh, John P., and Michael W. Traugott. "The Consequences of Validated and Self-Reported Voting Measures." *Public Opinion Quarterly* 45, no. 4 (Winter 1981): 519–35.

In an examination of the 1976 and 1978 American National Election Studies (NES) results, the authors found that some respondents misreported both their registration status and voting behavior. The percentages were 14 percentage points and 12 percentage points respectively for both cycles of the NES. The authors indicate that these findings are not at odds with the prior thirty years' data from the University of Michigan's Survey Research Center/Center for Political Studies (SRC/CPS). Historically, self-reported participation in the nation's political life has been in error in the range of 15 to 25 percent in relation to actually validated participation rates. The authors chose to examine a presidential election year, followed by a so-called off-year. Stating their results in another way, one in seven respondents misreported their registration or voting status. Regression models were used in the study of the survey data. Six tables provide breakdowns of the data. There are twelve references, several of which are from 1980.

84. Levy, Mark R. "Polling and the Presidential Election." In *Polling and the Democratic Consensus*, edited by L. John Martin, 85–96. *Annals of the American Academy of Political and Social Science*, edited by Richard D. Lambert, vol. 472. Beverly Hills, CA: Sage Publications, 1984.

The growth in importance and heightened role of polls and pollsters in presidential elections is traced. Focus is directed to the 1980 campaign, specifically on the use of polls by Democratic candidate President Carter. Pat Caddell served in the role as both pollster and campaign consultant. One section of the article deals with the debates between President Carter and then former Governor Reagan. The presentation is designed to show that the counsel of presidential pollsters, to quote Levy, "is often taken quite seriously." Other sections of the article include an overview of the major presidential pollsters from the early 1960s to the present, and a brief description of the nature of campaign polling. Innovations are described, particularly Reagan pollster Richard Wirthlin's tracking technique—one involving five hundred randomly selected voters who were telephoned across America every night starting in mid-October prior to the November election. Other developments include the use of focus groups and qualitative audience measurement. Consideration is given to the enhanced role of the pollster in campaigns—specifically, as a strategist. The examples of Caddell for Carter and Wirthlin for Reagan are described as pollster-strategists with each man having significant input into the decision-making process for the candidate of each of the major American political parties. The chapter has six footnotes.

85. McKean, Kevin. "The Fine Art of Reading Voters' Minds." *Discover* 5, no. 5 (May 1984): 66–69.

McKean deals with the issue that despite advances, polls in the political arena are still reporting inaccurate results from time to time. He suggests that polls are "not very good at predicting elections" and that they are only able to represent the facts from the "moment the survey is taken." It is also pointed out that unlike many other surveys, the political poll has a correct answer. McKean discusses key concepts such as randomness, courtesy bias, exit polls, and the controversy centered around the telephone straw poll. Four cartoon drawings, illustrated by Michael Witte, serve to highlight some polling situations. No references are included.

86.   Nelson, Allan D. "Political Implications of Modern Public Opinion Research." Ph.D. diss., University of Chicago, 1962. 489p.

This dissertation contains eleven chapters, three of which have a direct bearing on public opinion polls. Chapter 1 discusses the general character of public opinion research, covering basic elements and practical claims. Chapter 3 deals with public opinion polls and representative democracy. The subjects of tyranny, preferences, and strategies are reviewed. Chapter 10 considers the question of public opinion research as an instrument of democracy. Each chapter mentioned provides lengthy discussion of the issues with many points of view presented. The foundations of opinion polling are discussed, with considerable effort exerted to explain, query, and theorize on such topics as "values" in public opinion research, cognitive elements of opinion, the public's interests, and democratic "requirements" in relationship to scientific "values." Nelson's conclusion is twenty-four pages, ending with a call for opinion researchers to "give closer attention to our heritage of political theory." He also states that "it is likely that only the relatively simple and trivial facts of human existence can be known with the degree of certainty that the opinion researchers are wont to claim (at least by implication) for their findings." The work is highly footnoted along with an eighteen-page bibliography.

87.   Rinaldo, Matthew J. "The Use of Questionnaires and Public Opinion Polls by U.S. Congressmen to Determine Constituency Attitudes." Ph.D. diss., New York University, 1978. 176p.

At the time Rinaldo wrote this dissertation he was also a member of the U.S. House of Representatives from the 12th Congressional District of New Jersey. The dissertation was designed to test the following hypotheses: (1) polls are a major source of constituency attitude determination by House members; (2) election year use of polls are limited to swing vote evaluation; and (3) there is a difference in frequency of use of polls between urban/suburban and rural House members. Rinaldo found that of the 152 members who responded to his polling questionnaire, 81 percent or 123 members reported that they had used polls. At least eleven areas of poll data use were identified: (1) planning campaign strategy; (2) finding new groups where votes could be gained; (3) locating diversity of views by geography; (4) measuring the degree to which voters identify with the candidate; (5) finding important voter concerns; (6) identifying voters' candidate choices; (7) communicating with voters; (8) determining beliefs held by voters; (9) enhancing perception of voter participation in federal government; (10) keeping candidates' names in the public eye; and (11) helping decide legislative decisions. More than half the dissertation considers a trend survey of public opinion in the author's own congressional district taken during the 1974 general election. References are provided.

88.   Robinson, John P., and John A. Fleishman. "Ideological Trends in American Public Opinion." In *Polling and the Democratic Consensus*, edited by L. John Martin, 50–60. *Annals of the American Academy of Political and Social Science*, edited by Richard D. Lambert, Beverly Hills, CA: Sage Publications, 1984.

Four national survey organizations' survey data was considered in examining American ideological trends. The conclusions suggest that there is a trend in the direction of conservatism in terms of how people identify themselves ideologically, even though there are some specific issues—such as racial tolerance and feminism—in which attitudes are tending toward more liberal views. Ideological cohesiveness (i.e., what a person claims as an ideological position does not necessarily equate with votes on specific issues, individuals, or political party) is no more present in the 1980s than in the 1970s. In the words of the authors, "the meaning of the liberal-conservative dimension continues to be diffuse and diverse across the electorate." Figure 1 is a graph showing the ideological identification of voters from 1938–1983. Each of the four major types of survey instruments used in the study has its data plotted. These include: Gallup, 1938–1970; Roper, 1970–1983; Survey Research Center (SRC); Center for Political Studies (CPS); and the General Social Survey (GSS). Robinson and Fleishman write that Ronald Reagan's popularity may be more attributable to the clarity of his policy decisions than to the ideological foundations that these positions may have had. Although cohesiveness may not be increasing, professed ideology apparently continues to predict party affiliation and voting behavior. Nineteen footnotes are included.

89.   Robinson, John P., and Robert Meadow. *Polls Apart: A Report from the Kettering Foundation.* Cabin John, MD: Seven Locks Press, 1982. 183p.

Phillips Ruopp, in his foreword to *Polls Apart*, writes that the book examines "the conceptual and methodological problems of investigating and characterizing opinions on foreign policy issues, and the perceptions and values that lie behind them." Based on a series of "town meetings" conducted in ten American cities and cosponsored by the Bureau of Public Affairs of the U.S. Department of State and local foreign policy organizations, the polls taken before each meeting were sponsored and underwritten by the Charles F. Kettering Foundation. The book is divided into two main parts. The first deals with how foreign policy polls are used, problems with polls, and how foreign policy is made. Part 2 concerns how polls work (with regard to the four major foreign policy issues covered), a discussion of the ten-city study, poll question framing, and suggestions on how issue polls can be improved. There are four appendixes; the first covers the survey methods and questions used in the study. The bibliography has twenty-three items, but represents only those items which were not given full bibliographic citations in the notes found in the various chapters.

90.   Roll, Charles. "Private Opinion Polls." In *The Communications Revolution in Politics*, edited by Gerald Benjamin, 61–74. *Proceedings of The Academy of Political Science*, vol. 34, no. 4. New York: Academy of Political Science, 1982.

In 1980, privately commissioned opinion polls constituted $20 million in campaign expenditures—including all offices at all levels. Approaching ten years later, the figure is undoubtedly significantly higher, as polling has become even more widespread, with frequency of use probably having increased as well. Roll reviews a number of potential uses of private polls. The general media focus on polls has led to the increasing desire for speedy solutions to the problems faced by elected government officials. Roll maintains that more than anyone, it is the politicians themselves who are most affected by today's extensive polling. Presidents of the United States are described as demonstrating varying degrees of skill in both interpreting the results of the commissioned polls, as well as in the implementing of decisions based on these data. President Carter was the first U.S. president to have continuous and comprehensive private political polls during his term in office. Polls are used to indicate where problems may exist when following certain options. The author is concerned by the general lack of knowledge about polling techniques by the layman. He suggests that expectations about polls are too high, and that policies should not always be based on poll results—which at best show tendencies, fluidities, and approximations. Roll includes thirteen footnotes in the paper.

91. Roll, Charles W., Jr., and Albert H. Cantril. *Polls, Their Use and Misuse in Politics.* New York: Basic Books, 1972. Reprint. Cabin John, MD: Seven Locks Press, 1980. 177p.

The book was written to respond to what Bill Moyers, writing in the foreword, perceived to be a "dearth of understanding" about the meanings of polls and the techniques used to reach published results. The volume is a paperback edition of a work released eight years earlier. The Seven Locks Press edition has a forty-one page introduction titled "Trends in an Art-Science." The authors note in the introduction that their concern in the first edition continues, that of the "agenda of accountability" (the whole issue of the degree to which polls are accountable to their clients as well as to the general public) if and when polls are disclosed. Chapter 1 labels polling "The Fifth Estate," an acknowledgment of the significant role polls now command. The following six chapters cover unfortunate uses of polls in politics; positive uses; reliability; procedural issues; interpretation; and the place of public opinion polling in democratic environments. There are endnotes with each of the seven chapters.

92. Roper, Burns W. "Confused Voters Confuse Pollsters." *Psychology Today* 18, no. 10 (October 1984): 13.

In the "Crosstalk" column of *Psychology Today*, Burns W. Roper has, in a short four-paragraph article, discussed a problem of consequence to future political pollsters. As Roper says, "I'm not sure what's happening. And that concerns me most of all." He is referring to the failure of the polls to indicate the size of the Reagan victory in 1980 and "the tendency to overmeasure the front runner in 1982." Quoting Roper, "I think part of it may be increasingly conflicting pressures within any given voter." Expressing the thinking within the voter which Roper believes is impacting the poll results, he writes, "This part of me argues for this candidate, that part of me argues for his opponent. I am no longer bound by tradition or orthodoxy and so I'm not really sure what I'm gonna do next Tuesday [election day]." No references are included.

93. Rosenstone, Steven J. *Forecasting Presidential Elections.* New Haven, CT: Yale University Press, 1983. 211p.

Polls have long played a role in attempts to forecast political races— especially the presidential one. The book discusses poll use in forecasting, the methods employed, and how they are used by political strategists. Limitations of polls, the margin of error, and straw polls are also explored. The time period covered is from the 1948 election through

1980. Chapter 2 discusses "How Elections are Forecasted," with chapter 3 providing a "Theory of Elections." The work is footnoted throughout and there is a nine-page index. A short history of public opinion polls appears on pages 24–26. There are over twenty pages of references.

94.   Salwen, Michael B. "The Reporting of Public Opinion Polls during Presidential Years, 1968–1984." *Journalism Quarterly* 62, no. 2 (Summer 1985): 272–77.

Two hypotheses are tested: (1) "The reporting of needed methodological information in public opinion poll stories in daily metropolitan newspapers improved significantly during the presidential election years from 1968 to 1984"; and (2) "Daily metropolitan newspapers reported more needed methodological information in their own (in-house) polls than they did in wire-service and syndicated polls during the presidential election years from 1968 to 1984." The author analyzed 264 poll stories which appeared in the front sections of Detroit's two daily newspapers, the *News* and the *Free Press*. The results of the study support both hypotheses. It is suggested that increased awareness among journalists of the need to provide such data may be responsible for the change. The findings suggest that newspapers "invest more prestige, time and energy in their own polls than other polls." More than 72 percent of the in-house polls appeared on the front page, compared with 20 percent of the combined wire service and syndicated polls. There are sixteen footnotes.

95.   Sanoff, Alvin P., with Ron Scherer, Steve Hawkins, and Michael Bosc. "Are Pollsters Getting out of Hand?: Critics Are Raising Questions about the Importance and Reliability of Surveys That Shape Politics, Business." *U.S. News & World Report* 96, no. 18 (7 May 1984): 30–31.

Highlighted is the degree to which polls have become a part of our daily lives: in politics, in business, and in our social interactions. The use of polls by presidents, major corporations, and in particular, by marketing organizations is reviewed. The use of ever-increasing technology is addressed, with Burns Roper commenting, "Our technology is more and more sophisticated, and our accuracy is more and more off." One reason provided as a possible explanation is the rapidity with which moods are shifting and quickly making polls obsolete. Peter Hart is quoted as saying that in the 1984 presidential primary season polls had a "shelf life of 48 hours." The authors suggest that many do not understand the limits of surveys, which by their very nature capture only a "fleeting snapshot of public attitudes that frequently are in flux." Basic survey issues are covered such as order of questions asked, exact wording of questions, and sex of the interviewer. Exit polling is briefly discussed. No references are included.

96. Sudman, Seymour. "The Presidents and the Polls." *Public Opinion Quarterly* 46, no. 3 (Fall 1982): 301–10.

Through the eight United States presidencies since 1940, Sudman demonstrates the appropriate and inappropriate uses of public opinion research. The examples concentrate on all major uses and misuses of polls, rather than on the presidency of any particular individual, party affiliation, or length of time in office. Roosevelt was the first president to use polls in 1940. Truman had serious doubts about polls' accuracy in 1948, and history confirmed his viewpoint. There remains little evidence to determine Truman's use of polls. Eisenhower made limited use of opinion polls. Evidence suggests that poll results on attitudes toward Korea and Senator Joe McCarthy were made available to Eisenhower. Although Kennedy remained a skeptic toward polls, he nevertheless read carefully data produced by Harris, Gallup, and others. A 1960 poll showing 86 percent of the Cuban public opinion in urban areas as pro-Castro seems to have been overlooked prior to the Bay of Pigs invasion of 1961. It was believed by the advisors to the president that the Cuban population would rise up in revolution and join forces with the invaders. Johnson concentrated on trying to improve his image as his primary use of opinion polls. Carter is described as "not an effective president, nor did he use polls wisely." Reagan's use of polls has been "to tell him how to plan his strategies" in implementing his conservative policies. In the language of marketing Sudman states, "You can't get repeat purchases of a product that people don't like." Two of the eight references are from the 1980s.

97. Wilson, L.A., II. "Preference Revelation and Public Policy: Making Sense of Citizen Survey Data." *Public Administration Review* 43, no. 4 (July/August 1983): 335–42.

The research provides insight about the use and analysis of citizen surveys in local governments by, among others, budget decision makers. It attempts to deal with a recognized issue concerning the data from citizen surveys, namely whether or not the results reflect "real" preferences or "insincere preferences" (those expressed by individuals who mask their true preferences). At least two uses of such surveys are identified: (1) as a performance indicator; and (2) as a guide in the decision-making process of distributing monies to the various competing elements that constitute the budget. Wilson focuses on the question as to whether the survey results show sincere preferences for additional public spending. A major concern is that affirmative results may in fact be "quirks" generated by the research methodology employed. The author reports that both agency heads and elected officials, i.e., the budget advisers and decision makers, are greatly concerned about "preference revelation." The research undertaken by Wilson indicates that more than two-thirds of those who were in favor of additional spending for specific goods and services were also willing to bear the cost in the form of additional taxes. The importance of this article is the degree to which it demonstrates how far survey research has penetrated the political system, as well as the extent of survey analysis now being conducted on the local level. There are ten endnotes included.

6.2 LAW

98.   Crespi, Irving. "Surveys as Legal Evidence." *Public Opinion Quarterly* 51, no. 1 (Spring 1987): 84–91.

Crespi maintains that in order for survey data to be admitted in court, the rules of the legal system must be followed, rather than circumvented or ignored. The major stumbling block lies in differing understandings of what constitutes "truth." Scientific "truth" and legal "truths" may not be quite the same. Crespi uses about one-fourth of the article to clarify this point, documenting examples from actual cases. A discussion of the hearsay rule follows, with the observation that until recently survey data was excluded because of the hearsay rule. Viewing survey data as a "new kind of empirical information," many courts have accepted the data by applying existing legal criteria in new ways. A number of court cases are cited throughout the hearsay rule section. The last section deals with surveys and trademark litigation. Crespi stresses the need to consider legal principles when designing and analyzing a survey for use in litigation. The "Polaroid formula," which established eight criteria for determining the likelihood of purchasers' confusion with regard to trademark, is discussed. The legal citation to the case is provided, along with the citations to at least ten other cases throughout the trademark section. The author explains that in the American legal system decisions by individual courts may vary in the interpretation of the rules of evidence. No references are included.

99.   Dutka, Solomon. "Business Calls Opinion Surveys to Testify for the Defense." *Harvard Business Review* 58, no. 4 (July/August 1980): 40–42.

The uses by business of survey research in litigation include issues surrounding misleading advertising, efforts to gain rate increases by state regulatory bodies, credit card companies which are changing procedures, trademark cases involving logos and packaging, and graphic elements in trademark cases which may be confusingly alike. Efforts to include surveys as evidence began in the 1870s, but the first successful entry occurred in 1954. Dutka provides an overview of areas in the survey design which must be addressed for the successful use of the survey as legal evidence. These include: adequacy of the sample; questionnaire construction; pertinence of findings; conduct of the survey; documentation of all material; and the investigator's qualifications (someone who can withstand the rigors of cross-examination or a substitute expert witness other than the principal investigator). No references are included.

100.   Nietzel, Michael T., and Ronald C. Dillehay. "Psychologists as Consultants for Changes of Venue: The Use of Public Opinion Surveys." *Law and Human Behavior* 7, no. 4 (December 1983): 309–35.

This research reports on the use of public opinion polls as tools to assist legal efforts to have trials moved to another city and/or county—usually due to pretrial publicity. These polls are referred to as venue surveys and "include questions that gauge how many people have read or heard about a case, what they have read or heard, whether they have formed opinions, what these opinions are, and how they affect the way the case is generally perceived." The article relates the experiences of five capital murder trials, employing case history methodology. The authors cite four problems with the use of venue surveys: (1) judicial conservatism or the skepticism with which judges view the validity and admissibility of survey data; (2) problems such as the attitude-behavior inconsistencies of respondents; (3) sampling and survey construction difficulties (such as sample size which tends to be very small in venue surveys); and (4) deciding just how much prejudice is too much in a particular case. Nietzel and Dillehay would like to see more surveys of this kind conducted including and beyond venue cases, as a means of generating more adequate norms. Ten references (three from the 1980s) complete the article.

6.3 PRINT AND ELECTRONIC MEDIA

101.   Atkin, Charles K., and James Gaudino. "The Impact of Polling on the Mass Media." In *Polling and the Democratic Consensus*, edited by L. John Martin, 119–28. *Annals of the American Academy of Political and Social Science*, edited by Richard D. Lambert, vol. 472. Beverly Hills, CA: Sage Publications, 1984.

The record of the ever-increasing use of polling by the mass media is presented. This trend is evidenced by the greater occurrence of polling results in reporting and commentary; in their use in deciding story position and length; in editorializing; and in their means of quantifying news in what the authors describe as "the traditionally qualitative news profession." Polls are now providing us with "newsworthy" information, particularly in the political arena as election times draw closer. This tends to focus on the "horse-race" element of campaigns, with tremendous attention placed on election day coverage. Atkin and Gaudino describe the role of polling in editorial commentary and endorsement and also in the media's "adversarial relationship with government leaders." Critical issues raised include the challenge created by the "pseudo-event quality of polls." This situation can occur when the media creates news by conducting polls in order to make headlines. Another issue is the potentially deceptive nature of polling results in that not all are aware of the impact of question wording, interview method, and type of population sampled. Further, results geared for the general public are generated by simplified questionnaires with opinions measured crudely and the data superficially reviewed. The issue of interpretation of poll results is particularly problematical when dealing with uninformed opinions. Thirty-three footnotes complete the Atkin and Gaudino chapter.

102.   Broh, C. Anthony. "Horse-Race Journalism: Reporting the Polls in the 1976 Election." *Public Opinion Quarterly* 44, no. 4 (Winter 1980): 514–29.

Broh expresses some misgivings about the "horse-race" metaphor used by journalists. The author writes that "the search for excitement carries within it the danger of distortion." The horse-race image also has the capacity to cause the public to focus on irrelevant aspects of a campaign, such as trivia and media-created pseudo-events. This may cause substantive, complex, undebated issues of significance to be overlooked. The article deals specifically with the events and coverage or non-coverage of the 1976 presidential campaign of Jimmy Carter and Gerald Ford. The author writes about journalists who avoided predictions, reported only about certain segments in samples, made questionable comparisons of poll results, and generally questioned the validity of polling. Broh describes journalistic inaccuracies in reporting polls and continues by citing an example in which relevant data is simply ignored. The concern here is about journalists who wish to create a spectacle—one which tends to enhance the image of the campaign as a sporting event, a betting one at that, i.e., the horse race. Two tables accompany the text. There are twenty-two references, one from the 1980s.

103. Broh, C. Anthony. "Polls, Pols and Parties." *Journal of Politics* 45, no. 3 (August 1983): 732–44.

The increased use of public opinion polling on television during the presidential campaigns of 1972, 1976, and 1980 is reviewed. Broh maintains that polling on television strengthens a trend toward direct representation in United States presidential elections. He suggests that this trend has had the effect of increasing the importance of television. Polling has permitted the networks to provide "professional commentary on the meaning of each electoral contest." Television commentators thereby become more astute interpreters of electoral opinion. In the primary contests, Broh states that after the early primaries, those that follow are "likely to use the televised poll results" when deciding both issues and choice of candidates. A table shows the number of states with presidential primaries from 1948 through 1980, and the percentage of convention delegates from those states. A graph displays the number of poll reports on evening network news during the campaigns of 1972, 1976, and 1980. Additional graphs show poll stories cumulated by position in the newscasts, and another by month of telecast. A final table indicates the number of national and state polls on the evening news during the same years as above. Thirty-two references accompany the article.

104. Crespi, Irving. "Polls as Journalism." *Public Opinion Quarterly* 44, no. 4 (Winter 1980); 462–76.

The twenty-four years of personal experience, beginning in 1956, which Crespi draws on are the basis for an examination of the close financial and institutional relationship between public opinion polls and journalism. Crespi argues that many of the strengths and weaknesses of public opinion polls are derived from this association with journalism. The author maintains that a systematic analysis is necessary in order to find effective means to modify weaknesses and build on strengths. Crespi discusses the challenges that frequent academic polling encounters, as well as the serious limitations posed by government sponsorship. Further review emphasizes the difficulties created by private political polling, along with advocacy polling. Each shortcoming is designed to highlight the necessity of media polling. The author examines a number of areas in detail, including the origins of the polling-journalism association, the role of the editor, the consideration of newsworthiness and timeliness, and objectivity. Other areas discussed are journalistic efforts at avoiding the abstract, dealing with fast-breaking news, human interest stories, and the challenges of space constraints. There are thirty-one references provided.

105.   Gollin, Albert E. "Exploring the Liaison between Polling and the Press." *Public Opinion Quarterly* 44, no. 4 (Winter 1980): 445–61.

The level of participation by the press in the endeavor of polling is one issue addressed here. Other issues discussed are the so-called pseudo-events which the media is able to create through the use of polls, the politics of public opinion, and the role that polling has come to play in contemporary society. The article begins with the role that polls played in the 1980 presidential campaign, most notably in the efforts of U.S. Congressman John Anderson. The article concludes with a call for the media to draw on the practical knowledge and theoretical foundation which public opinion research has established, and to slow down the use of polling until better prepared to utilize polling techniques. Gollin served as guest editor for this issue of *Public Opinion Quarterly* which is titled *Polls and the News Media: A Symposium.* He explains some of the subjects he sought to have addressed by the contributors to this issue, including a historical overview of the liaison between polling and the press. There are sixty-seven references, with nineteen from 1980.

106.   Gollin, Albert E. "Polling and the News Media." *Public Opinion Quarterly* 51, no. 4, pt. 2 (Winter 1987): S86–S94.

The relationship between the news media and polling are considered in sections of this article titled "The Mass Media Encounter Polls"; "New Polls: Strengths, Problems, Risks"; and "Regulating Polls and Educating the News Media." Gollin describes one of the major triumphs of the last fifty years as that of the quantitative approach. A table shows the number of polls conducted by CBS News, the *New York Times* Polls, and those conducted jointly between 1975 and 1986. It is noted that CBS pioneered in exit polling. The data is provided to show the overall trend, which has steadily expanded. One of the concerns expressed by politicians, among others, is that the media may be trying to change the public agenda or "make news" rather than report it. The issue of exit polling is discussed, with references to articles by Seymour Sudman and J. Ronald Milavsky, et al. The challenges faced by the American Association for Public Opinion Research (AAPOR) to provide standards for all of the conditions in which polling is conducted are outlined. The AAPOR's Code of Professional Ethics and Practices was not binding on AAPOR members as individuals until 1986—even though the first effort in this direction began in 1947. The article closes with the view that the improvement and continued strengthening of professional standards will continue to be as important in the next fifty years as it has been in the first half century. Twenty-two references are provided; nearly all represent literature from the 1980s.

107. Graber, Doris A. *Processing the News: How People Tame the Information Tide.* Longman Professional Studies in Political Communication and Policy. New York: Longman, 1984. 241p.

This book is based on a year-long, multiwave panel study of twenty-one residents of Evanston, Illinois. The participants were selected on the basis of different interest in and access to the news. The study is modeled on Robert Lane's work in 1957 and 1958 which led to a book titled *Political Idealogy: Why the American Common Man Believes What He Does.* Lane studied fifteen blue-collar working men in a medium-sized town in the eastern United States. It is within the context of Graber's study that public opinion polls and survey research are mentioned, with critiques of survey research and entries on polls in relation to presidential elections. There are more than twenty-two references indexed which are of interest to this annotated bibliography. While these references are scattered throughout the text, their relationship to how the news is processed continues to be an area of concern. The author provides some specific advice, calling for greater attention with regard to closed questions because they can "provide cues leading to specific schemas and hence predetermine the nature of answers." This lowers the validity of the answers. Graber calls for more extensive use of open-ended questions. Here the risk is one of generating unwarranted "don't know" answers due to the absence of the cues provided in closed questions. Word choice also receives critique. There is a fifteen-page cumulative bibliography at the end of the book.

108. Hicks, Ronald G., and Michael P. Dunne. "'Do-It-Yourself'
      Polling: A Case Study and Critique." *Newspaper Research
      Journal* 1, no. 2 (February 1980): 46–52.

The discussion presented concerns the "Insta-poll" system and two
newspapers' experiences with it. The newspapers are the Baton Rouge,
Louisiana, *Morning Advocate* and *State Times*, a morning daily and an
afternoon daily under common ownership with circulations of 65,000
and 43,000 respectively. The authors review topic selection, sample
selection, the telephone system, and experiences with and a critique of
the system. Insta-poll is a semiautomated polling system with three
telephone lines linked to three tape recorders. Two part-time employees
were hired to operate the system. The authors believe that new technology of this type should be used by newspapers as a means to engage
in "do-it-yourself" polling at the local level. Hicks and Dunne recommend that more traditional sample designs be employed, that American
Association for Public Opinion Research (AAPOR) Standards of
Disclosure be complied with, and that weekly polling not be the goal, as
this tends to reduce the value of the effort. Additionally, the authors suggest that newspapers should not provide advance publicity for the next
poll as spontaneity may be affected (along with the potential for distorting actual public opinion). Eight endnotes complete the article.

109. Ismach, Arnold H. "Polling as a News-Gathering Tool." In
      Polling and the Democratic Consensus, edited by L. John Martin,
      106–118. *Annals of the American Academy of Political and Social
      Science*, edited by Richard D. Lambert, vol. 472. Beverly Hills,
      CA: Sage Publications, 1984.

By the mid-1980s as many as five to six hundred news organizations
regularly or occasionally conducted polls and other quantitative studies.
The year 1967 is considered as the beginning of in-house newspaper
polling research. Prior to 1967, commercially produced syndicated polls
were the staple products for most newspapers. Today, in-house polling is
growing in breadth and depth, including both behavioral and attitudinal
studies covering a wide range of subjects. Philip Meyer is credited with
the introduction of this new genre. In his 1973 book called *Precision
Journalism*, he provides justifications and suggestions for establishing
such in-house polling research units. Ismach discusses the training needs
for poll researchers and explains efforts in schools of journalism, and in-
house approaches. About one-half of the article discusses various major
polling projects by the largest newspapers, along with a number of
smaller endeavors being conducted in a variety of other publishing

houses. In a section titled "A Balance Sheet," Ismach outlines eight areas of criticism of in-house newspaper polls that have been brought to trade and professional meetings. The author suggests that the continuing inclination toward interpretative and investigative journalism which is enhanced by statistical presentations is likely to ensure the continuance of in-house users' polls. There are thirty-nine footnotes.

110. Kovach, Bill. "A User's View of the Polls." *Public Opinion Quarterly* 44, no. 4 (Winter 1980): 567–71.

As Washington editor of the *New York Times*, Kovach has had extensive experience with polls—both for internal use and for public reporting. The *New York Times* is apparently making significant use of polls in their decision-making process, e.g., in deciding what stories to run and how many reporters to assign. Polls are used to "check our perception of the relative importance of the issues, to discover—through open-ended questions—issues which otherwise might have escaped our attention, and to test suspicious or tentative notions about public attitudes and behavior." Exit polls have permitted newspapers to have a story first instead of always being preceded by television. Kovach praises polls as having made journalists more knowledgeable, more understanding, and more confident in story selection and approach. He is concerned that excessive polling could "fundamentally frustrate the democratic process." Tom Winship, editor of the *Boston Globe*, is cited in response to such concerns as having pulled poll reporting from the front page in 1978. Organizations with their own polling units tend to overlook or ignore other polls, suggests Kovach. No references are included.

111. Ladd, Everett Carll. "Polling and the Press: The Clash of Institutional Imperatives." *Public Opinion Quarterly* 44, no. 4 (Winter 1980): 574–84.

Ladd raises the question as to whether opinion research improves the democratic process. Among his many examples citing the differing needs of the press and opinion research, the following is of particular note: reporting calls for relatively clear and unambiguous conclusions—opinion research tends to reveal "tentativeness, ambivalence, uncertainty, and lack of information or awareness." Interestingly, Ladd agrees with and quotes Burns W. Roper in a footnote, suggesting that adding a "wholly misleading plus-or-minus-3-percent-error statement" be dismissed. Quoting Michael Wheeler, Ladd agrees that it is an error for the press to report poll results as though "each American holds a firm opinion on every topic." The issue of the challenge of showing through polls that opinion is complex, layered, and intertwined is highlighted. Ladd is concerned with the levels of inaccuracy in press reporting of poll results. He believes that the United States should not pass laws restricting polling, but that a new organization be established to provide commentary on public opinion questions. The new organization should be separate and independent from the press and polling firms, reporting at similar times on similar issues to those discussed through the print and electronic media channels. Ten references (three from 1980) complete the research.

112.   Miller, M. Mark, and Robert Hurd. "Conformity to AAPOR Standards in Newspaper Reporting of Public Opinion Polls." *Public Opinion Quarterly* 46, no. 2 (Summer 1982): 243–49.

The American Association for Public Opinion Research (AAPOR) Standards of Disclosure require the following items to be included with survey results: sample size; sponsor name; wording—all words of all questions; sampling error—percentage error; definition of population sampled—age group, type, etc.; interview methodology—telephone, in-person, mail; timing—when conducted; and an explanation as to how a sample was created when less than the total is used. The study undertaken was conducted using the AAPOR standards to determine the degree to which newspapers responded to the public's need for methodological information about the public opinion poll results they are reading. Three newspapers were selected: the *Chicago Tribune*, the *Los Angeles Times*, and the *Atlanta Constitution*. Each was chosen because indexing was available for the period under review, and each used "public opinion polls" (or a synonym) as a heading. The author suggests that editors do not see methodological details for poll results as "automatically worthy of highly valued news space"—even though they "should generally be included...." Five of the seven references are from the 1980s.

113.   Paletz, David L., Jonathan Y. Short, Helen Baker, Barbara Cookman Campbell, Richard J. Cooper, and Rochelle M. Oeslander. "Polls in the Media: Content, Credibility, and Consequences." *Public Opinion Quarterly* 44, no. 4 (Winter 1980): 495–513.

The main question that the authors sought to address was: "What is represented as public opinion by the news media?" To answer the question, the researchers examined every poll reported in the *New York Times* and on the evening news programs of NBC and CBS during the years

1973, 1975, and 1977. The years were selected to avoid election-related polls. NBC and CBS were chosen because they were the leading networks during the study period; the *New York Times* was selected as the closest aspirant to a national newspaper with significant prestige and influence. The findings of the study suggest that the interests of sponsoring organizations of public opinion polls have a significant impact on the subject dealt with. When polls deal specifically with policy-relevant issues, many of the questions do not concern policy per se, and rarely call for responses to complex trade-off issues. Also, the selection of forced-choice answer formats limits the respondents' range of possibilities when selecting answers. In summary, the authors found that current public opinion polls are flawed to the degree that they are inappropriate guides for public policy. However, pollsters are claiming to be able to say what Americans are thinking about. A thirty-three item list of references is provided with approximately one-third from *New York Times* articles.

114. Patrick, William Lawrence. "Network Television News and Public Opinion Polls." Ph.D. diss., Ohio University, 1975. 241p.

Divided into five major sections, the dissertation includes a history of public opinion polls, the results of personal interviews with network news personnel and pollsters, purpose and methods of the research, and recommendations for the use of public opinion polls by network television news. The network news personnel included executives in the network news divisions and producers of news programs. The pollsters included are those whose national public polls are regularly used by the networks. Patrick explores the questions of how and why networks use polls and what impact they are having on programming. The level at which polls are authorized and how they fit within corporate networks are analyzed. The author hypothesizes that "poll material is utilized not only as news content but also as an input to the news decision making process." His findings indicate that polls "serve as agenda-setting devices shaping the editorial stance of some news and public affairs presentations." Another finding was that television networks rely "almost exclusively" on telephone sampling and interviewing. Three major critics of public opinion polls, the news, and their relationship are discussed. The three critics are Herbert Blumer, a sociologist; Herbert Schiller, a professor of communications; and Daniel Boorstin, a historian [and former Librarian of Congress]. Patrick suggests further study in the area of the impact of polls. The bibliography extends to six pages.

115. Rippey, John N. "Use of Polls as a Reporting Tool." *Journalism Quarterly* 57, no. 4 (Winter 1980): 642–46, 721.

A mail survey of 817 daily newspapers in the United States was conducted by Rippey in the summer of 1978. The names of the newspapers selected were taken from the *Editor & Publisher Yearbook* (1977) and represented almost half of the U.S. daily newspapers. More than one-third of the newspapers reported that they had used polls to gather information for news stories. A statement that preceded the questionnaire made it clear that systematic survey research was the subject of interest, and that only internally generated polls were of concern, rather than Gallup, Harris, or other syndicated material. The results indicate that some editors believe that poll stories have an effect on community decision making. "There is an overwhelming acceptance of the idea that polling is a valid news gathering technique," states Rippey in the discussion section of the article. An increasing number of editors believe accurate polls can be completed within sensible cost parameters. The larger the circulation of a daily newspaper, the more likely it is to have conducted survey research, and that the subjects of the survey extend beyond the scope of only election-related issues. The author has included four footnotes.

116. Roper, Burns W. "The Media and the Polls: A Boxscore." *Public Opinion* 3, no. 1A (February/March 1980): 46–49.

Journalism's impact on polling is the subject of Roper's address which was presented at a program titled "Polling on the Issues." The National Council on Public Polls and the Charles F. Kettering Foundation sponsored the program. Roper focuses on eight negative and two positive effects of journalism on polling. These are, in the order presented: (1) newspeople in the 1930s, 1940s, and 1950s viewed polling as competition and an invasion of their function and prerogatives; (2) little critical judgement or discrimination was used in what was reported; (3) newspeople are made "survey experts" after a two- to six-week course instead of using experienced veterans; (4) sampling error is overstressed without attention to other errors, such as impact of question wording; (5) newspeople are now in the position of making news instead of reporting what others said or did; (6) media pushes its own in-house polls; (7) speed is the number one criteria, making a poll older than four days not worthy of being reported; (8) complex issues are oversimplified into questions of ten to fifteen words; (9) the speed requirements of the media are forcing nonmedia polls to quicken their processing and reporting time; and (10) media acceptance of polls has led to the broad awareness and acceptance of polling. (The first eight items listed were viewed as journalism's negative effects on polling; the last two were seen as positive.) Roper would like to see question wording reported as well as conflicting or contrary poll results. No references are included.

117. Stovall, James Glen, and Jacqueline H. Solomon. "The Poll as a News Event in the 1980 Presidential Campaign." *Public Opinion Quarterly* 48, no. 3 (Fall 1984): 615–23.

The "precision journalism" movement created an environment in which the use of polls seemed very logical. Using a content analysis of fifty daily newspapers, the authors sought to examine the coverage of the 1980 presidential election campaign. A number of questions about public opinion polls as news events were examined. Stovall and Solomon found that public opinion polls are important in presidential election news coverage. There is a tendency for the "horserace" element to be focused upon—rather than using polls to examine issues. Newspaper editors were less likely to focus as much attention on a poll story as on other campaign stories. The authors suggest that past failures to predict or forecast election outcomes may have damaged the value of public opinion polls as news stories. Also described are the difficulties and confusions which editors might experience when attempting to interpret election campaign poll data. Four tables provide some of the data generated, including types of news events in 1980, polls as news events in 1980, newspaper coverage of various poll stories, and the newspaper coverage of the last two weeks of the 1980 presidential election campaign. Twenty-one references accompany the text.

118. Sudman, Seymour. "The Network Polls: A Critical Review." *Public Opinion Quarterly* 47, no. 4 (Winter 1983): 490–96.

Sudman reviews the work of CBS, NBC, and ABC polls, which are described and evaluated according to the quality of selection of topics, sample designs, sample execution, interviewers and sample cooperation, questions and questionnaire design, analysis, reporting of limitations, and archiving. In 1967 CBS began to conduct its own polling, with design and financial assistance from the *New York Times*. NBC started polling in-house in 1973 and collaborated with the Associated Press from 1978 to 1983. ABC established its own polling unit in 1981 and works with the *Washington Post*. The major reason for the establishment of these units is to provide election coverage and postelection analysis. The author confines his evaluation to traditional topics in public policy polls and refers readers to Mark R. Levy's article (Item No. 133) on exit and other election day polls. In his conclusion Sudman maintains that network polls are "reasonably competent" and that the results of the polls are a rich source of material for secondary analysis. Weaknesses of the network polls are reported to be in "areas of questionnaire testing and in analysis of results." A table lists the topics covered by the network polls which were selected for this study. One reference is supplied.

119.   Von Hoffman, Nicholas. "Public Opinion Polls: Newspapers Making Their Own News?" *Public Opinion Quarterly* 44, no. 4 (Winter 1980): 572–73.

Nicholas Von Hoffman writes a syndicated column for King Features. In this article he raises a question concerning "checkbook journalism." Newspapers and the electronic media are essentially purchasing the "right to cover an event" when they buy Gallup, Harris, or other polls. The author's argument is that starting around 1975, major newspaper and television networks began conducting and commissioning their own polls, thus creating news "events" at will. As Von Hoffman suggests, this gives the corporations that operate news entities "the power to make every day election day." Blending theater with politics and government has produced a sometimes entertaining "soap opera," but Von Hoffman wonders about the appropriateness of this news event generating business. He suggests that politicians should treat poll results as "harmless hullabaloo," as he maintains the population at large has learned to do. No references are included.

120.   Wheeler, Michael. "Reining in Horserace Journalism" *Public Opinion* 3, no. 1A (February/March 1980): 41–45.

The role of newspapers and television poll reporting is discussed from a critical standpoint, with a number of suggestions provided. The article begins by citing the limitations of space and time the media provides to polls. Although press releases are usually 750 words, they may be reduced to a few paragraphs by the media. Other constraints include economic factors—few can afford their own polling organizations—and the media's need for drama. Wheeler cites six of what he calls the "worst sins": (1) reporting poll results as though firm opinions were held on every topic; (2) failure to distinguish between voter and public opinion; (3) the dubious practice of asking questions with "if the election were held today" phrases; (4) journalists' failure to clarify in political campaigns candidates that are most likely to gain support as time goes on; (5) lack of sufficient issue polling by the press; and (6) the failure to acknowledge varying intensities of opinion. The author observes that polling organizations which disapprove of press treatment can withdraw from providing poll results to the offending source, but even though there is precedent for it, the practice is rare. The interpretation of polling data is something Wheeler believes polling organizations should be doing—Gallup takes the opposite view. The author seems to suggest that a standard for analysis should be developed, but that enforcement would be difficult. There are four footnotes included.

6.4 EDUCATION

121. Fuqua, Dale R., Bruce W. Hartman, and Darine F. Brown. "Survey Research in Higher Education." *Research in Higher Education: Journal of the Association for Institutional Research* 17, no. 1 (1982): 69–80.
Guidelines for selecting and applying incentives to increase survey response were determined through a reanalysis of educational survey research results. In summary, the findings are: (1) follow-ups increase response rates; (2) preliminary contact by postcard, letter or telephone call produces higher return rates; (3) personalizing the survey request offers no advantage; (4) third class postage is as effective as first class; (5) a monetary incentive up to 25 cents generates higher response rates; and (6) white or the least expensive color paper is recommended. The studies reanalyzed were drawn from nine professional journals, for a total of thirty-nine appropriate studies dealing with the mail survey as the data collection tool. The authors comment that textbooks in educational research provide little or no guidance in the area of survey research methodology. Three tables indicate journals and theses utilizing the survey method and incentive clusters found in the various studies reviewed. Forty-two pre-1980 references are included.

122. Walker, John E. "Local Opinion Polling for Educators: The Benefits of Polls and How to Conduct Them." *Education Digest* 53, no. 4 (December 1987): 26–29. Condensed from the *Journal of Educational Public Relations* 9 (First Quarter, 1987): 10–14.
The purpose of this article is to briefly highlight how to modify a "Gallup-type" poll for use in a local school environment. The author

offers specific suggestions as to modifications which should be completed, and enumerates another eight steps to pursue for obtaining useful poll results. These include advice on which polling method to use; the suggested population and size for telephone polls; who to use as interviewers; interview preparation; how to generate the names of the appropriate poll population; response processing; report writing; and the issue of the possible annual occurrence of the poll. Several educational organizations are cited which can serve as poll information resources. No references are included.

6.5 ADDITIONAL STUDIES

123. Dalbey, Gordon. "Of Pollsters and Prophets." *Christian Century* 101, no. 28 (26 September 1984): 862–63.

Dalbey's article is a rebuttal to a newspaper column which appeared in the *Los Angeles Times* by John Dart, and was titled "US Religious Leaders Depend on Poll Data." The Dart article, according to Dalbey, referred to "more than 17,000 religious leaders [that] receive Gallup's monthly newsletter." The *Christian Century* article refers to "the desperate effort to meld secular and religious 'information systems.'" The crux of the argument presented by Dalbey is that Christians should form their positions based on the "Word of God" and that there is no place for surveying "what others want" and that "gathering data to support your position" is misplaced and inappropriate. No references are provided.

124. McKillip, Jack. "Surveying Needs." Chap. 6 in *Need Analysis: Tools for the Human Services and Education*, 70–85. Applied Social Research Methods Series, edited by Leonard Bickman, vol. 10. Newbury Park, CA: Sage Publications, 1987.

As a means of determining the needs of subgroups of the selected population, surveying has shown itself to be a popular approach. The chapter discusses the choice of techniques available, question format, the use and coding of open-ended questions, and an array of procedures associated with different types of surveys. The chapter does not consider large sample "technical" surveys which the author maintains require expert assistance. Specifically reviewed are training, client, key information, and citizen surveys. A brief consideration of the strengths and weaknesses of surveys concludes the chapter. The volume includes cumulative chapter references and a four-page index.

125. Schmidt, Casper. "The Use of the Gallup Poll as a Psychohistorical Tool." *Journal of Psychohistory* 10, no 2 (Fall 1982): 141–62.

Schmidt considers the value of the Gallup Poll as a psychohistorical tool. He views the following items as drawbacks: sampling error; results only indicate the conscious part of the opinion process; imperfect methodology; and the short-sightedness experienced by all participants within a group, or, to use Schmidt's language, the "inescapable psychological blindness...." Schmidt sees polls as part of the process of working toward "group solidarity." He believes that polls are "most profitably used as raw data." The interpretations proposed by pollsters are part of the poll results, and Schmidt maintains that these require analysis as much as do the statistical findings. In reviewing the polling literature, the author found three areas in which pro and con arguments exist. These are: (1) polls do not measure anything—at least nothing of consequence; (2) statistical problems are such that the results should be dismissed; and (3) public opinion is manipulated by those in public relations, and business and political leaders. Schmidt writes in response to the above three points of view that polls usually measure what they set out to, that methodology exists to create valid statistics, and, finally, that the "paranoid-conspiracy" theory may be only partially correct, i.e., polls can be manipulated—but the opinion remains true. Twenty-nine endnotes are included in the article.

126. "Unions Are Turning to Polls to Read the Rank and File: Members Answer Surveys on Everything from Pension Plans to Trade Deficits." *Business Week*, no. 2865 (22 October 1984): 66, 70.

The article has no byline and is under the column subject heading of "Labor." The basic reason labor seems to be turning to polls is to address the frequent criticism that union leadership does not know what the rank and file membership really wants. Polls are used to evaluate what new services should be offered by the unions to their membership. By conducting more broadly based polls of nonunion members, unions are learning more effective positions to take, thus becoming "more capable adversaries." Larger unions are hiring in-house pollsters; others are using less well-known polling organizations, thereby cutting the fees by as much as 50 percent or more. No references are included.

7. Exit Polling and Election Projection

127. Abrams, Floyd. "Press Practices, Polling Restrictions, Public Opinion and First Amendment Guarantees." *Public Opinion Quarterly* 49, no. 1 (Spring 1985): 15–18.

This short article focuses on the issue of exit polling, specifically the law in the state of Washington which makes it a misdemeanor level criminal offense to conduct an exit poll within three hundred feet of the voting station in any direction. Abrams, a lawyer with a New York firm who was cocounsel in the Pentagon papers case in the early 1970s, specializes in First Amendment cases. Representing the *New York Times*, the Everett *Herald* (which is owned by the Washington Post Company), and broadcasters, Abrams has filed suit in federal court in the state of Washington seeking to stop the interference with the collection of exit polling data. Abrams argues that on strictly legal grounds, that is constitutional grounds, the action by the state of Washington (and other locations which have adopted similar measures) is constitutional. He seems to suggest, however, that the issue is one of policy rather than law (i.e., broadcasters choosing for reasons of ethical policy to conduct business in certain ways, rather than being mandated by law to desist from certain practices). No references are included.

128. Busch, Ronald J., and Joel A. Lieske. "Does Time of Voting Affect Exit Poll Results?" *Public Opinion Quarterly* 49, no. 1 (Spring 1985): 94–104.

The explanations provided for pursuing this topic include the need to better understand when different groups of people vote, to improve forecasting capabilities, and to better understand election day voting constraints. The tool used to research these needs was the exit poll. The critical question is whether or not exit pollsters must poll all day or will a morning or afternoon suffice to yield adequate data. Busch and Lieske maintain that day-long interviewing is necessary to avoid sampling bias, thereby producing a nonrepresentative cross section of the voting electorate. The employment status of the voter significantly affects when s/he votes. Retirees, the unemployed, and professionals are the groups most likely to differ in their voting patterns from those who are job-centered. They are also the least affected by constraints as to when they can vote. The authors stress that since different groups vote at different times, a particular issue or candidate might receive varying responses from these groups, and therefore the morning or afternoon only exit poll might miss a substantial change in the vote outcome. The text includes three tables. The twelve references include five from the 1980s.

129.   Calmes, Jacqueline. "Method Sought to Restrict Broadcast Vote Predictions: Exit Polls Targeted." *Congressional Quarterly Weekly Report* 42, no. 10 (10 March 1984): 565–66.

The various congressional means which have been proposed to hinder, reduce, or eliminate exit polling are explored. National television net-works—ABC, CBS, and NBC are cited—use election-day polling to predict results. Critics charge that this practice makes voters feel that their votes do not seem to matter, and social scientists suggest that voter turnout drops as a result. First Amendment rights protecting the press probably prohibit any legal restriction on the press, leaving voluntary means as the other possible option. However, some states are using election codes to limit access to voters by electronic media. The networks, through exit polls, are able to interview over many hours, and are able to project election results within a number of hours—and long before the polls close according to Rep. Timothy E. Wirth, D-Colo. Washington and Wyoming passed laws in 1983 that specifically ban exit polling within three hundred feet of the polls. The networks, along with the *New York Times* and the Washington Post Company's *Everett* (Wash.) *Daily Herald*, are challenging the Washington law as a violation of the First Amendment protection of freedom of the press. No references are included.

130.   Epstein, Laurily K., and Gerald Strom. "Election Night Projections and West Coast Turnout." *American Politics Quarterly* 9, no. 4 (October 1981): 479–91.

It may be suggested that this article, by Epstein from the NBC Election Unit and Strom from the University of Illinois at Chicago Circle, was written at least partially to address the criticism NBC received in 1980 for making an early presidential projection, which was followed by the early concession by President Carter. The main question is: Does an early projection inhibit Western state citizens from voting (thereby hurting local politicians and issues which therefore go unaddressed by some of the voters)? The findings of the authors are that the decision to vote is not affected by information received on election day, and that "declines in participation generally help incumbent members of Congress." The latter is in reference to Representatives James Corman (California) and Al Ullman (Oregon) who believed that their defeats were the product of the early presidential projection in 1980. The authors cite the fact that presidential voting has been declining since 1960. Those most likely to vote are older people, suburban residents, high earners, the well educated, and those with "prestigious" occupations. Epstein and Strom provide some possible reasons for voter decline in their discussion section. Included are: (1) decline of the political party—rise of professional campaign workers; (2) information by television news—rather than from neighborhood precinct; and (3) the separating of local and state elections from the presidential election in many areas—forcing people to vote more frequently or to choose the most salient election in which to participate. Four of the nine references are from the 1980s.

131. Epstein, Laurily, and Gerald Strom. "Survey Research and Election Night Projections." *Public Opinion* 7, no. 1 (February/March 1984): 48–50.

About sixty percent of the article focuses on the work of John Jackson, the principal investigator of a 1981 survey conducted by the Survey Research Center (SRC) at the University of Michigan. Two national election samples were reinterviewed to determine the effects of early projections on voting behavior. In the 1980 election, Jackson believes voter turnout was reduced by 6 to 12 percent. Epstein and Strom's reevaluation using the same data suggested the figure to be closer to 0.2 percent. In 1984 Epstein was a polling consultant to NBC News; Strom was associate professor of political science at the University of Illinois at Chicago [Circle]. The authors believe that survey research cannot adequately address the question of measuring the magnitude of media effects. The article contains eight footnotes.

132. Jackson, John E. "Election Night Reporting and Voter Turnout." *American Journal of Political Science* 27, no. 4 (November 1983): 615–35.

This article is based on the 1980 Presidential Election Study which determined the time of day people voted, whether they heard election night news, and at what hour that news was heard. Jackson shows that many people heard projections of the presidential election outcome prior to the closing of local polls. An analysis of the data demonstrates that hearing the projection news decreased the likelihood of voting among those who had not yet cast their ballots, and that this tendency was greater among Republicans than Democrats. Interestingly, Republicans are more likely to vote late on election day. Broadly speaking, Jackson reports that the determination to vote is based on the individual's "perception of the value of their vote in determining the election's outcome." Also discussed are the different types of election outcomes: those which appear lopsided, those which are close, and those in which prior expectations differ from reported projections. Apparently, each case produces somewhat differing responses and therefore impact varyingly on voting behavior. Analysis suggests that lopsided contests appear to be only modestly affected by confirming election day projections. Close elections will probably not generate sufficiently early projections to alter voting behavior, and where a "one-sided election" is projected which turns into a close contest, some may be encouraged to vote who might not have otherwise. Six references (all from the 1980s) are included.

133.   Levy, Mark R. "The Methodology and Performance of Election Day Polls." *Public Opinion Quarterly* 47, no. 1 (Spring 1983): 54–67.

The article considers perhaps the most controversial type of political polling, i.e., the exit or election day poll. Methodological details are covered, and the performance of such survey research approaches is considered. The 1980 presidential election is the basis for this study—an election in which eighty-three million Americans voted, with thirty-six thousand voters responding to three different election day surveys in voting districts across the country. The first known exit poll by the "major media" was in 1967. Prior to this approach, preelection surveys from selected precincts were relied upon. Some of the difficulties encountered were problems with "screening" to identify likely voters and late shifts in voter behavior potentially missed by publication declines for the survey data. Levy considers the work of four major polls: ABC, CBS, NBC, and the *Los Angeles Times*. Discussions focus on sample design, questionnaires, field work, data manipulation, the use of exit polls, and poll performance. Levy states that the exit polls examined in his article were conducted with a "degree of meticulousness which compares favorably to the highest standards of commercial and academic research." He is quick to caution that some election day polls produce a quality of field work which "remains a continuing source of concern." Twelve references (three from the 1980s) complete the research.

134. Salant, Richard. "Projections and Exit Polls." *Public Opinion Quarterly* 49, no. 1 (Spring 1985): 9–15.

According to Salant, the fundamental issue is the extent to which professional journalists allow public opinion polls and majority votes control what they report and what they do not report. Salant's basic credo is that journalists must report facts when they are known. He is against exit polling for the purposes of projecting a winner because of concerns of the dangers of people lying, not responding, or perhaps even the potential for "dirty tricks," i.e., manipulation. The value of exit polling in ascertaining demographics as well as perhaps determining the mandate of an election are suggested. Projections by the networks began at CBS during election night in 1962. Salant suggests that the real debate about projections in a presidential election year concerns the effect on nonpresidential candidates—with the no-show effect possibly hurting candidates in California, Oregon, Washington, Alaska, and Hawaii. (The author discounts this point of view and suggests that those who do not vote "foolishly disenfranchise themselves.") Salant cites the journalists' imperative to report what s/he knows, except in cases of true national security or in an individual's right to privacy—stating again that if a news organization has the data, that data should be made public (with the proviso of waiting for state polls in the region under consideration to close). This article is part of a section titled "Early Calls of Election Results and Exit Polls: Pros, Cons, and Constitutional Considerations" (pages 1–18). No references are included.

135. Sudman, Seymour. "Do Exit Polls Influence Voting Behavior?" *Public Opinion Quarterly* 50, no. 3 (Fall 1986): 331–39.

The reason exit polls have become such an issue is explained by Sudman in the first paragraph: data is collected, analyzed, and the results are discussed on national television while the election is still in progress. The author summarizes studies which have examined the relationship between exit polls and voting behavior. Two types of studies are reviewed—the macro approach compares total voter turnout in different areas or elections, while the micro approach uses surveys of individual voters and nonvoters and ascertains from the respondents whether or not they viewed the election evening news. The data indicates that "there is a possibility of a small decrease ranging from 1 to 5 percent in total vote in congressional districts where polls close significantly later than 8 PM

EST in those elections where the exit polls suggest a clear winner when previously the race had been considered close." Sudman explains that this is the best level of accuracy now possible. The major criticism of existing micro-level studies is the small sample size used, thus leading to unstable results. Macro data can be hampered by the impact of the following: the factor of the weather (not controlled for in existing studies); the candidates involved influence turnout; and the redistricting of congressional districts hindering long-term analysis. The author includes eleven references, eight from the 1980s.

136. Tannenbaum, Percy H., and Leslie J. Kostrich, with assistance from Eric R.A.N. Smith, and Michael Berg. "The Exit Poll Alternatives." Chap. 5 in *Turned-On TV/Turned-Off Voters: Policy Options for Election Projections*, 133–55. People and Communication, vol. 15. Beverly Hills, CA: Sage Publications, 1983.

The book deals with the issue of media election projections which are made prior to the closing of voting stations in certain parts of the country. The project grew out of the 1980 presidential campaign in which President Carter conceded to Ronald Reagan early in the evening (9:50 P.M.) with voters in some Western states, Hawaii, and Alaska still in line at polling stations. Chapter 5 is of particular interest in that it addresses exit poll alternatives. The issue of the legality thereof is briefly discussed, along with a number of possible solutions. The idea of a contact prohibition near voting sites is discussed from the point of view of effectiveness, the cost of implementation, and the political and legal aspects of the likelihood of such an approach. Two types of boycott of exit polls are covered—a government-sponsored approach, and a nonlegislated approach. The author again covers the costs, effectiveness, and likelihood of these methods. Chapter 7 briefly deals with state-level action in response to exit polls (pages 199–201). The book does not have an index. There are notes at the end of each chapter, with cumulative references at the end of the volume.

137. U.S. Congress. House. Task Force on Elections of the House Committee on Administration, Subcommittee on Telecommunications, Consumer Protection, and Finance of the Committee on Energy and Commerce. *Election Day Practices and Election Projections: Hearings.* 97th Cong., 1st and 2d sess., 1982. Washington, DC: U.S. Government Printing Office, 1982. 177p.

The testimony of Mitch Farris of Atkinson-Farris Communications and John E. Jackson, a professor with the Center for Political Studies (CPS),

Institute for Social Research (ISR), at the University of Michigan, speaks directly to the issue of exit polling. The Farris testimony appears on pages 94 through 108, with an accompanying statement on pages 108 through 110. The Jackson testimony appears on pages 110 through 117 with an accompanying statement on pages 117 through 122. Atkinson-Farris Communications is a research and consulting firm whose clients include major broadcast organizations. Mr. Farris, in his testimony before the House Task Force on Elections, describes the accuracy of the science of exit polling as "razor-sharp." Farris calls for self-regulation of the polling industry, clearly without the intervention of congressional legislation. Professor Jackson discusses findings which indicate "that people's likelihood of voting is related to their perception of the value of their vote in determining the election's outcome. Events that alter that perceived value alter turnout." In his prepared statement Jackson writes about early projections stating, "Overall turnout will be substantially reduced in an election where new and unexpected information that one candidate has an early and decisive lead in the electoral college is reported to the public before the polls close." No references are included.

138.　Wolfinger, Raymond, and Peter Linquiti. "Tuning In and Turning Out." *Public Opinion* 4, no. 1 (February/March 1981): 56–60.
In 1964, 1972, and 1980 there were presidential election landslides. The issue is whether television networks should pronounce the winner of the presidential election before the polls close in all the states. The authors examine each of the many issues which have been raised on the topic, and conclude that unless all other factors which might influence voter turnout are also addressed, there is certainly no logical reason to prevent the media from continuing its work. The 1972 and 1974 elections receive special analysis. A popular solution discussed is that of closing all polls at the same time all over the country. The issue of the changing time zones is covered as well as a proposal to have election day fall on a Sunday. Exit polling is mentioned, along with attempts by various states to limit the practice by restricting how close to the voting station exit polls can be conducted. As the authors note, if exit polling is severely hampered, television networks could always employ telephone interviewing, although the results might be subject to considerable error caused by those who claimed they voted but in fact did not. The article includes three tables, a Brian Basset cartoon, and thirteen endnotes.

8. Pollsters

139. Bonafede, Dom. "Campaign Pollsters—Candidates Won't Leave Home without Them." *National Journal* 16, no. 21 (26 May 1984): 1042–46.

The campaigns of the 1984 presidential candidates are covered. Each candidate and his pollster is reviewed. All the candidates have an in-house pollster with the notable exception of Jesse Jackson. The polls are used to measure voter attitudes, determine national issues, contribute to campaign strategy, evaluate the candidate's relative strengths within particular constituencies, and determine the allocation of campaign resources. The polls also help decide where a candidate will go and how frequently return trips will be made. Pollsters Dotty Lynch, Richard B. Wirthlin, Peter D. Hart, William R. Hamilton, Robert M. Teeter, and Patrick H. Caddell contribute thoughts about polling and the roles they have played for their respective candidates. Reference is made to the role the media plays in both conducting its own polls and in the reporting of the findings of the polls of others. Significantly, Wirthlin observes that a "rise in the polls can get a candidate more funds and more media coverage, particularly during the primaries." The categories of polling organizations are identified: national public opinion and market researchers, political pollsters, and media pollsters. No references are included.

140. Dye, Thomas R., and L. Harmon Zeigler. *American Politics in the Media Age.* Monterey, CA: Brooks/Cole Publishing Company, 1983. 476p.

The Dye and Zeigler book is designed as an introduction to American government with a "special focus on the political role of the news media." Two short sections review a number of the elements of polling. In the first section titled "Public Opinion and the Pollsters" (pages 155–57), Dye and Zeigler focus on the "dismal record in predicting election outcomes" and proceed to cite a number of possible explanations. In the second section titled "Image Makers and Pollsters as Policy Advisors" (pages 219–20), the Reagan and Carter presidential race of 1980 is discussed—specifically comparing Richard Wirthlin and Peter Dailey for Reagan with Patrick Caddell and Gerald Rafshoon for Carter.

141. Goldhaber, Gerald M. "A Pollsters' Sampler." *Public Opinion* 7, no. 3 (June/July 1984): 47–50, 53.

Considered are the views of seven leading practitioners, from both public and private polling organizations, on a number of issues such as sample size of polls, voter turnout estimates, and the pollster as data-gatherer or strategist. The pollsters consulted are Patrick Caddell, Peter Hart, Robert Teeter, Richard Wirthlin, George Gallup, Albert Cantril, and Charles Roll. The author of this article was then chairman of the Department of Communication at the State University of New York at Buffalo. Each respondent answered a number of questions, e.g.: (1) What sample size do they use for most of their polls? (2) How do they deal with the problem of estimating voter turnout? and (3) Should the pollster be just a data-gatherer or also a strategist? There were additional subquestions within each major category. No references are included.

142. Ladd, Everett C., and G. Donald Ferree. "Were the Pollsters Really Wrong?" *Public Opinion* 3, no. 6 (December/January 1981): 13–20.

The "wrong" in the title refers to the 1980 presidential election and the preponderance of the mistaken "calling" of the election by the major polls. The article is based on the following four propositions: (1) "Election polling in 1980 did not present any special problems of 'approximation'"; (2) "The record of the polls in 'calling' the 1980 presidential election was basically an 'average' one"; (3) "There are new challenges to election polling in the 'Age of Dealignment'"; and (4) "Too much emphasis is placed on election polling." Also included is a summary of polling methodology from four major national polling organizations, namely, CBS/*New York Times*, Gallup, ABC/Harris, and NBC/AP. Another page provides survey questions from each of the above organizations, along with data in terms of percentages for each of the three candidates (Reagan, Carter, and Anderson). Ten endnotes are provided.

143. Lanouette, William J. "Candidates Turn to Their Pollsters for Advice on Campaign Strategy." *National Journal* 12, no. 42 (18 October 1980): 1741–43.

The author discusses the role of the pollster in presidential campaigns, comparing and contrasting the pollsters involved with the major 1980 presidential candidates. Carter used the polling services of Patrick H. Caddell; Reagan's pollster in 1980 was Richard B. Wirthlin; and Anderson had two pollsters—Mark Penn and Douglas E. Schoen. The relative importance attached to polls and thereby the pollster in each organization was somewhat different. Caddell's work was used to shape the themes of the campaign and to guide the manner in which campaign funds were spent. Wirthlin updates polling data daily—preferably by 9 A.M.—and then spends the remainder of the day making suggestions to, and answering questions from, the campaign staff. Due to a lack of local and state organization, Anderson's pollster, Mark Penn, relies on state-wide public polls such as the California Poll, and is cautious about the credibility of national polls, citing the fact that the election is a collection of simultaneous statewide races. No references are included.

144. Sabato, Larry J. "The Pols and the Polls." Chap. 2 in *The Rise of Political Consultants: New Ways of Winning Elections*, 68–110. New York: Basic Books, 1981.

This book is divided into two parts: "Political Consultants and Their Wares" and "Democracy and the New Campaign Technology." Chapter 2 of Part 1 is of most relevance to this annotated bibliography. Sabato takes a critical look at polls and pollsters, examining roots, roles, and practices. Potential sources of error are discussed concluding with the view that polls are "far less 'scientific' and reliable than is commonly believed." The author discusses the variety and costs of surveys. A ten-page essay relates the works of a wide range of pollsters who have contributed their efforts in campaigns for those seeking the presidency. Polling is described by Richard Wirthlin, Reagan's chief pollster, as "the science of ABC—almost being certain." The remainder of the chapter deals with "Mines and Mistakes: Sources of Error in Polls." Issues addressed are prejudice and question bias; construction, analysis, and interpretation; and problems with interviewers and respondents. Approximately 11 percent of what reviewer David Broder described as a potential "standard reference" book in the area of political consultants is devoted to polls and pollsters. Other major areas covered include media consultants, direct mail, and political consultants, parties, and PACs. Chapter 2 has 107 endnotes.

9. Administration and Design

9.1 ADMINISTRATION

145. Prewitt, Kenneth. "Management of Survey Organizations." Chap.
     4 in *Handbook of Survey Research*, edited by Peter H. Rossi,
     James D. Wright, and Andy B. Anderson, 123–44. Quantitative
     Studies in Social Relations, consulting editor Peter H. Rossi. New
     York: Academic Press, 1983.

The management and goals of survey research organizations are
examined by the former director of the National Opinion Research
Center (NORC). Prewitt was NORC director from 1976 through
September 1979. In reviewing goals, the author discusses prestige, sur-
vival, and growth of survey research organizations. He suggests that
larger organizations are "more vulnerable" to surges and declines in the
volume of business which are caused by the "nature of the funding world
[and] are not under the control of the organization." Prewitt considers the
"management issue" by examining the managerial task and then
reviewing the nature of the various employee groups which help achieve
the management goals. The first group considered is the field staff, followed by the technical staff, the senior professional staff, and finally, the
senior management. In his "Personal Postscript" the idea to which
Prewitt frequently returns is the complexity of the modern environment.
He views modern empirical science and in-depth analytical demands
placed by society as the driving forces which will transform survey
research management in the future. Eight pre-1980 references are provided.

9.2 DESIGN

146.   Labaw, Patricia J. *Advanced Questionnaire Design*. Cambridge, MA: Abt Books, 1981. 183p.

Labaw prefaces the book with the observation that it is an "extension and expansion of issues covered in Stanley Payne's *The Art of Asking Questions* [1951]." While Payne concentrates on the wording of single questions, Labaw focuses more on overall questionnaire design. Question wording is covered by Labaw in a seven-page chapter. The thirty-year span between the publication of the Payne and Labaw volumes has seen a marked increase in knowledge in the areas of psychology, communication studies, and questionnaire research. It follows that this volume reflects these changes with the inclusion of chapters which deal with consciousness, the role of behavior, limitations of personality theory, and routing to break up mind sets and avoid position effect. There are chapters dealing with hypotheses and how to develop them, questionnaire structure, question formulation, and a sample questionnaire. The work has been written by a general practitioner of survey research who is in business with Michael A. Rappeport, whose works are cited four times in the Labaw bibliography. He is the cocopyright holder with Labaw of *Advanced Questionnaire Design*.

147.   Sudman, Seymour, and Norman M. Bradburn. *Asking Questions: A Practical Guide to Questionnaire Design*. Jossey–Bass Series in Social and Behavioral Sciences. 1st ed. San Francisco, CA: Jossey-Bass Publishers, 1982. 397p.

As the title indicates, this is a resource book advising readers how to order, format, and design questionnaires from the initial stages to the final product. Sudman is a former president of the American Association for Public Opinion Research (AAPOR); Bradburn is the director of the National Opinion Research Center (NORC). The book is dedicated to Stanley Payne whose work *The Art of Asking Questions* (1951) is the perennially referenced tool in this area. Chapter 1 explains why wording of questions is important and provides examples. It also sets the stage for the rest of the work with a definition of the survey interview. Chapters 2 through 7 cover the major issues in constructing scales or writing individual questions with areas such as the following: threatening and nonthreatening questions, measuring knowledge, formulating questions, and recording responses. The remaining four chapters examine the order of the questionnaire, the format to use, types of mail and telephone surveys, and supplies a checklist of what to do from start to finish. Each chapter closes with a short additional reading section. The book is designed to be both a textbook and a reference manual. A four-part "Resource" section contains a fifteen-page glossary, two sample questionnaires, and a sample survey. A seven-page list of references precedes the eleven-plus pages of indexing.

9.3 INSTRUMENT LENGTH

148. Herzog, A. Regula, and Jerald G. Bachman. "Effects of Questionnaire Length on Response Quality." *Public Opinion Quarterly* 45, no. 4 (Winter 1981): 549–59.

The study reported was designed to examine whether survey length impacts respondents in negative ways, such as terminating the interview, giving uniform answers, or answering differently from earlier in a survey. The study data shows that people do tend to answer the last parts of long surveys in "stereotypical ways" as indicated by "straight-line or almost-straight-line responding." Stated differently, respondents begin to answer in a uniform manner as a means of coping with a situation that has overtaxed their motivation levels. Herzog and Bachman state that even at the end of a two-hour-plus questionnaire some item sets did not conform to the straight-line answering approach, and even those item sets that may be so affected may not influence the overall bias in correlation because of the restriction of the problem to essentially the same question sets. One way to counter this challenge when long questionnaires are administered is to divide the questions into parts and then alternate the subset question order. This approach would permit checking for, and controlling of, any distortions that might occur due to late placement in the questionnaire. Ten references are listed, one of which is dated 1980.

149.   Layne, Ben H., and Dennis N. Thompson. "Questionnaire Page
        Length and Return Rate." *Journal of Social Psychology* 113, no. 2
        (April 1981): 291–92.
The research undertaken was to determine whether people react to the
number of items asked in a questionnaire or whether they react to the
number of pages. The response rate was tested when the page length was
varied while keeping the item number the same. Thirty items were placed
on one page, and for another group, the items were spread over three
pages. A follow-up letter was employed for half of each of the above
categories. Four hundred questionnaires were mailed, with 111 returned
for a 27.75 percent return rate. The data suggests that there is no
statistically significant difference between the return rates of the long or
short lengths, with or without the follow-up letter. The authors conclude
that short questionnaires will not increase response rates, but that follow-
up letters might help to increase them. No references are included.

9.4 INCENTIVES

150.   Hubbard, Raymond, and Eldon L. Little. "Promised Contributions
        to Charity and Mail Survey Responses: Replication with
        Extension." *Public Opinion Quarterly* 52, no. 2 (Summer 1988):
        223–30.
Promises of charitable contributions by the survey sponsor did not
achieve much in the way of increasing returns and may even have the
opposite effect. By contrast, offering a cash prize seems to stimulate
response. The authors reason that if the prize is viewed as sufficiently
worthy, a larger degree of cooperation in responses will be forthcoming.
In conclusion, Hubbard and Little advise that the study was not identical
to two prior studies on the same subject in two ways: the approach to
listing the charities was different, and there was commercial content in
the survey, perhaps influencing the respondents' altruistic thoughts.
There are sixteen references as well as a table showing response rates by
type of incentive.

151. Mizes, J. Scott, E. Louis Fleece, and Cindy Roos. "Incentives for Increasing Return Rates: Magnitude Levels, Response Bias, and [sic] Format." *Public Opinion Quarterly* 48, no. 4 (Winter 1984): 794–800.

Previous studies had focused on the effects incentives of $1 or less. This study compared the effects of $5 and $1 incentives on mail return rate. The $5 and $1 monetary incentive achieved an increased return rate of 21.1 percent. Another approach researched was the "Answer Check" method, which has the survey answer blanks printed on the reverse side of the check. This means the questionnaire responses travel through the Federal Reserve System and become canceled checks. This latter approach increased return rates by 19.2 percent on $5 answer checks. The authors summarize their findings as follows: (1) response rates are significantly increased by financial incentives; (2) increasing the dollar incentive reaches a point of diminishing return which may still be a considerable distance from the ideal 100 percent return rate; (3) biased results do not appear to be a factor resulting from incentives; and (4) an Answer Check does not help, and in fact may reduce the response rate. A table shows the varying options tried by the researchers, along with the question and response rates. Nine references are provided, three from the 1980s.

9.5 COMPUTERS

152. Allen, D.F. "Computers Versus Scanners: An Experiment in Nontraditional Forms of Survey Administration." *Journal of College Student Personnel* 28, no. 3 (May 1987): 266–73.

The administration of a computer survey was compared with that of a machine-readable paper survey. The paper survey was an optically scanned questionnaire. The author found that the computer respondents provided a wider array of responses, responded at a lower rate, and were more positive about the survey instrument than were the noncomputer respondents. The computer option provided greater ease in programming and processing of the data. Allen maintains that the administrative gains achieved through the computer survey exceed the losses with respect to the lower response rate. A sample of 249 sophomores was used in the experiment, with 125 students in the computer group and 124 students in the scanner group. The article contains a table of the means and standard deviations found for each group charted for each of the twelve questions asked. There are nine references, four from the 1980s.

153.   Karweit, Nancy, and Edmund D. Meyers, Jr. "Computers in Survey Research." Chap. 11 in *Handbook of Survey Research*, edited by Peter H. Rossi, James D. Wright, and Andy B. Anderson, 379–414. Quantitative Studies in Social Relations, consulting editor Peter H. Rossi. New York: Academic Press, 1983.

The authors place importance on four themes, namely: (1) the need to differentiate the roles played by the investigators and the computing staff; (2) the need for consultation with computing staff; (3) the importance of record keeping, including the written documentation of decisions taken during the research process; and (4) the encouragement of viewing computers as tools for activities beyond statistical analysis of data. Karweit and Meyers suggest that previous treatments of the subject have narrowly focused on the statistical processing of computers. To provide a different approach, the authors begin with the first steps of a survey, namely the instrument design, and work progressively through to the writing of the final report indicating how computing can be employed at each step of the process. These various steps include sampling, field monitoring, coding and editing, data capture, data cleaning, scale-index construction, database organization, data retrieval, statistical analysis, and documentation. Three figures are used and a number of tables appear throughout the chapter. Twenty-nine references are drawn primarily from the 1970s.

10. Measurement and Scaling

10.1 MEASUREMENT

154. Alwin, Duane F., and Jon A. Krosnick. "The Measurement of Values in Surveys: A Comparison of Ratings and Rankings." *Public Opinion Quarterly* 49, no. 4 (Winter 1985): 535–52.

The literature dealing with value measurement through ratings and rankings is reviewed at the beginning of the article. The experimental study that follows compares the two approaches using a split-ballot measuring the parental orientations toward children as part of the 1980 General Social Survey (GSS). The authors observe that the data indicates that although ranking methods have been the approach of choice in the past, rating techniques are shown to be as effective. Alwin and Krosnick hesitate to make generalizable recommendations, citing the need to select a measurement approach best suited to the particular study under consideration. The comparison of ratings and rankings measurement approaches concentrates on the ordering of aggregate value preferences and the measuring of individual differences in latent value preferences. The two methods are shown to be similar in regard to ordering the aggregate preferences of the sample. The differences lie with the latent variable structure underlying the measures. Five tables supplement the text, along with fifty-eight references (eleven from the 1980s).

155. Anderson, Andy B., Alexander Basilevsky, and Derek P.J. Hum. "Measurement: Theory and Techniques." Chap. 7 in *Handbook of Survey Research*, edited by Peter H. Rossi, James D. Wright, and Andy B. Anderson, 231–87. Quantitative Studies in Social Relations, consulting editor Peter H. Rossi. New York: Academic Press, 1983.

The chapter deals with the measurement of attitudes, opinions, and related matters—the "perplexing" concepts of social science which "prove troublesome" when applied to the task of measurement. The authors identify four areas in measurement: (1) the philosophical, or those belonging to epistemology and the philosophy of science; (2) the classical measurement theory, found mostly in the psychometric literature, and focused upon reliability and validity; (3) the theory of measurement, concerned with developing formal models of measurement by those working in the area of mathematical psychology; and (4) the development of "specific techniques for constructing measurements, that is, methods for obtaining measurements of unobserved variables from responses to questions." The next section of the chapter discusses the basic concepts and definitions of measurement theory, along with consideration of relational systems and meaningful statements and statistics. Most of the chapter is devoted to a discussion of twenty different scaling techniques (including those of Thurstone, Likert, and Guttman), magnitude scaling, and factor analysis. A number of the sections employ complex mathematics as part of the explanations. There are 129 references which conclude the review of measurement options, with items dating as far back as 1901 and as recent as 1981.

156. Andrews, Frank M. "Construct Validity and Error Components of Survey Measures: A Structural Modeling Approach." *Public Opinion Quarterly* 48, no. 2 (Summer 1984): 409–42.

The study uses structural modeling of data from special supplements to regular surveys to produce estimates of construct validity, method effects, and residual error for a wide set of measures obtained from five national surveys and one organizational survey with a total of 7,706 respondents. The estimates suggest valid variance on the order of 50 to 83 percent, methods effects variance from 0 to 7 percent, and residual variance from 14 to 48 percent, with the qualifiers that a general population sample is used, and that the survey be conducted by a "respected survey organization." The use of multivariate analysis enabled the researcher to make the evaluation that more than two-thirds of the differences in measurement quality could be attributed to thirteen survey design characteristics. Respondent characteristics were also responsible for some portion of the measurement quality. The author believes that there are several benefits from this research. These include: (1) measuring modeling techniques can be successfully used and with a modest increase in survey item numbers (10 to 20); and (2) the possibility that through use, the technique will yield surveys with higher quality measures. There are six tables and one figure with the text. There are fifty-four references (eleven from the 1980s).

157. Armenakis, Achilles A., M. Ronald Buckley, and Arthur G. Bedeian. "Survey Research Measurement Issues in Evaluating Change: A Laboratory Investigation." *Applied Psychological Measurement* 10, no. 2 (June 1986): 147–57.

The researchers sought to determine factors which effect temporal survey responses. Laboratory methodology (using videotape technology, random respondent assignment, exact stimuli replication, and systematic time interval variation for three, four, and eight weeks in pretest-posttest designs) was used to examine two research questions related to scale recalibration (beta change) in temporal survey research. The first research question addressed deals with the appropriate measurement interval for temporal survey research involving the pretest and posttest designs. The second concerns the use of retrospective designs. A total of four hundred students participated in the research involving a thirty-nine-item survey instrument and the viewing of a videotape at different times during the academic term. The authors defend the laboratory setting for the research, citing the degree to which experimental control can be maintained, and the near impossibility of sustaining comparable control in a field setting. The major conclusion of the study is that time interval does not contribute to scale recalibration in pretest-posttest designs. The text includes three tables, one figure, and twenty-four references; nine of the references are from the 1980s.

158. Bohrnstedt, George W. "Measurement." Chap. 3 in *Handbook of Survey Research*, edited by Peter H. Rossi, James D. Wright, and Andy B. Anderson, 70–121. Quantitative Studies in Social Relations, consulting editor Peter H. Rossi. New York: Academic Press, 1983.

In the introduction Bohrnstedt points out that survey researchers have long neglected the issues of reliability and validity in the literature. Citing this, along with the few examples in which efforts were made to include measurement as a topic, the author proceeds to supply a fifty-page formal treatment of measurement and error theory. Measurement is discussed in a number of sections which include the following: "Platonic and Classical True Scores"; "Reliability and Validity Defined"; "The Effect of Unreliability on Statistical Estimates"; "Reliability as a Function of the Number of Independent Measures"; "Types of Reliability"; "Factor Analysis and Internal Consistency"; and "Validity." There are many figures and tables employed to demonstrate points in a number of the sections. The mathematics used are advanced in nature. The *Handbook* is intended for use as a graduate-level textbook. There are 108 references at the end of the chapter.

159. Duncan, Otis Dudley. "Rasch Measurement in Survey Research: Further Examples and Discussion." Chap. 12 in *Surveying Subjective Phenomena*, edited by Charles F. Turner, and Elizabeth Martin, vol. 2, pt. 4, 367–403. Panel on Survey Measurement of Subjective Phenomena, Committee on National Statistics, Commission on Behavioral and Social Sciences and Education, National Research Council. New York: Russell Sage Foundation, 1984.

The author advises the reader that Volume 1, Section 6.4, of the work edited by Turner and Martin (Item No. 165), should be read prior to reading this chapter. Duncan further suggests reviewing the works by Rasch dealing with models in psychometrics, so that the "rationale and motivation of Rasch's approach" is understood. The chapter begins with the consideration of a four-item scale, followed by two examples of multidimensional structures, an experiment in survey design, and a final section dealing with ordered polytomous variables. There are ten tables and many examples of statistical formulae throughout the chapter. The level of statistics knowledge needed to comprehend the material is at the advanced stage.

160. Lessler, Judith T. "Measurement Error in Surveys." Chap. 13 in *Surveying Subjective Phenomena*, edited by Charles F. Turner, and Elizabeth Martin, vol. 2, pt. 4, 405–40. Panel on Survey Measurement of Subjective Phenomena, Committee on National Statistics, Commission on Behavioral and Social Sciences and Education, National Research Council. New York: Russell Sage Foundation, 1984.

The first section of the chapter provides a definition of survey measurement and documents three cases of survey variable measurement. The author continues with varying definitions of what constitutes measurement error, with the next section covering the assessment of the extent of errors of measurement and their impact on survey estimates. The assessment of bias follows, with subsections dealing with general procedures, procedures for special sources of error, and procedures for adjusting for effects of bias in a survey measurement process. The last major section discusses assessing the impact of measurement variability, with subsections covering bias in the usual sample estimates of variance in the presence of measurement variability, use of repeat measurements, use of interpenetrated samples, and combination methods. The chapter concludes with an examination of methods used to adjust for response error. One table is provided along with numerous statistical formulae. Advanced statistics constitutes the largest percentage of the presentation as is clear from the nature of the three pages of references.

161. Martin, Elizabeth. "Surveys as Social Indicators: Problems in Monitoring Trends." Chap. 16 in *Handbook of Survey Research*, edited by Peter H. Rossi, James D. Wright, and Andy B. Anderson, 677–743. Quantitative Studies in Social Relations, consulting editor Peter H. Rossi. New York: Academic Press, 1983.

Two "puzzles" in the area of trend monitoring are discussed: assessing trends in criminal victimization and confidence in American institutions. As the author clarifies, noncomparable measurements can hinder trend estimates. Most of the chapter discusses in detail the sources of noncomparability at each point of the survey leading to the sought-after data. Martin hopes to highlight sources of noncomparability with a view to correcting the problem with practical solutions. A series of recommendations is provided in the last section of the chapter. The first area covered deals with "Constructing a New Baseline for Future Measurement of Change." The second covers "Replicating Baseline Surveys," and the last reviews "Analysis of Trends Based on Secondary Sources of Data." Eight tables illustrate the text. The list of references at the end of the chapter has 120 entries, 75 percent of which are from the 1970s. About 30 percent of the journal articles are from *Public Opinion Quarterly*.

162. Norpoth, Helmut, and Milton Lodge. "The Difference between Attitudes and Nonattitudes in the Mass Public: Just Measurements?" *American Journal of Political Science* 29, no. 2 (May 1985): 291–307.

The assessment of the role of "nonattitudes" in survey research is the challenge undertaken. Some maintain that nonattitudes are responsible for the "instability" and "low coherence" of responses to policy issues in mass surveys. Others maintain that the measurement instruments are to blame for the previous shortcomings. Authors Norpoth and Lodge used magnitude scaling to obtain multiple measures, using latent variables proposed a measurement model, and finally, using LISREL, estimated the response reliabilities jointly for four policy issues, party identification, and liberal-conservative self-location. The authors found that the political sophistication of the resondents makes a considerable difference for the reliability and structure of political attitude responses. Great constraint and higher response reliabilities were exhibited by the sophisticated half of the sample. Norpoth and Lodge maintain that their findings reject the hypothesis that fallible measurement instruments are solely responsible for response error, with nonattitudes held accountable for these shortcomings. Thirty-six references accompany the article, along with several figures and three tables.

163.   Stolzenberg, Ross M., and Kenneth C. Land. "Causal Modeling and Survey Research." Chap. 15 in *Handbook of Survey Research*, edited by Peter H. Rossi, James D. Wright, and Andy B. Anderson, 613–75. Quantitative Studies in Social Relations, consulting editor Peter H. Rossi. New York: Academic Press, 1983.

Some basic principles of causal inference in nonexperimental contexts which underlie causal modeling are discussed, along with linear, nonlinear, additive, and nonadditive recursive causal models. A set of techniques is developed which enables the measurement of the causal effects in each of the models described. The last section deals with nonrecursive models. The authors assume that the reader can understand elementary statistics, linear regression, elementary calculus, and matrix algebra. Seven figures and five tables illustrate textual points. Eighty-eight references conclude the chapter, with 50 percent from the 1970s, 25 percent from the 1960s, and the remaining 25 percent from earlier years—one from 1875.

164.   Turner, Charles F., and Elizabeth Martin, eds. *Survey of Subjective Phenomena: Summary Report*. Panel on Survey Measurement of Subjective Phenomena, Committee on National Statistics, Assembly of Behavioral and Social Sciences, National Research Council. Washington, DC: National Academy Press, 1981. 97p.

This summary report is intended for nonspecialists, i.e., the general public. The full study report and a set of technical papers commissioned by the panel are available separately. The summary report is divided into three parts: introduction, summary of findings, and recommendations, followed by notes, references, and separate statements. The introduction differentiates between objective and subjective phenomena, discusses subjectivity and social "facts," provides the background of the study, and places surveys in context within the continuum of measurement errors in other sciences and possible alternatives to surveys. The survey findings section reviews the uses and abuses of surveys, measurement as applied to subjective phenomena, survey measurement as a psychosocial process, and provides concluding observations. The final section suggests four specific ways to improve the public's understanding of surveys and polls, six ways to upgrade current survey practice, and eight approaches to advance survey measurement and the scientific use of survey data. In total, eighteen recommendations are stated and explained. A list of 151 references is supplied. Three "Separate Statements" conclude the volume. They provide criticisms or points of omission as viewed by the author of each of the named statements. The report is not indexed.

165.   Turner, Charles F., and Elizabeth Martin, eds. *Surveying Subjective Phenomena,* vol. 1. Panel on Survey Measurement of Subjective Phenomena, Committee on National Statistics, Commission on Behavioral and Social Sciences and Education, National Research Council. New York: Russell Sage Foundation, 1984. 494p.

Volume 1 is the product of the Panel on Survey Measurement of Subjective Phenomena which was convened in January 1980, and met in five plenary sessions through February 1981. Most of the participants were active in collecting or analyzing survey data, but they varied considerably in type of organizational background and philosophical viewpoint. Page vi attributes major portions of Volume 1 to the various contributors although they are not so acknowledged in the "Contents." The page opposite each new chapter beginning provides a "responsibility" statement. There are five major parts in this volume: (1) "Background"; (2) "Uses and Abuses of Surveys"; (3) "Measurement Issues"; (4) "The Survey Interview Process"; and (5) "Improving Survey Measurement of Subjective Phenomena." Eight appendixes cover almost one hundred pages, which are followed by nearly forty pages of references. Name and subject indexes conclude the volume. The panel members and their institutional affiliations are listed on a prefatory page. The first of the two-volume set with this title should be viewed as providing summary information, with

Volume 2 supplying in-depth material on many of the topics covered in Volume 1.

166. Turner, Charles F., and Elizabeth Martin, eds. *Surveying Subjective Phenomena,* vol. 2. Panel on Survey Measurement of Subjective Phenomena, Committee on National Statistics, Commission on Behavioral and Social Sciences and Education, National Research Council. New York: Russell Sage Foundation, 1984. 617p.

Volume 2 of this two-volume set contains the individual reports undertaken on special studies by members of the Panel on Survey Measurement of Subjective Phenomena and others. The presentations in Volume 2 are designed to provide a fuller, deeper coverage of many of the topics treated summarily in Volume 1. As with the first volume, Volume 2 is divided into five main parts: (1) "Measurement of Subjective Phenomena in the Social Sciences"; (2) "Quasi-Facts"; (3) "Nonsampling Sources of Variability"; (4) "Some Statistical Models for Error and Structure in Survey Data"; and (5) "Putting Survey Measurements in Context." Name and subject indexes follow for the whole of Volume 2. Among the opening pages of the volume is a list of contributors which provides institutional affiliations of the authors included in Volume 2. There are nine contributions of particular interest to this work; these are listed below in order of appearance. Each chapter has been separately considered, and can be found under the following item numbers in this annotated bibliography.

Contents:

Part I,	Chapter 3:	The Use of Survey Data in Basic Research in the Social Sciences (Presser—Item No. 42).
Part III,	Chapter 7:	Why Do Surveys Disagree? Some Preliminary Hypotheses and Some Disagreeable Examples (Turner—Item No. 329).
Part III,	Chapter 8:	Nonattitudes: A Review and Evaluation (Smith—Item No. 297).
Part III,	Chapter 9:	Social Desirability and Survey Measurement: Analysis of Survey Question Form Across Organizations and Over Time (Converse and Schuman—Item No. 173).
Part IV,	Chapter 11:	Some Statistical Models for Analyzing Why Surveys Disagree (Clogg—Item No. 314).

10.2 SCALING

167. Lodge, Milton. *Magnitude Scaling, Quantitative Measurement of Opinions.* Sage University Paper series on Quantitative Applications in the Social Sciences, edited by John L. Sullivan, Number 07-025. Beverly Hills, CA: Sage Publications, 1981. 87p.

There are eight chapters, the first of which is an introduction to the magnitude scaling of social judgements. The final chapter seeks to demonstrate the benefits of magnitude scaling over the commonly used category scaling approach. Other chapters examine psychophysics, the validation of magnitude scaling, the applications of magnitude scaling for survey research, the direct magnitude scaling of political judgments, the comparison of category and magnitude scales of social opinion, and the considerations involved in employing magnitude scaling in research projects. There are several major arguments that are raised which may explain category scaling's continued preeminence. These include the ways to compare survey results with earlier research, some of which may date back to the 1930s, and the other major aspect is cost–magnitude scaling requires more interview time. On the other hand, categorical scaling seldom provides quantitative measurement of opinion strength. Approximately three pages of endnotes are included along with fifty-seven references.

168. Lodge, Milton, and Bernard Tursky. "On the Magnitude Scaling of Public Opinion in Survey Research." *American Journal of Political Science* 25, no. 2 (May 1981): 376–419.

The quantitative measurement of the intensity of people's impressions, preferences, and judgments can be achieved through category scaling and magnitude scaling. The authors believe magnitude scaling to be the superior approach, and provide this "Workshop" as a means to describe scaling in terms of costs, benefits, and procedural requirements. Major sections of the article include a discussion of the "magnitude scaling and validation of political judgments," "research decisions," and "the relative utility of magnitude over category scales." General procedures for use in survey research are outlined, along with discussions of response modalities, survey protocol, multiple sections dealing with varying calibration topics, stimulus-type magnitude scales, and elements of the challenges faced in the scale-building approach. The text is accompanied by four figures, four tables, and forty-nine pre-1980 references.

169.   McIver, John P., and Edward G. Carmines. *Unidimensional Scaling*. Sage University Paper series on Quantitative Applications in the Social Sciences, edited by John L. Sullivan, Number 07-024. Beverly Hills, CA: Sage Publications, 1981. 96p.

This entry in the Sage University Papers series provides an introduction to Thurstone scaling, Likert scaling, Guttman scaling, and unfolding theory. It is suitable for both undergraduates and beginning graduate students. The work is designed to be used by those individuals seeking to apply the material to practical scaling issues. Examples are used throughout the monograph. Unidimensional scaling techniques are used in the social sciences in the study of attitudes, preferences, and perceptions. The chapter dealing with Thurstone scaling discusses "The Law of Comparative Judgment" and reviews the limitations of Thurstone scaling. Likert scale construction is explained in another chapter, along with criticism of the approach. Guttman scaling is introduced in one chapter with a follow-up chapter considering a number of issues concerning this scaling technique, such as too many respondents, missing data, and errors. Coombs's unidimensional unfolding model is the subject of the last chapter, with the major features of the model highlighted. The contents pages serve as the subject access, as an index is not provided. Four-and-one-half pages of references are given.

11. Questions

11.1 FORM

170. Aldrich, John H., Richard G. Niemi, George Rabinowitz, and David W. Rohde. "The Measurement of Public Opinion about Public Policy: A Report on Some New Issue Question Formats." *American Journal of Political Science* 26, no. 2 (May 1982): 391–414.

Writing in a column headed "The Workshop," the authors discuss problems associated with current measures, in particular the seven-point scales. They cite difficulties in interpretation, in an excessive number of responses in the middle category, and in the failure to allow for respondent ambiguity. Also discussed are problems of status quo, labeling, reliability, location, and intensity. Two new formats are reviewed as alternatives: the "branching" format and the "ambiguity" format. The branching format apparently resolves the middle-category problems and assists with the interpretation issues. The ambiguity format permits the respondent to answer in ranges as well as at specific points on the issue scale. The ambiguity format adds little to the cost of the survey; the branching format requires longer interview time. Another approach, the "status quo-government involvement" format, is discussed, but the authors found this the "least impressive" of the new formats considered. The National Election Study (NES) Research and Development Survey used a telephone survey of an initial 280 respondents to test the various formats. Test questions appear in the appendix. Two of the references are from the 1980s; ten are from earlier years.

171.   Blankenship, Albert Breneman. "The Influence of the Question
        Form upon the Response in a Public Opinion Poll." Ph.D. diss.,
        Columbia University, 1940. Offprinted from *The Psychological
        Record* 3, no. 23 (March 1940): 345–422.

The issue of "leading" or "loaded" questions as a biasing element was
raised early in the nation's experience with polling. Blankenship sought
to answer seven questions concerning the nature of question wording: (1)
Are results influenced by question form? (2) Of five question forms employed, which is the most useful in predicting the results of elections? (3)
Given two samples of voters, which question form consistently yields the
highest response? (4) Which question form enables the respondent to
answer freely without influence or interference from the question wording? (5) Which wording generates the smallest number of "don't know"
responses? (6) Does question wording influence the next question asked,
and if so, how does it affect consistency and "don't know" answers? and
(7) Of the questions used in this study, which one is considered to be the
best? A study was conducted in Irvington, New Jersey with three
thousand interviews. A pool of at least fifteen hundred registered voters
was sought, and the Irvington registration list indicated 50 percent
registration. The study concludes that the only certain indication is that
further tests in the same community using different issues, similar tests
elsewhere, and national replication are necessary before reaching any
conclusion. References are provided.

172.   Converse, Jean M. "Strong Arguments and Weak Evidence: The
        Open/Closed Questioning Controversy of the 1940s." *Public
        Opinion Quarterly* 48, no. 1B (Spring 1984): 267–82.

The debate about open/closed questioning and interviewing developed
during World War II. The opposing points of view were held between
groups of commercial and academic researchers working for the federal
government. Converse traces the organizational rivalry and discusses
methodological issues. The author suggests that the effect of the debate
was mostly institutional, and argues that the methodological questions
remain both unresolved and unexplored from the "scientific" standpoint.
Converse reviews the origins of the rivalry, discusses the practical use of
both formats during the 1930s and 1940s, and traces the path of the controversy during these years. Little published research on the open/closed
issue was produced during this period. There seems to have been considerable discussion at meetings such as the American Association for Public Opinion Research's (AAPOR) meeting following the 1948 election
polling failures, as well as other smaller meetings held to review the

causes and consequences of what are described as "sympathetic post-mortem's." The personal interviews cited in the bibliography are to be housed in an AAPOR archive at the University of Chicago. There are seventy references.

173. Converse, Jean M., and Howard Schuman. "The Manner of Inquiry: An Analysis of Survey Question Form across Organizations and over Time." Chap. 10 in *Surveying Subjective Phenomena*, edited by Charles F. Turner, and Elizabeth Martin, vol. 2, pt. 3, 283–316. Panel on Survey Measurement of Subjective Phenomena, Committee on National Statistics, Commission on Behavioral and Social Sciences and Education, National Research Council. New York: Russell Sage Foundation, 1984.

The form of questions used by four major surveys are compared, with two of the studies comparing practice over time. The Gallup Poll and the Harris Survey were chosen as representatives of commercial organizations; the General Social Survey (GSS) of the National Opinion Research Center (NORC) and the National Election Study (NES) of the Institute for Social Research (ISR) were chosen to represent academic institutions. All questions received a designation in a twenty-one.category detailed code, the main elements of which include closed, quasi-closed, and open questions. Other areas of interest include the level of language difficulty and the percentage of "no opinion" responses. A summary of the practice by the four surveys during the early 1970s indicates that similaries exist on five question forms: "1. Concentration on closed questions, 2. Substantial use of the two-way choice, 3. Minor use of multiple arguments, 4. Negligible use of checklists, and 5. Negligible use of intensity measures." The language skill level of all the surveys is designed to be comprehensible to high school graduates. The Gallup Poll and the NES permitted comparison over time and showed that the Gallup Poll (probably due to Gallup's personal influence) changed very little, whereas the NES changed question format many times—perhaps reflecting the many analysts associated with the ISR over the years. Several appendixes show the classification of the questions and the distribution of question form. Notes and references complete the chapter.

174.   Davis, Todd M., and James E. McLean. "Simplifying Ranking
        Tasks in Survey Research: A Method and Example." *Psy-
        chological Reports* 62, no. 3 (June 1988): 987–92.

The method described involves the respondent considering a number of
options, two at a time, thereby generating a set of ranked options. The
example cited was a comprehensive survey of financing options available for a school district in Alabama. Several tables illustrate the "paired-
comparison options" and the "ordered paired-comparison options." This
approach permits choices among alternatives which can be presented to
decision makers in the form of a list of priorities, and it can also be used
to allow respondents to rank or select among unpleasant alternatives.
Other tables include "proportion matrix" and "matrix." One figure illus-
trates a "reverse options scale." There are seven references, one from the
1980s.

175.   Geer, John G. "What Do Open-Ended Questions Measure?"
        Public Opinion Quarterly 52, no. 3 ((Fall 1988): 365–71.

Survey data from the University of Michigan's Center for Political
Studies (CPS), generated through the National Election Studies (NES),
was analyzed from 1952 through 1984. Geer found that only a small percentage of the respondents was unable to answer open-ended questions,
and he suggests that these people may be apolitical. The author maintains
that the record shows that open-ended questions do accurately measure
the concerns which are important to the public. Although the format adds
costs to surveys and may be difficult to code, it does reflect respondents'
attitudes rather than just their ability to express a response. The
educational level of respondents was examined to see if this factor had a
bearing on the category that failed to respond to the open-ended questions. The study led Geer to suggest that it is not education or ability to
articulate, but rather that some people "simply had nothing to say."
Looking for other possible explanations, respondent inhibition or nervousness is cited. The study was not able to examine such a factor, as the
"conditions of the interview" section for the interviewer does not contain
any questions which relate to inhibition or nervousness on the part of the
respondent. Eight references, six of which are from the 1980s, are listed.

176. Krosnick, Jon A., and Duane F. Alwin. "A Test of the Form-Resistant Correlation Hypothesis: Ratings, Rankings, and the Measurement of Values." *Public Opinion Quarterly* 52, no. 4 (Winter 1988): 526–38.

As part of the 1980 General Social Survey (GSS), the National Opinion Research Center (NORC) sampled 1,468 adults, one-third of whom were asked to respond to a question on desired child qualities adapted from M.L. Kohn's *Class and Conformity: A Study in Values* (1969). Using the data, authors Krosnick and Alwin confirmed their hypothesis that discrepancies between the rating and ranking results were to some degree the result of nondifferentiation in response to the rating measures. Their evidence agrees with other approaches which suggest that ranking is the more fruitful approach when measuring values. The discussion phase of the article seems to be providing yet another alternative explanation for the results achieved, rather than one tested for, and therefore the potential subject for further research. The challenge is whether or not nondifferentiators do in fact value each quality equally in the survey question. If so, and these individuals are forced to rank, then their responses may have little or no validity. The text includes three tables. Twenty-eight references are included, with half the entries from the 1980s.

177. Miller, Peter V. "Alternative Question Forms for Attitude Scale Questions in Telephone Interviews." *Public Opinion Quarterly* 48, no. 4 (Winter 1984): 766–78.

The "folklore of experience" used in ordinary survey practice is the focus of this article. More specifically, it is Miller's attempt to bring scientific research to bear on one of the elements in this folklore: namely, whether it is necessary or appropriate to use a two-step question format when conducting telephone interviews without the benefit of visual aids developed for face-to-face interviews. The one-step question involves the interviewer presenting the "response categories in the questions through verbal description." The alternative method has the respondent answer in two stages, the first to a general statement of affect. The second stage is a more specific query which permits the interviewer to place the respondent on the scale. Miller tested the two approaches with a study sample of 4,300 families queried about health data. The health data was compared with information gathered through in-person interviews by the U.S. Bureau of the Census. The author found the similarity of the results using the two question forms to be "impressive." Miller suggests that the data does not support the argument that seven-point scale questions need to be broken down into components when conducting telephone surveys, with the qualifier that this applies when the responses can be converted to a numerical scale. Twelve references (three from 1980) complete the article.

178. Parker, Robert Nash, and Rudy Fenwick. "The Pareto Curve and Its Utility for Open-Ended Income Distributions in Survey Research." *Social Forces: An International Journal of Social Research 61*, no. 3 (March 1983): 872–85.

The Pareto Curve is derived from Pareto's Law of Income Distribution, which is cited and explained in the article, along with recommendations for the use of Pareto's Curve as a solution to the challenge of the open-ended income category problem. Two methods for estimating the midpoint of open-ended categories in income distributions are compared. The choice of the approach selected is shown to have "substantial effects on analyses in which income is the dependent variable." The authors recommend that survey researchers use the two category, rather than the four category method, as this method produces more accurate estimates. The median midpoint estimator is recommended, rather than the mean estimator, because of greater accuracy. Also, the median estimator will be smaller than the median estimate. The authors maintain that survey researchers should reassess the need to include the way in which the open-ended problem was resolved in their work. Three tables are included, along with an appendix showing the variety of categorical income distributions employed in the studies considered. There are thirty-three references provided, nine from the 1980s.

179. Petty, Richard E., Greg A. Rennier, and John T. Cacioppo. "Assertion Versus Interrogation Format in Opinion Formats: Questions Enhance Thoughtful Responding." *Public Opinion Quarterly* 51, no. 4 (Winter 1987): 481–94.

The research conducted by the three authors clearly shows that greater item-relevant thinking is generated through the use of the interrogation format than the assertion format. With research by others indicating that thoughtful attitudes are more likely to be predictive of behavior, the authors suggest that the interrogation format is to be preferred—but with a qualifier. The qualifier is that the interrogation format focuses on cognitive dimensions, rather than affective dimensions. For political polls which focus on cognitive elements, the use of the interrogation format may serve to reduce the role of affect in evaluation of candidates. Petty, Rennier, and Cacioppo view the exploration of question format impact on elicited opinions as a source for future research. The reported research was conducted through interviews with ninety-one undergraduate students who completed a survey on one of two supposedly new consumer products. Forty-two students completed a survey on a new disposable razor product, and on another day forty-nine students completed a survey about a new calculator. Variables manipulated were question format and strong versus weak background statements about the product. The interrogation format produced more polarized opinions in response to both surveys. One table, one figure, and two appendixes containing the strong/weak statements and the questionnaire are included. Twenty references are supplied.

180. Schuman, Howard, and Jacqueline Scott. "Problems in the Use of Survey Questions to Measure Public Opinion." *Science* 236, no. 4804 (22 May 1987): 957–59.

Schuman and Scott, writing while associated with the Survey Research Center (SRC), Institute for Social Research (ISR) at the University of Michigan, suggest that both open and closed questions used in sample interview surveys have limitations. The authors report on two experiments designed to show how difficult it is to infer "relative orderings of public choices" using either question type. Open questions call for the respondent to answer in his/her own words from alternatives they construct. Closed questions call for the respondent to select from a list of offered alternatives. The conclusion of the researchers is that these question types can be used successfully to study "responses over time and differences across social categories." Two tables show the answers given by percentage in each experiment conducted. There are nine endnotes.

181. Schuman, Howard, and Stanley Presser. "Public Opinion and Public Ignorance: The Fine Line between Attitudes and Nonattitudes." *American Journal of Sociology* 85, no. 5 (March 1980): 1214–25.

This research was designed to probe the issue of nonattitudes versus attitudes, and to determine if differences between the two as reported in survey research may, in fact, be the result of the question format used. Approximately 30 percent of the group surveyed for this study were willing to provide an opinion concerning a proposed law—one they knew nothing about, and to which "don't know" (DK) was not an "explicit option." When the DK option is "fully legitimized for both interviewers and respondents by being read as part of the question," this becomes the choice of 90 percent or more of those questioned. Another study cited by Schuman and Presser found the DK note to be 93 percent

[Bishop, et al (in press)]. Schuman and Presser found that people with more education were more willing to show ignorance by selecting the DK choice. The authors believe that this finding is a product of those with education being more able to distinguish between difficult versus impossible questions. However, even in the most educated category between 20 to 25 percent of the respondents gave opinions on matters that were unknown to them. Schuman and Presser recommend using the DK filters when trying to measure "informed opinion" on public issues. Investigators seeking greater understanding about "underlying dispositions" are advised to omit the DK option or are discouraged from using it. Ten references (one from 1980) accompany the article.

182.　Schuman, Howard, and Stanley Presser. *Questions and Answers in Attitude Surveys: Experiments on Question Form, Wording, and Context.* Quantitative Studies in Social Relations, consulting editor Peter H. Rossi. New York: Academic Press, 1981. 370p.

This book reports on the investigations which have been made using various kinds of questions in surveys—particularly those examining "subjective phenomena," i.e., those dealing with attitudes, opinions, beliefs, values, preferences, etc. The goal of the work is to determine the way in which attitude question formulation affects the result. The authors have focused on a small number of important ways in which the form of the question varies. Schuman and Presser suggest reading the first chapter on scope and method as the starting point. Beyond that, the chapters can be read in any order, as each can stand alone. There are twelve chapters which cover the entire gamut of issues from question order and response order to tone of wording. Other topics considered include open versus closed questions, the assessment of "no opinion," attitudes and nonattitudes, the balanced question, attitude strength, and "passionate attitudes." The final chapter addresses some broader themes and problems utilizing the results of the foregoing chapters. There are four appendixes and eleven pages of references.

11.2 WORDING

183. Bishop, George F. "Experiments with the Middle Response Alternative in Survey Questions." *Public Opinion Quarterly* 51, no. 2 (Summer 1987): 220–32.

The middle response alternative changes considerably any survey interpretation which might be made concerning the spectrum of opinion on a subject. The middle option tends to attract people who may be uncertain about the other possible choices available. Bishop discovered that just mentioning the middle alternative as an option draws people to select the choice significantly more frequently than when it is not mentioned at all (even when not explicitly offered as a choice with the questions). People are significantly more likely to select the middle response when it is explicitly offered as part of the question. The position of the middle alternative—middle or last—has a bearing on the results. The author also explains that those individuals who select the middle response alternative would not necessarily respond to the question in the same manner as other respondents if they were forced to select sides on issues. The experiments were conducted in conjunction with the Greater Cincinnati Survey, a telephone survey run by the University of Cincinnati's Behavioral Sciences Laboratory. Several tables are included along with an appendix which provides the wording of the questions used in the split-ballot experiments. Several 1980s references complete the article.

184. Klopfer, Frederick J., and Theodore M. Madden. "The Middlemost Choice on Attitude Items: Ambivalence, Neutrality, or Uncertainty?" *Personality and Social Psychology Bulletin* 6, no. 1 (March 1980): 97–101.

Ambivalence, neutrality, and uncertainty are three processes which can lead to the selection of the middlemost response in a survey. The authors state that Likert-type items in attitude scales usually have middlemost response options which reflect indecision on the part of the respondent. Klopfer and Madden believe that by understanding the underlying concept used by respondents who frequently select middlemost responses, greater depth will be provided to the data. The researchers tested four different versions of the middlemost response. Each of four groups was provided with a different definition of the middlemost response, with the results indicating that there were only marginal differences in the responses. The data does indicate that in certain cases the definitional variation did make a difference, as in the case of attitudes toward capital punishment. The authors stress the need to carefully select the appropriate attitude scale as well as to carefully define the middlemost response option. A table shows the mean and standard deviations for response use under the four conditions defined with the two scales. Nine references complete the article.

185.   Pace, C. Robert, and Jack Friedlander. "The Meaning of Response Categories: How Often Is 'Occasionally,' 'Often,' and 'Very Often'?" *Research in Higher Education: Journal of the Association for Institutional Research* 17, no. 3 (1982): 267–81.

The inquiry undertaken was to determine if "occasionally," "often," and "very often" had different meanings for individuals, and to ascertain if these differences were influenced by alternative settings (in this case colleges and universities). The authors found that six generalizations emerged from their work: (1) the topic or subject of the survey determines the differences in frequency definition; (2) regardless of the subject or topic, there are wide differences in the meaning attributed to the above categories; (3) "the group data show clear modal differences between occasionally and often and between often and very often"; (4) the modal differences exist across all topics and at all institutions; (5) the difference in the meaning of each of the response categories is very small between institutions, including different types of institutions; and (6) separate norms need not be developed for different types of institutions. Four tables are included, along with thirteen references (two from the 1980s).

186.   Peterson, Robert A. "Asking the Age Question: A Research Note." *Public Opinion Quarterly* 48, no. 1B (Spring 1984): 379–83.

The research undertaken sought to empirically investigate a question which many practitioners face routinely: How does one best ask the question of the respondent's age and ensure not only accuracy but also avoid an unacceptable level of refusals? Peterson used four formats: (1) How old are you? (2) What is your age? (3) In what year were you born? and (4) Are you...18–24 years of age, 25–34, 35–49, 50–64, 65 or older? All four formats yielded uniformly high levels of reporting accuracy. The refusal rates were significantly different among the different question formats. Overall, 4.8 percent of the 1,260 individuals questioned refused to answer an age question. The question "How old are you?" generated the response with the highest accuracy (98.7 percent), as compared with the lowest accuracy for the category question (95.1 percent). The "How old are you?" format also had the highest refusal rate (9.7 percent), while the category format had the smallest percentage that refused to answer (1.1 percent). Peterson addresses the question of "Which format is best?" by saying that it is dependent upon the needs of the researcher and decision maker. There are six pre-1980 references.

187. Presser, Stanley, and Howard Schuman. "The Measurement of a Middle Position in Attitude Surveys." *Public Opinion Quarterly* 44, no. 1 (Spring 1980): 70–85.

In order to determine the effects of offering or omitting a middle alternative in forced-choice attitude questions, the authors conducted five split-ballot experiments, along with replications, in a number of national surveys. Presser and Schuman found that by offering an explicit middle alternative the percentage of respondents increased to somewhere between 10 and 20 percent, with most of the change arising from a decline in the polar positions. The intensity of the opinion held is one factor that may distinguish those affected by question form from those who are not. Form effect is apparently unrelated to education and information. For those with a weak leaning position, the question form probably structures the respondents' decision making. Respondents may perceive or make different assumptions about the information that is being called for—according to which question form (with/without middle position) is asked. It appears that Stanley L. Payne's work titled *The Art of Asking Questions* (1951) may be accurate when he suggests using the middle alternative to find which people are "leaning" on the issue, and to omit it in cases in which clear convictions are sought. There are fifteen references.

188. Smith, Tom W. "That Which We Call Welfare by Any Other Name Would Smell Sweeter: An Analysis of the Impact of Question Wording on Response Patterns." *Public Opinion Quarterly* 51, no. 1 (Spring 1987): 75–83.

The research was undertaken for the General Social Survey (GSS) with experiments conducted in 1982, 1984, and 1985. Differences in results were noted between "welfare," "assistance for the poor," and "caring for the poor," when examining spending priority scales. When examining the terminology and results from other survey organizations, using terms such as "the unemployed," "food stamps," or other similar terms used in connection with "welfare" or "the poor," Smith found that response effects were large, similar in degree, and continued across time. The results cut across all the survey organizations examined. The word "welfare" consistently generates much more negative evaluations than does "the poor." One explanation for this may be the association in the minds of respondents of "welfare" with minorities, and that it may be a "code word for racism." Alternately or additionally, "welfare" may be viewed as a wasteful program. The results of this study indicate the need for linguistic sensitivity when writing survey questions. The study also indicates that multiple approaches to an issue may be required to properly gauge the public's attitude toward it—in this case public assistance. Four tables show the study data from 1982 through 1985. There are twelve references provided, half from the 1980s.

11.3 FILTER QUESTIONS AND CONTEXT

189. Bishop, George F., Robert Oldendick, and Alfred Tuchfarber. "Effects of Filter Questions in Public Opinion Survey." *Public Opinion Quarterly* 47, no. 4 (Winter 1983): 528–46.

The research examined the effects of using filter questions and found that they can make a significant difference in the percentage of "don't know" (DK) responses. Filter questions, which seek to determine interest level, reading, and thinking about an issue, tend to screen out more individuals than asking whether or not the person has an opinion on an issue. As the degree of abstractness or remoteness of the issue increases, so too does the impact of the question wording effect. The more obscure or unfamiliar the issue, the more likely is it that the DK responses will be increased by the use of a filter. The conclusions that are drawn from surveys using filter questions regarding the distribution of public opinion on an issue are likely to be somewhat different had the same survey been completed without filter questions. A concern that the researchers express is that although individuals may be excluded from particular questions or sets of questions by filter questions, it is not clear why or what aspect within the filter question they may have responded to. One solution would be to ask "what they had in mind" in seeking to determine whether it was an attitude toward the object, the attitude toward the policy situation, or other possibilities. The issue of some words used in questions having multidimensional meanings is addressed. The text is accompanied by seven tables, and fourteen references (four from the 1980s).

190. Bishop, George F., Robert W. Oldendick, and Alfred J. Tuchfarber. "Experiments in Filtering Political Opinions." *Political Behavior* 4, no. 4 (1980): 339–69.

The use of a filter question can reduce opinion giving from 20 to 25 percent. The issue content is a factor in this percentage. The filter question proved to be an effective means of removing respondents who felt that "they should have an opinion." The authors suggest that the less familiar respondents are with an issue, the more useful the filter question is in removing the uninformed or uninterested. Other issues addressed are the impact of the level of education and the interest in politics of respondents in relation to the impact of the filter question. Additionally, the possible altering of public opinion by the experience of being measured through surveys is examined. The researchers also became aware that not only may question wording be the subject of continuing research needs, but also question meaning to those of differing educational levels and involvement in politics may have to come under greater scrutiny. Experimenting with identically worded versions of the filters generated differing results based on varying degrees of the above mentioned variables. The appendix provides the questions in the four experiments undertaken. Notes and references are provided, along with seven tables.

191. Files, James A. "Filter Questions Can Screen Out Uninformed Responses." *Public Relations Journal* 40, no. 7 (July 1984): 8–9.

The use of filter questions is discussed, with experimental data cited suggesting that their use may increase the "don't know" or "no opinion" response by 20 to 25 percent. The Bishop, Oldendick, and Tuchfarber article titled "Effects of Filter Questions in Public Opinion Surveys" (Item No. 189) is cited, with Files summarizing the significant points. In closing, Files suggests that substantial questions remain to be resolved, and therefore he maintains that filter questions should be used cautiously. No references are included.

192. Loftus, Elizabeth F., and Wesley Marburger. "Since the Eruption of Mt. St. Helens, Has Anyone Beaten You Up? Improving the Accuracy of Retrospective Reports with Landmark Events." *Memory & Cognition* 11, no. 2 (March 1983): 114–20.

It is common for people to report that past events happened more recently than they actually did. This phenomena is referred to as "forward telescoping." One method for countering this tendency is to use landmark events to mark the beginning of a reference period. Another approach is to ask the interviewees to provide their own personal landmarks. The researchers found in a series of five experiments that the use of landmarks did improve the accuracy of retrospective reports when either a public or private landmark was used. Loftus and Marburger raise the question as to just exactly what constitutes a landmark event, with one problem being that some large surveys may be conducted over many months. The specific use to which the authors utilized this technique involved data on crime victimization gathered at six-month intervals through personal interviews from thousands of households via the National Crime Survey (NCS). The general approach is adaptable to many areas, including health, consumer behavior, and memories from childhood and early life experiences. A single reference note is followed by sixteen references, all but one of which are pre-1980 items.

193. Schuman, Howard, Graham Kalton, and Jacob Ludwig. "Context and Contiguity in Survey Questionnaires." *Public Opinion Quarterly* 47, no. 1 (Spring 1983): 112–15.

The research study discussed concerns the extent to which context effects may be due to placing questions in contiguous positions, with no questions in between, as contrasted with the questions appearing distributed throughout a questionnaire. The original experiment using a split-ballot format was conducted by Hyman and Sheatsley in 1948; the questions asked concerned a Communist reporter item and an American reporter item with one question asked first, followed by the other for one-half of the sample. The question order was reversed for the other half. A new experiment using the split-ballot format was conducted in 1981 using three randomly assigned forms in a Survey Research Center (SRC) national telephone survey. The original context effect was successfully replicated. The authors regard the problem of context as a "matter of real substantive importance, rather than a technical issue of interest only to questionnaire specialists." There are three references. Two of them are from the 1980s.

194.   Sudman, Seymour, Adam Finn, and Linda Lannom. "The Use of Bounded Recall Procedures in Single Interviews." *Public Opinion Quarterly* 48, no. 2 (Summer 1984): 520–24.

The problem of telescoping and procedures to overcome it are discussed. Telescoping is the tendency of respondents to report behavior at a different time than when it occurred, usually that an event occurred more recently than it actually did. The memory errors are the subject of this study which employs a method developed in 1964 by John Neter and Joseph Waksberg. The method, called bounded recall, is an attempt to overcome these errors, and uses an initial interview with a panel to report events over a specified period of time. This data is not included in estimates, but serves as a "bound" on respondent memory. Then, over successive months, the interviewer asks about events that have occurred since the previous interview. With the data from previous interviews in hand, the interviewer can determine when the respondent has a memory error and delete the incorrect report from estimates. Sudman, Finn, and Lannom went one stage further and reduced the method to a single interview using bounded recall. In the two attempts reported, the application of the procedure was very effective in reducing telescoping. The researchers suggest that the next step should be to conduct the study where simultaneous validation information is available. There are several tables with the article, along with seven references, two from the 1980s.

11.4 ORDER AND ORDER EFFECTS

195.   Bishop, George F. "Context Effects on Self-Perceptions of Interest in Government and Public Affairs." Chap. 10 in *Social Information Processing and Survey Methodology*, edited by Hans-J. Hippler, Norbert Schwarz, and Seymour Sudman, 179–99. Recent Research in Psychology. New York: Springer-Verlag, 1987.

Bishop discusses the conditional inference model developed by Wyer and Hartwick to explain question order and context effects on people's self-perceptions of their interest in government and public affairs. The model suggests that it is not so much how recent the information is, but rather the relevancy of the information so far as how respondents answer questions. The author also found how difficult it is to measure people's interest in government and public affairs without changing their self-perception. The author poses this question for further research: To what degree are people's attitudes, perceptions, and opinions changed in the process of measuring them, and are there some individuals who are more easily affected than others? A series of three experiments was conducted as part of the Greater Cincinnati Survey, conducted by the Behavioral Sciences Laboratory at the University of Cincinnati. Using telephone surveys, a number of questions were asked in one of six possible order patterns and buffer conditions. In the second experiment, the buffer was larger. In the third experiment the buffer was larger than in the previous two experiments. In this discussion the "buffer" refers to other questions in the survey not related to government and public affairs. Following a page of ten footnotes, there are twelve references.

196.   Bishop, George F., Robert W. Oldendick, and Alfred J. Tuchfarber. "Interest in Political Campaigns: The Influence of Question Order and Electoral Context." *Political Behavior* 6, no. 2 (1984): 159–69.

The article addresses the question of whether it makes a difference in what order certain questions are asked in a survey dealing with a political campaign, and also if the context of the question has a bearing on the answer. The researchers found that both where and when a question is asked has a decided impact on the respondent. Those individuals who were asked about their interest in a political campaign, immediately after being asked whether or not they voted, were more likely to indicate interest in the campaign—especially if they claimed they had voted. The reverse question order produced responses claiming less interest in the campaign. As time passes from the actual occurrence of the political campaign, better-educated respondents are more likely to be "pressured by a social norm" and continue to be affected by the question order effect. Suggestions for countering these effects in the National Election Study (NES) include asking such questions in multiple locations in the NES interview schedule, with a preference by the article authors toward a random arrangement (within the required limitations that related items be in blocks). Three tables accompany the text, along with notes and nine references.

197. Bishop, George F., Robert W., Oldendick, and Alfred J. Tuchfarber. "Political Information Processing: Question Order and Context Effects." *Political Behavior* 4, no. 2 (1982): 177–200.

The community of researchers is challenged to develop a new information-processing model of human memory to better explain the phenomena that are discussed in this article. The root of the problem is that changes in question order and context may be responsible for apparent trends or shifts in the distribution of a number of indicators in long-existing, time-series election surveys, such as those from the Center for Political Studies (CPS) and the Survey Research Center (SRC) [of the University of Michigan]. The authors discuss Daryl Bem's self-perception theory as a means of explaining the cognitive processes underlying order and context effects. Two experiments were conducted in an attempt to evaluate these issues; both employed the telephone survey approach. The authors conclude that there are no "correct" locations to pose questions about interest in political campaigns or in government and public affairs. The work confirms that respondents tend to answer these questions in terms of the information that is most available to them in memory. The agenda-setting function of the mass media is reviewed, along with its impact on respondents' survey answers. "Feeling thermometers," widely used in causal analysis of electoral behavior, may also be susceptible to question order effects. In concluding, the authors note that psychological states of respondents are often changed simply by the process of having opinions measured in surveys. The 1980s references number six; there are twenty-eight references in total.

198. Bishop, George F., Robert W. Oldendick, and Alfred J. Tuchfarber. "What Must My Interest in Politics Be If I Just Told You 'I Don't Know'?" *Public Opinion Quarterly* 48, no. 2 (Summer 1984): 510–19.

Survey respondents who answered "I don't know" to questions about their congressman's record were then asked what his/her views were on their own interests in government and public affairs. The result is that when questioned in the foregoing order, these respondents are much less likely to think that they follow public affairs than if the question order is reversed. The researchers also found that buffer questions on unrelated topics do not eliminate or significantly reduce this contextual effect. Earlier research indicates that people tend to respond with the "first thing that comes to mind from their most relevant, recent experience"— relevant experience depends largely on the context in which the question is posed. The conclusion to the article indicates that what is really needed is a theory of the question-and-answer process in which the meaning of the questions to the respondents is addressed. The issue of how questions are interpreted by respondents is the fundamental issue. Eleven references, including eight from the 1980s, accompany the text, along with three tables.

199.   Crespi, Irving, and Dwight Morris. "Question Order Effect and the Measurement of Candidate Preference in the 1982 Connecticut Elections." *Public Opinion Quarterly* 48, no. 3 (Fall 1984): 578–91.

The *New York Times* (NYT) and the *Hartford Courant* (HC) published poll results that were in conflict as to who was ahead in the 1982 campaign for United States Senator from Connecticut, incumbent Senator Lowell Weicker or Democratic challenger Toby Moffett. The NYT reported that Moffett was narrowly ahead, while the HC reported a Weicker sixteen-point lead. The polls from each newspaper also measured the standing of the candidates for governor, with both showing incumbent Democratic Governor William O'Neill "comfortably" in the lead against rival Republican Lewis Rome. The authors' hypothesis was that when two contests are measured in the same poll, the question order will affect the standing of the candidates. A poll using a split-sample design verified this hypothesis. Crespi and Morris examine the role that question order has in relation to party identification, candidate preference, political ideology, and education. The results of the study substantiate the view that the order in which candidates are listed on voting ballots can affect voting behavior. The text includes nine tables and nineteen references (four in the 1980s).

200.   Lickteig, Carl W. "Informational Salience Effects on Attitudinal Inference and Expression: Context Effect in Survey Research." Ph.D. diss., University of Louisville, 1984. 139p.

The dissertation examines the effect of the specific-general sequencing of related items as contrasted with a cross-typical range of attitudinal issues. Context effects are explored with respect to their responsibility for false survey research results. Lickteig found that while respondents were generally not affected by the specific-general arrangements, they may report "somewhat more favorable" attitudes with this approach. When more unusual salience manipulations were tested, significant attitudinal shifts may be produced. A discussion of the findings in relation to survey research specifically, and to attitudinal research in general, concludes the study. References are included.

201. McClendon, McKee J., and David J. O'Brien. "Question-Order Effects on the Determinants of Subjective Well-Being." *Public Opinion Quarterly* 52, no. 3 (Fall 1988): 351–64.

Questions using the part-whole format are shown to be particularly vulnerable to question-order effects. Part-whole combinations of questions involve a general question which is "intended to contain or summarize one or more specific questions." Order effects found with the married group were not found with the unmarried group in a 1982 telephone survey (known as the Akron Area Survey) sponsored by the Department of Sociology at the University of Akron. A split-ballot experiment was used. The authors' analysis indicates that the order of the general and specific items in a survey can substantially affect conclusions relating to the effects of unmeasured variables. A suggestion is made that further research should focus on possible variation in context effects across social groups. A figure demonstrates the manner in which the questions were asked in the Akron experiment, leading from the specific domain to the general (with the alternate version of general-first, leading to specific explained). Other tables concentrate on the results obtained from the married persons. A twenty-seven-item list of references includes nineteen from the 1980s.

202. McFarland, Sam G. "Effects of Question Order on Survey Responses." *Public Opinion Quarterly* 45, no. 2 (Summer 1981): 208–15.

In the discussion section of the article, McFarland observes that the effects of question order are consistent no matter what the sex or educational attainment of the respondents. Therefore, the issue of question order is significant when dealing with a special segment of the population or when conducting a general population survey. In a statewide (Kentucky) random survey, two question orders were employed. Four questions dealing with general interest in politics and religion, and general evaluations of the gravity of the economic and energy situations were asked. The first two questions call for respondents' interest, while the latter called for discriminating judgments. These four questions either preceded or followed a series of specific questions depending upon the question order the respondent received. The author found that respondents showed significantly greater interest in politics and religion when the general questions followed the specific questions, whereas the evaluations of the economic and energy situations were little altered by question order. McFarland suggests that interest is more easily influenced than evaluation in this question order experiment. He continues by observing that the more specific the question content, and the more concrete the response is therefore required to be—to that degree the influence of question order will also be less a factor. There are eighteen pre-1980 references.

203.   Sigelman, Lee. "Question-Order Effects on Presidential Popularity." *Public Opinion Quarterly* 45, no. 2 (Summer 1981): 199–207.

Sigelman seeks to evaluate a concern expressed by Darcy and Schramm (*American Political Science Review*, 1979) which expresses the view that the Gallup presidential popularity question used for more than forty years may be affected by question-order bias. Darcy and Schramm "without evidence to the contrary" assume that a consistency effect invalidates these Gallup survey results. The Gallup question at issue reads: "Do you approve or disapprove of the way that _____ is handling his job as President?" Using a methodological experiment, Sigelman tested the following hypotheses: When the Gallup presidential popularity question (1) "is preceded by negatively charged items, presidential popularity tends to be biased downward"; (2) "is asked very early in an interview, it tends to elicit more favorable evaluations than when it is asked late"; and (3) "is asked very early in an interview, it tends to elicit less opinionation than when it is asked late." Opinionation refers to the willingness to evaluate the president, whether positively or negatively. The author found that the order in which the question is presented "does not significantly affect the direction of response, but it does affect opinionation." The author supplies eight pre-1980 cited references.

11.5 MISCELLANEOUS

204. Bishop, George F., Robert W. Oldendick, and Alfred J. Tuchfarber. "Effects of Presenting One Versus Two Sides of an Issue in Survey Questions." *Public Opinion Quarterly* 46, no. 1 (Spring 1982): 69–85.

The research concerns whether it is appropriate to ask a simple question with no alternative provided or whether the alternative is necessary to generate a realistic picture of public opinion. The authors set up means to determine the effects of one-sided questions versus questions with two sides of the issue presented. Prior research by many different survey researchers indicates that providing a second substantive alternative reduces the percentage of respondents who will choose the first alternative from a single-sided form. The authors found that it is no easy challenge to decide what the alternative or other side of each issue should be. The question form effects depend upon the respondents' educational level. In the view of the article researchers, theory building in the form of an information-processing model of the survey instrument is the way to more adequately deal with form challenges (rather than attempting further methodological improvements). The data gathered reinforces many previous findings that survey results can vary greatly depending upon question wording and format. Study data and question formats are displayed in four tables. Complete question variations employed are found in the appendix. There are twenty-one references, five of which are from the 1980s.

205. Converse, Jean M., and Stanley Presser. *Survey Questions: Handcrafting the Standardized Questionnaire.* Sage University Paper series on Quantitative Applications in the Social Sciences, edited by John L. Sullivan, and Richard G. Niemi, no. 63. Beverly Hills, CA: Sage Publications, 1986. 80p.

Focusing on research, exploration, and pretesting, this volume is designed for practitioners and teachers of survey research. Emphasis is placed on face-to-face and telephone interviewing situations, rather than on written questionnaires. The book is directed primarily toward the general public rather than the well-educated or "intensely motivated" individual. The volume is divided into three chapters. Chapter 1 explores the art and experience elements, covering what the authors describe as a "litany of cautions," including the "enduring counsel for simplicity." The next chapter reviews the empirical findings, discussing topics such as using specific questions, question order, and the "no opinion" option. Chapter 3 reviews pilot work and pretesting (including strategies, purposes, and phrases). A call to heed the advice of available experts— namely critics, colleagues, and interviewers—is suggested. Converse and Presser believe that each survey must be "custom-built" to the needs of each research project, employing the guidelines developed from both the artistic and the social scientific means available, as well as with practical guidance from experienced researchers. Four pages of references are provided.

206. Gilbert, D.A. "Creating an Index of Public Opinion Questions." *Behavioral & Social Sciences Librarian* 3, no. 4 (Summer 1984): 77–80.

The reasoning behind the compilation of the *American Public Opinion Index* (APOI) is considered. The *APOI* collects the questions used for scientifically drawn samples of the general public. The results must be available to any researcher for inclusion in the annually produced volume. For the 1981 volume more than two hundred surveys from national, state, and local populations are included. An estimated ten thousand questions, as well as the responses offered, are entered under a wide variety of subject headings. The index provides the information necessary to retrieve the complete polling results. Gilbert observes that a great deal of the survey research conducted in the United States is not available to the general public, as many of the market, product, and political polls are conducted by private companies for the exclusive use of their clients. The author also believes that both the complexity and the overwhelming amount of data currently being generated are some of the reasons for not attempting to develop a single source of polling information for the nation which would cover national, state, and local efforts. No references are included.

207. Kenney, Patrick J., and Tom W. Rice. "The Evaporating Independents: Removing the 'Independent' Option from the NES Party Identification Question." *Public Opinion Quarterly* 52, no. 2 (Summer 1988): 231–39.

The subject of experimentation in this study revolves around what happens when the "Independent" option is removed. This was done by varying the wording in the National Election Study (NES) question which classically read: "Generally speaking, do you think of yourself as a Republican, a Democrat, an Independent, or what?" In two surveys of

Vermont residents, when the Independent choice is omitted, the percentage of "self-identified independents" drops significantly. The impact is also related to the age of the respondents. Younger respondents chose the Independent option to a much greater degree than older respondents when specifically included as a choice. When omitted, more older respondents opted to identify as Independents. Roper Organization and NES nationwide survey data subjected to similar analysis support the findings of Kenney and Rice from the Vermont studies. If the Independent option had been left out of the NES questions over the last twenty years, the authors theorize that the percentage of nonpartisans would have remained more stable (as it is apparently the large influx of young members of the electorate who steer toward the Independent label when given such an option). Twenty-one references are included, with twelve from the 1980s.

208. Smith, Tom W. "The Art of Asking Questions, 1936–1985." *Public Opinion Quarterly* 51, no. 4, pt. 2 (Winter 1987): S95–S108.

The surveys reviewed for this article are public opinion polls, which Smith explains as being "public" in these four ways: (1) the samples used are from the American general adult population; (2) the surveys are conducted for mass media or by the mass media; (3) the results are regularly made available to the public; and (4) the surveys deal with public "matters," such as what people would like/would not like government to do, and their feelings about leaders and candidates. After fifty years, Smith finds that surveys of public opinion continue to serve the role of monitoring society and measuring "the pulse of democracy." The author observes that knowledge questions are relatively rare and in decline and that behavioral inquiries are seldom made. Polls examine people's opinion, while gathering some basic background information about the respondent. Polls are described as "reactive" to history in general and to current events in particular. Topics are covered when they are considered newsworthy. Poll language has moved away from the natural language of the early years to larger surveys with more categories, longer questions, and generally more questions. Open-ended questions are in decline, and show cards are in more frequent use in face-to-face interviews. Likert scales and scalometers have specialized the communication format of surveys and moved them further from natural language format. Seven references are included.

209.   Smith, Tom W. "Recalling Attitudes: An Analysis of Retrospective Questions on the 1982 GSS." *Public Opinion Quarterly*
48, no. 3 (Fall 1984): 639–49.

The General Social Surveys (GSS) are used to explore the requests that
are made of respondents to recall attributes, events, behaviors, and attitudes from the recent and distant past. Research in cognitive psychology
indicates that error is created through forgetting and memory distortion.
There is a marked tendency to omit facts, associate events or behavior
with a different time frame than when it really occurred, and also to
create consistency or a standard pattern that can cause distortion through
the changing of facts. Bias therefore becomes a feature of attitude recall.
The author suggests that attitude recall at best is a questionable basis for
social science research to build on. Smith uses the phrase "hazardous
enterprise" to describe attitude recall, and discusses the effect of the
"good old days" image in which the respondent overstates the
pleasantness of the past and the degree of traditionalism (along with the
problem of telescoping in which the actual occurrence of events is
shifted closer to the present). Due to these shortcomings, Smith believes
that the reliability of attitude is seriously undermined. The text includes
several tables, an appendix of question wordings, and thirty-two
references (eight from the 1980s).

12. Sampling

12.1 RESPONDENT SELECTION

210. Adler, Kenneth P. "Polling the Attentive Public." In *Polling and the Democratic Consensus*, edited by L. John Martin, 143–54. *Annals of the American Academy of Political and Social Science*, edited by Richard D. Lambert, vol. 472. Beverly Hills, CA: Sage Publications, 1984.

The "attentive public" is often a small group which is particularly interested in the problem at hand, while the general public may have little or no interest in the subject. Adler demonstrates that the attentives are drawn from all segments of the population, thereby making the group more representative of the general public than, for example, the group comprising the best educated. The attentives are more likely to be politically involved, and their views are more likely to predict policy decisions. Additionally, the attentives are more likely to reflect current political trends than their counterparts in the best-educated group. The argument is that public opinion polls can be misleading when the general public is polled on issues of little or no concern or about which little knowledge or information is held. Adler identifies six techniques which have been used to isolate four major groups—the interested, the informed, the involved, and the influential. He briefly explains the shortcomings of each technique before discussing the value of the attentive public as a tool for analysis. Gabriel Almond is credited with coining the term "attentive public" in 1950, with further analysis, empirical scrutiny, and application by Donald Devine in the work titled *The Attentive Public: Polyarchial Democracy* (1970). The Adler article contains seventeen footnotes.

211. Czaja, Ronald, Johnny Blair, and Jutta P. Sebestik. "Respondent Selection in a Telephone Survey: A Comparison of Three Techniques." *Journal of Marketing Research* 19, no. 3 (August 1982): 381–85.

The purpose of the study is to determine the cooperation rates and respondent/household characteristics of the (Leslie) Kish procedure and two versions of the (Verling C.) Troldahl–(Roy E.) Carter–(Barbara E.) Bryant [T–C–B] procedure. One of the two versions of the T–C–B asks for the number of women and one requesting the number of men. The Kish procedure, when selecting respondents by telephone survey, requires the interviewer to determine all of the eligible respondents within a household, list them by sex, and within sex groupings to list oldest to youngest. Once listed, the interviewer uses a random number table to determine which person should be interviewed. Typically, only one individual is interviewed per household. The T–C–B approach was developed out of a concern that the Kish procedure calls for two questions to be asked: (1) "How many persons 18 years or older live in your household, counting yourself?" and (2) "How many of them are men?" A four selection matrix rotated randomly over the sample enables the interviewer to quickly make a selection. Bryant suggested modifying the matrix sequence to accommodate changing household patterns and the higher refusal rate among men. No major differences in cooperation rates were found between the methods, nor were bias differences noted. The different matrix assignment (T–C–B [men] and T–C–B [women]) did generate different interview rates. For this reason, the researchers preferred the T–C–B (women) and Kish procedures over the T–C–B (men) approach. A table shows the T–C–B matrix choices, and three other tables clarify in percentage terms the study findings. Four pre-1980 references are provided.

212. Hagan, Dan E., and Charlotte Meier Collier. "Must Respondent Selection Procedures for Telephone Surveys Be Invasive?" *Public Opinion Quarterly* 47, no. 4 (Winter 1983): 547–56.

The purpose of the study was to see if noninvasive telephone surveying could be conducted without impairing results or altering the nature of the respondent sample selected. The authors sought to study the question through the use of two procedures. The first procedure asked two household composition questions as a technique in selecting random respondents. The alternative approach did not ask preliminary questions. The results indicate that there were fewer refusals with the alternative approach. The data also shows that the demographic profile of the sample generated without the preliminary questions was not compromised. As the authors suggest, the alternative mode of respondent selection places a lesser burden on the respondent, while at the same time saving the survey research organization money (because it is most likely that the interview will be shorter). The Kish procedure and the Troldahl–Carter procedure are discussed as alternative methods used in the past for generating random respondent samples. The benefits and shortcomings of each approach are briefly reviewed. Three tables explore comparisons of the Troldahl–Carter procedure with those of the alternative procedure discussed by Hagan and Collier. Five references are provided (two are from the 1980s).

213. Rothbart, George S., Michelle Fine, and Seymour Sudman. "On Finding and Interviewing the Needles in the Haystack: The Use of Multiplicity Sampling." *Public Opinion Quarterly* 46, no. 3 (Fall 1982): 408–21.

Multiplicity sampling, in the case described in the article, yielded twice the number that conventional sampling would have, but was even higher for blacks and Mexican–Americans than for whites (the case involved Vietnam era veterans). The larger local network size, for the minorities mentioned, provided uniquely effective opportunities to employ multiplicity sampling. The authors cite, among other reasons, the general tendency of minority group members to be localized—and therefore not distant from their families. These characteristics permit the surveying of rare populations to a greater degree than might otherwise be thought. It would also include other minority groups that share the proclivity to have high local network size, (i.e., Jews). Although the interviewing process which uses multiplicity sampling is longer due to the need for special information that is required, the overall screening cost savings to the organization conducting the survey is substantial when compared with standard methods. A discussion of the survey results in relation to yield, kinship, and ethnicity follows. Fifteen pre-1980 references complete the article.

214. Salmon, Charles T., and John Spicer Nichols. "The Next-Birthday Method of Respondent Selection." *Public Opinion Quarterly* 47, no. 2 (Summer 1983): 270–76.

Four methods for selecting telephone survey respondents within a household unit are discussed. These are the Troldahl–Carter, male/female alternation, next-birthday, and whoever answers methods. The researchers suggest that the next-birthday method is relatively efficient for selecting a sample that is representative of all household members. The study was conducted in Kentucky by a professional interviewing firm with a total of 230 interviews completed after contacting 416 households. The issue here concerns how respondents are selected from within the household members once a household has been contacted. The Troldahl–Carter method, in the original configuration, excludes 2 to 3 percent of the population due to a false assumption on the part of the researchers. Subsequent modifications have addressed the oversight. The method of permitting whoever answers the telephone to be the respondent yields a disproportionately high number of older women. The male/female method has several shortcomings, including the requirement to eliminate households from the sample if a member of the predetermined sex is not present, and the approach is not age factored— which again means that more older people are represented in such a sample. The next-birthday method calls for the interviewer to speak to the person who has the next birthday in that household. Three tables and six pre-1980 references are present.

215. Sudman, Seymour. "Applied Sampling." Chap. 5 in *Handbook of Survey Research*, edited by Peter H. Rossi, James D. Wright, and Andy B. Anderson, 145–94. Quantitative Studies in Social Relations, consulting editor Peter H. Rossi. New York: Academic Press, 1983.

The material for this chapter is drawn mostly from Sudman's book titled *Applied Sampling* (1976). The selection and evaluation of survey research samples are covered in the *Handbook* chapter. There are twenty-six sections in addition to the introduction, including: "Inappropriate Sample Design"; "A Credibility Scale"; "Simple Random Sampling"; "Systematic Sampling"; "The Use of Telephone Directories and Random Digit Dialing" (RDD); and "Appropriate and Inappropriate Uses of Stratification." Sudman emphasizes the large number of issues which come into play when considering survey sampling. The pages covering the subject of stratified sampling—variances differing between strata, and costs differing by strata—involve considerations employing advanced mathematics. The additional reading section for chapter 5 lists six bibliographies, three journals, and six textbooks which might be useful for further information. Another eight items are cited which deal with special topics covered in the Sudman chapter. Nine tables are used to highlight examples of sample surveying. Thirty-eight references are listed.

216. Traugott, Michael W. "The Importance of Persistence in Respondent Selection for Preelection Surveys." *Public Opinion Quarterly* 51, no. 1 (Spring 1987): 48–57.

The importance of persistence when contacting designated respondents lies in measurement differences in levels of support for political parties and candidates which can arise with less than diligent efforts. Samples which are comprised of first-call respondents only, include more Democrats; with further calling persistence the number of Republicans increases. The author suggests that although the sample size used for the study is small, some variations in public opinion polls may be the result of the respondent selection techniques employed. Additionally, party identification data may not be comparable across different surveys because of differing techniques and methodologies employed to collect the data. The context for this study was the 1984 presidential campaign between Republican Ronald Reagan and Democrat Walter Mondale. Overall 745 interviews were conducted with a response rate of 65 percent; 39 percent of the interviews were obtained within two calls, 57 percent within three calls, 68 percent within four calls, 92 percent within ten calls, and 96 percent within fifteen calls. The most difficult-to-reach respondents received as many as thirty calls. Three tables provide analyses of the data by age, sex, educational level, and race. An appendix reproduces the result codes employed. There are five references (two from the 1980s).

217. Traugott, Michael W., Robert M. Groves, and James M. Lepkowski. "Using Dual Frame Designs to Reduce Nonresponse in Telephone Surveys." *Public Opinion Quarterly* 51, no. 4 (Winter 1987): 522–39.

Dual frame designs use two sets of frames to locate the desired population. Separate samples are drawn from the frames and combined in analysis to calculate the overall population boundaries. The researchers conducted three surveys of telephone households which were selected by two methods: (1) standard random digit dialing (RDD) techniques; and (2) commercially purchased lists of telephone numbers. The RDD sample received "cold contact" interviews. The list frame samples were sent letters in advance, and the listed household name was used in the introduction. The advance letter was found to increase response rates. The use of the household name led to no discernible difference in response rates. The use of the telephone directory frame increased response rates as well as the productivity of the interviewer. The list frame covers about three-fourths of the telephone household population. When RDD and list frame samples are combined, survey design is improved, response rates are higher, and overall the survey is financially more cost-effective. The authors suggest further research using different percentages of the sample which receive the advance letter and possibly varying the sample design in other ways, e.g., using the names and addresses from a list frame. Six tables are provided along with twenty references.

12.2 SAMPLE SIZE

218.   Hinkle, Dennis E., and J. Dale Oliver. "How Large Should the Sample Be? A Question with No Simple Answer? Or..." *Educational and Psychological Measurement* 43, no. 4 (Winter 1983): 253–57.

The question of what size the sample should be is unanswerable unless the question of the effect size is considered. Hinkle and Oliver focus attention on the complexity of the initial question, and at the same time attempt to simplify the answer once the effect size has been determined. The authors have developed tables which provide the appropriate sample size for these values: (1) the level of significance; (2) the power of the statistical test; (3) the estimated variance—standardized in the Effect Size (ES); and (4) the ES. The authors cite J. Cohen's *Statistical Power Analysis for the Behavioral Sciences* (New York: Academic Press, 1969, p. 9), for a definition of ES: "the degree to which the phenomenon exists." A table provides the "Sample Sizes for Varying Numbers of Treatment Levels and Effects Sizes to be Detected." Seventeen references, three from the 1980s, are included.

219.   Hinkle, Dennis E., J. Dale Oliver, and Charles A. Hinkle. "How Large Should the Sample Be? Part II—The One-Sample Case for Survey Research." *Educational and Psychological Measurement* 45, no. 2 (Summer 1985): 271–80.

This is a follow-up article which addresses the sample size question for one-sample case survey research projects. The authors suggest that the one-sample case is the general one encountered in survey research. There are five tables in the article which address varying survey situations with differing ranges of effect size and levels of power. The authors review other considerations which need to be addressed when determining the sample size. One assumption is that simple random sampling is the method used—other approaches would require adjustments to the tables presented. The tables assume a 100 percent response rate, with over sampling suggested as a means to meet the sample size requirements. A common response rate is 40 to 50 percent. Follow-up of nonrespondents is recommended in order to "assure an adequate sample which is free from response bias." The authors caution that "the enclosed tables are not appropriate for determining the sample sizes necessary for effect sizes for differences between these subclassifications [white and nonwhite, rural, suburban and urban respondents] of respondents." Eleven references are provided, two from the 1980s.

220. Milton, Sande. "A Sample Size Formula for Multiple Regression Studies." *Public Opinion Quarterly* 50, no. 1 (Spring 1986): 112–18.

The formula presented is designed to avoid the "rules of thumb" techniques used to determine the minimum sample size in regression studies. Milton views these techniques as inadequate because they are subject to change and interpretation by their users, and by their very nature they are less than satisfactory. A presentation of the sample size formula follows, along with considerations of its use with stratified and cluster samples. The author maintains that the formula is easier to use than existing formulae based on statistical power. Milton views the application of the formula as one of the researcher's tools to maximize available resources. Several tables assist in sample size determination. There are eighteen references (two from the 1980s).

221. Wunsch, Daniel R. "Survey Research: Determining Sample Size and Representative Response." *Business Education Forum* 40, no. 5 (February 1986): 31–34.

The purpose of the presentation is to assist researchers, educate students, and advise research evaluators how to determine appropriate sample sizes and to ascertain how representative the response rate is by means of a table. One table shows the sample size by population number and percentage of confidence in a plus or minus figure from one to ten. For example, a sample of one hundred individuals with eighty respondents yields a confidence level of plus or minus 5 percent. A second table graphically compares sample and respondent characteristics. The table is designed to deal with the issue of respondent bias. The article appears in a section called "Forum Feature: Action Research in Business Education," edited by Kenneth W. Brown. There are six references, one from the 1980s.

12.3 SUBGROUPS AND SPECIAL POPULATIONS

222.   Blair, Johnny, and Ronald Czaja. "Locating a Special Population Using Random Digit Dialing." *Public Opinion Quarterly* 46, no. 4 (Winter 1982): 585–90.

A modification of a procedure developed by Joseph Waksburg (a two-stage method of selecting equal probability samples of the general population using random digit dialing) is used to locate special populations which cluster geographically. When geographic proximity is known, telephone area code(s) and prefix combinations can be defined as Primary Sampling Units (PSU) and be used to select a sample which will have probabilities proportionate to the number of the subpopulation within each PSU. The article discusses an example of the method using a national telephone survey conducted at the Survey Research Laboratory (SRL) at the University of Illinois, Urbana–Champaign. In a 1978 study conducted by the SRL, which was limited to the one hundred largest Standard Metropolitan Statistical Areas (SMSA), 34 percent of the working primary telephone numbers were identified as compared to the standard for national surveys of between 22 and 24 percent. It is suggested by Blair and Czaja that the method described in the article is effective for reaching special populations which are highly clustered, such as with some racial groups. A table and four pre-1980 references are provided.

223.   Davis, Todd McLin. "Detecting Subgroups in Survey Research." *Psychological Reports* 59, no. 2, pt. 2 (October 1986): 751–60.

The purpose of this research was to determine whether cluster analysis can be used effectively to determine interaction between subgroups within a survey sample. The author suggests that when the data is in the form of coded categories, cluster analysis is particularly effective. Two fictitious data sets were generated for the experiment. The article appendix supplies the format of the ten-item questionnaire employed.

Two sets of data were used: random and contrived. The clustering procedures were successful in identifying the structure of the contrived data set. The author suggests that cluster analysis would be useful in situations in which presurvey investigation is limited or nonexistent, "leaving the survey open to bias from unrevealed subcultures." Several figures display the results using the random and contrived data. A table compares clusters and selected questionnaire items. Nine of the references are from the 1980s, the other three are from the 1970s.

224. Himmelfarb, Harold S., R. Michael Loar, and Susan H. Mott. "Sampling by Ethnic Surnames: The Case of American Jews." *Public Opinion Quarterly* 47, no. 2 (Summer 1983): 247–60.

The article covers alternative means of establishing a sample when dealing with numerically small minorities other than by using standard probability sampling. Two methods are covered: (1) the creation of a sample through distinctive surnames; and (2) the creation of a sample through the use of organization membership lists. The 1974 estimate of the American Jewish population was between 2.6 percent and 2.8 percent nationally. One handicap for the organization lists, so far as survey researchers are concerned, is that only about half of all adult Jews are affiliated with the organizations from which the lists are drawn. The researchers conclude that a fairly representative sample can be created using individuals with distinctive Jewish names (DJN). The differences between those with DJNs and those without were very slight and considerably less than those sample members generated from the organization list. There are caveats to the findings, which include: (1) geographic differences were not considered as this was a national sample; (2) DJNs lists imply the use of an existing source such as a telephone directory; and (3) Jewish women married to men not born Jewish are likely to be underrepresented due to the absence of a Jewish surname. The authors suggest the technique has applicability for Greek-Americans, Chinese-Americans, and Korean-Americans. Eighteen references (two from the 1980s) complete the article.

225. Sudman, Seymour. "Efficient Screening Methods for the Sampling of Geographically Clustered Special Populations." *Journal of Marketing Research* 22, no. 1 (February 1985): 20–29.

The methods for reaching careful probability samples for special populations are described by Sudman. Screening costs will continue to be a significant factor in the overall cost of gathering information, but alternative procedures are shown to have difficulties and shortcomings.

As a timely inexpensive alternative, the author cites lists for locating the areas where special populations can be found. One such list source is Gale Research Company's *Encyclopedia of Associations*. The article discusses procedures when zero segments are not known in advance; when face-to-face screening is required; the use of combined methods; situations which call for telephone screening but face-to-face interviewing; and finally, variations in density of special populations in nonzero clusters. Cost formulae are presented throughout and require advanced mathematical knowledge for comprehension. A summary listing five alternative methods for reducing screening costs is provided for cases which involve clustered special populations. Four tables and seven references (one from the 1980s) are included.

226.   Tourangeau, Roger, and A. Wade Smith. "Finding Subgroups for Surveys." *Public Opinion Quarterly* 49, no. 3 (Fall 1985): 351–65.

Sampling statisticians seek to increase the "take" rate during the screening operation and to keep the costs of screening interviews to a minimum. The take rate refers to the percentage of screeners which produce members of the eligible population. The subgroup spoken of here is a national sample of blacks, generated as part of an experiment with the General Social Survey (GSS) of 1982. Two methods of sample selection were used. One employed area probability sampling with the selection probability for an area proportional to the number of its black population. The alternate method sampled extra dwelling units in areas selected for the regular GSS. The article refers to the first approach as "The Black Frame" and the second as "The Black Oversample." The black frame is more cost efficient than the alternative mentioned, although less so statistically. The black frame has a higher take rate and includes a larger number of cases. The two samples were much the same so far as response rates were concerned, with about 97 percent of the screeners completed; 71 percent of the households with eligible respondents had interviews conducted. Three tables accompany the text, along with seven references (two from the 1980s).

12.4 NONRESPONSE

227. Aiken, Lewis R. "The Problem of Nonresponse in Survey Research." *Journal of Experimental Education* 56, no. 3 (Spring 1988): 116–19.

The challenge of small proportions of responses or returns in educational research employing survey methods is considered. Aiken confirms a 1985 finding by Hartman, Fugua, and Jenkins (*Journal of Experimental Education*, 1986) that "over 50 percent of research papers and dissertations in education are reports of investigations in which some type of survey methodology has been employed." Aiken considers nonresponse primarily in relation to mail surveys. Article sections include discussions of sample size determination; estimating population parameters from sample statistics; remedies for nonresponse; interval estimation; and a test of the difference between proportions and means. Advanced statistics are used to explain the various national and empirical procedures suggested to deal with nonresponse in survey research. Nine references are provided, seven from the 1980s.

228. Daniel, Wayne W., Brian Schott, Fred C. Atkins, and Alpheus Davis. "An Adjustment for Nonresponse in Sample Surveys." *Educational and Psychological Measurement* 42, no. 1 (Spring 1982): 57–67.

The use of Bayes's theorem in adjusting for nonresponse bias is explored by simulating a mail survey of hospitals in the United States. Using six hundred hospitals with information on five known variables, Bayes's formula correctly predicted the status of ninety-two of the one hundred "non-respondents" with respect to a sixth variable. The authors suggest that further research is needed involving a real survey in which the accuracy of the predictions could be determined. Varying levels of nonresponse will be necessary to adequately test the approach (17 percent was used in the simulated survey). The researchers would also like to vary the number of characteristics and determine the level of predictive accuracy, thereby establishing a minimum number of characteristics needed. The use of Bayes's theorem has potential in estimating missing data in partially completed questionnaires. Bayes's theorem is expressed mathematically, along with an example, and a table showing the number-of-admissions/characteristics matrix. There are forty-three pre-1980 references.

229.   DeMaio, Theresa J. "Refusals: Who, Where and Why." *Public Opinion Quarterly* 44, no. 2 (Summer 1980): 223–33.

The older and predominately middle-class portions of the sample, among households that have not been previously surveyed, are where the refusals occurred. Geographically, Westerners and urban residents are the most likely to refuse. In order of frequency cited, privacy concerns, postsurvey experience, and the knowledge that participation is voluntary are the primary reasons for refusals. DeMaio is with the U.S. Bureau of the Census and is interested in studying the characteristics of refusers to determine means to appeal to those individuals and to develop procedures that will reduce their numbers. Of particular interest to DeMaio was the effect of the Privacy Act, and whether it played a role in the decision-making process of the refuser. The Privacy Act "requires explicit notification of potential respondents that participation in the survey is voluntary, and that no penalties are involved in refusal." To measure the impact of the Privacy Act, information was obtained from the refusals as to why they were not cooperating. The data suggests that the Privacy Act is not the primary reason for refusal, and, in fact, the author states that other Census Bureau research indicates that refusals have not increased significantly since the act went into effect. There are four tables and twelve pre-1980 references.

230.   Pearl, Dennis K., and David Fairley. "Testing for the Potential for Nonresponse Bias in Sample Surveys." *Public Opinion Quarterly* 49, no. 4 (Winter 1985): 553–60.

As the authors explain, nonresponse bias results if there is a difference between the preferences of those who do not respond and those responders on whom the estimates are based. Pearl and Fairley propose a technique to establish the size of the nonresponse problem—a technique which provides a statistical hypothesis test for association between issue preference and opinion strength. The authors use an example which appeared in the *Columbus Dispatch* [Ohio] newspaper. Two mail surveys were conducted one week before the election to determine voter preference for the position of Columbus mayor. Measures taken in some surveys to determine strength of opinion (such as checking the length of time needed for each response or sending multiple mailings) are difficult if not impossible when short time spans exist between poll mailings and when the results are due. This could mean that strength of opinion becomes an uncorrected source of bias. Following the authors' statistical test, if bias is detected, the accuracy of the poll results may be in serious doubt, and if published, would reflect biases leading to questions of the validity of the data. There are three tables provided, along with fourteen references (two from the 1980s).

231.   Steeh, Charlotte G. "Trends in Nonresponse Rates, 1952–1979." *Public Opinion Quarterly* 45, no. 1 (Spring 1981): 40–57.
As the title suggests, the author examines twenty-seven years of survey responses. Considered are the results of the National Election Studies (NES) and the Surveys of Consumer Attitudes conducted by the Survey Research Center (SRC) of the University of Michigan. A systematic documentation of the nonresponse rates in the sample surveys was conducted. The analysis shows that there have been substantial increases in total nonresponse. The increase is largely due to respondents who refuse to be interviewed. The trend toward increasing nonresponse is related to the level of urbanization. Varying theories are cited to explain this trend, including those suggested in 1974 by the American Statistics Association (ASA), which cites concerns over privacy, confidentiality, and disillusionment with, and overexposure to, survey research as primary reasons for increasing refusal rates. A report by House and Wolf (*Journal of Personality and Social Psychology*, 1978) is cited in which large city dwellers are shown to be less helpful and trusting than people living elsewhere. Imputation is suggested as a means by which some sample deficiencies created by nonresponse can be overcome. Steeh concludes that further research into the characteristics of nonrespondents is the most effective way to overcome the challenges posed by these individuals. Twenty-one references are provided.

232.   Stinchcombe, Arthur L., Calvin Jones, and Paul Sheatsley. "Nonresponse Bias for Attitude Questions." *Public Opinion Quarterly* 45, no. 3 (Fall 1981): 359–75.
With 20 to 30 percent of a designated sample either never contacted or, once contacted, never interviewed, the issue of nonresponse bias in sample surveys using probability methods is investigated. Using telephone surveys with a list sample of a rural population, the researchers found that refusals created much more bias than inaccessibility. Several suggestions are made as to how error estimates for surveys could be improved. First, the authors believe that more resources should be spent in trying to convert refusals than into finding difficult-to-reach respondents. In the rural population studied, the difficult-to-reach individuals were not attitudinally distinct. The authors also found the characteristic of being less accessible less consistent than the predisposition to refuse. Second, the authors suggest that researchers adopt a

"Temporary Refusal" variable, and that the number of respondents who refused and the number who were never reached should be reported to the client. The authors state that the "accuracy of estimation of nonresponse bias depends on the number of converted refusers who finally get interviewed," and that "bias depends less on the response rate overall, than on the number of refusers who are not converted." There are five pre-1980 references included.

12.5 OTHER SAMPLING RESEARCH

233.   Assael, Henry, and John Keon. "Nonsampling vs. Sampling Errors in Survey Research." *Journal of Marketing: A Quarterly Publication of the American Marketing Association* 46, no. 2 (Spring 1982): 114–23.

By examining and empirically comparing elements of total survey error for a number of survey designs and data collection methods, the authors conclude that nonsampling error contributes to a much larger degree than random sampling error to total survey error. Within the parameters of the sample of small businesses studied, the following conclusions were reached: (1) mail and "drop-off techniques" are the most effective in reducing nonsampling error; (2) efforts to make large samples as a means to reduce random sampling error may be "misplaced"; (3) selecting personal interviewing as a preferred option may be "misplaced"; and (4) the authors recommend using validated nonresponse bias to measure nonresponse error. Total survey error measurement is presented mathematically in the first section of the article; a discussion of data collection and survey design follows, emphasizing analysis of results. The results analysis section contains discussions of random sampling error versus nonsampling error, prealert techniques, follow-up techniques, and second delivery. The article includes four tables, one figure, and an appendix dealing with unbiased estimates of mean squared error for total survey error, nonsampling error, and sampling error. One of the twenty-seven references is drawn from the 1980s.

234. Frankel, Martin. "Sampling Theory." Chap. 2 in *Handbook of Survey Research*, edited by Peter H. Rossi, James D. Wright, and Andy B. Anderson, 21–67. Quantitative Studies in Social Relations, consulting editor Peter H. Rossi. New York: Academic Press, 1983.

Survey sampling theory concerns the methods and techniques of selecting samples in which the "results may be projected to larger populations." It was the introduction of probability sampling into survey research which shifted survey research more in the direction of science than art. Frankel discusses statistical inference in relation to population and element and covers the sample, sample design, probability samples, and nonprobability samples. A number of mathematical formulae are introduced to illustrate the topics discussed. The development of the sample design, along with design effect and related concepts, are the next subjects of concern. The major areas of the chapter are stratified sampling, cluster sampling, and the consideration of advanced topics, including unequal size cluster sampling with stratification, simple replicated (interpenetrating) subsampling, and several other areas. A full understanding of the chapter contents will require an understanding of statistical theory which entails more than an elementary knowledge of mathematics. A twenty-five item bibliography is divided into three groups: "Elementary," "Applied," and "Mathematical Theory."

235. Hess, Irene. *Sampling for Social Research Surveys, 1947–1980*. Ann Arbor, MI: Survey Research Center, Institute for Social Research, The University of Michigan, 1985. 294p.

The Survey Research Center (SRC) at the University of Michigan is the setting for the experiences in survey sampling described here. The thirty-three-year period covered reviews sampling practices from the origin of SRC and presents more extensive information than is available through summary statements which accompany archivally held data. A variety of sample designs and implementing methodologies are covered, as well as the sampling procedures used in a number of specialized situations. The sampling practices employed in ongoing personal interview surveys in a national sample of counties are discussed. There are nine chapters, related references, ten appendixes, and a glossary. The topics considered include (1) the multipurpose, flexible sample of counties from the 1970s and early 1980s; (2) personal interview surveys and the sampling procedures used to obtain samples of housing units and household members; (3) household samples for ongoing research programs; (4) the means by which sample counties may be supplemented to expand samples of rare populations; (5) the study of congressional elections through the use of a sample of congressional districts; (6) the SRC county sample and nonresidential populations; (7) sample surveys using the telephone; (8) state and local area household samples; and (9) other survey samples including various medical and educational research projects. A collaboration with the Mershon Center at the Ohio State University began in 1972 and has continued into the 1980s; it involves SRC's participation in five research projects. The appendixes provide some specifics of sample selection, examples of roles of the interviewers in household sampling, and data on household composition as well as nonsampling error information. A glossary of technical terms used in the book has over forty-five entries. The Hess book concludes with 145 selected references, 17 percent (or 24) from the early 1980s; 35 percent (or 49) from the 1970s; 23 percent (or 33) from the 1960s; 17 percent (or 24) from the 1950s; and 8 percent (or 11) from the 1940s. There are a few undated items suggesting long runs of certain serial titles.

236. Kalton, Graham. *Introduction to Survey Sampling.* Sage University Paper series on Quantitative Applications in the Social Sciences, edited by John L. Sullivan, and Richard G. Niemi, 07-035. Beverly Hills, CA: Sage Publications, 1983. 96p.

The Sage University Paper by Kalton presents a broad overview of survey sampling with a wide range of techniques described. The volume is designed for the beginning reader who has some knowledge of elementary statistics and as a refresher for those with a modest familiarity with sampling theory. Kalton begins with simple random sampling and progresses to systematic sampling, stratification, and cluster and multistage sampling. The next topic addressed is probability proportional to size sampling followed by other probability designs. Sampling frames, nonresponse, survey analysis, and sample size are then presented. Two examples are given, one dealing with a national face-to-face interview survey, the other for a telephone interview survey. The last chapter deals with nonprobability sampling. In the concluding remarks Kalton cites thirteen authors whose works treat many of the subjects covered in much greater detail. There are thirty-nine references, six from the 1980s.

13. Interviewing

13.1 TELEPHONE INTERVIEWING

237. Bergsten, Jane Williams, Michael F. Weeks, and Fred A. Bryan. "Effects of an Advance Telephone Call in a Personal Interview Survey." *Public Opinion Quarterly* 48, no. 3 (Fall 1984): 650–57.
As part of a survey involving senior citizens, an experiment was conducted to determine the effects of a telephone call placed in advance (for purposes of scheduling an appointment for a personal interview). The authors found that, for surveys involving senior citizens, the additional telephone call did not greatly increase the refusal rate. A significant element is the cost savings to the research team—refusals by telephone are less expensive than refusals for in-person interviews. Prior to any contact with the respondents by telephone, there was an advance mailing designed to pave the way for the interviewer. The authors cite research showing that letters sent in advance can significantly reduce the refusal rate in telephone surveys. If the experiment were to be replicated, the authors suggest a refusal rate increase of about 1 percent for the advance telephone call sample versus a no-telephone call sample. Three tables provide breakdowns of the data. The authors indicate that they were able to find only two previous studies investigating advance telephone call effects—both from the 1960s and indicating conflicting results. Four references are provided.

238. Miller, Peter V., and Charles F. Cannell. "A Study of Experimental Techniques for Telephone Interviewing." *Public Opinion Quarterly* 46, no. 2 (Summer 1982): 250–69.
Face-to-face interviewing techniques have had a longer period of development than telephone interviewing techniques. The authors found

that the simple transference of techniques from one approach to the other does not work well. The different communication patterns and respondent motives, as well as the lack of visual cues, all call for other solutions before optimal telephone interviews can be achieved. The interviewing techniques used from face-to-face experience include commitment, instructions, and feedback. The experimental procedures followed involved two different combinations of the techniques mentioned. The techniques were designed to clarify the tasks of the survey and to provide motivation to complete the tasks well. On the whole, the interviewing techniques tried in this experiment had weaker effects when used over the telephone than in person. The authors speculate that the nonverbal cues of the interviewer and the obvious lack of visual cues may account for the reduced impact of the commitment and instructions procedures used in the telephone survey experiments. There are several tables with the text along with thirty-six references (one is from 1980, others are all pre-1980).

239. Oksenberg, Lois, Lerita Coleman, and Charles F. Cannell. "Interviewers' Voices and Refusal Rates in Telephone Surveys." *Public Opinion Quarterly* 50, no. 1 (Spring 1986): 97–111.

The issue of the interviewers' vocal characteristics on refusal rates in telephone interviews is addressed. Interviewers working on a continuing monthly survey at the University of Michigan's Survey Research Center (SRC) were experiencing refusal rates ranging from 6 to 42 percent. The article cites and briefly describes the results of a long series of research studies on paralanguage and language attitudes. Three objectives for this study were derived from the literature. They were: "(1) Can vocal qualities of telephone interviewers be judged reliable? (2) Do ratings of vocal qualities correlate with perceptions of desirable and undesirable personal attributes? and (3) Is there a relation between these characteristics and rate of refusals?" The researchers believe that all three goals were achieved. They found that "higher pitch, greater variation in pitch, loudness, faster rate of speaking, clearer and more distinct pronunciation, and good speaking skills were all associated with attractiveness...and with higher perceived social class." Interviewers with these characteristics had low refusal rates. The article has six figures and tables and twenty-five references (two from the 1980s).

240. Quinn, Robert P., Barbara A. Gutek, and Jeffrey T. Walsh. "Telephone Interviewing: A Reappraisal and a Field Experiment." *Basic and Applied Social Psychology* 1, no. 2 (1980): 127–53.

A content analysis of a number of survey research textbooks was conducted to determine the treatment of telephone interviewing as an option for the researcher. The authors found, with a few cited exceptions, that textbooks in the field either fail to mention telephone interviewing or suggest that the method is only useful for simple issues involving a few questions. The authors also examined twenty-five empirical evaluations of telephone interviewing that made favorable observations relative to face-to-face interviewing in relation to length of interview, response rates, quality of data, and cost. Some limitations exist in the research to date, which led the article authors to conduct a field experiment to compare telephone and face-to-face interviewing. Face-to-face interviews were found to be "significantly longer" than telephone interviews. While response rates for men and women were the same for each method, the sex of the interviewer played a role in that male interviewers achieved "somewhat higher response rates with the telephone method." The experiment suggests that the quality of data on sensitive issues, as well as overall data quality, make telephone interviewing a cost effective and efficient method. There are forty-one pre-1980 references.

241. Sharf, Donald J., and Mark E. Lehman. "Relationship between the Speech Characteristics and Effectiveness of Telephone Interviewers." *Journal of Phonetics* 12, no. 3 (July 1984): 219–28.

The study measured the degree to which success was achieved by telephone interviewers in relationship to acoustic measures of speech, listener ratings of pitch, loudness, and rate of speaking. Six telephone interviewers were selected. The six had high and low rates of success in completing survey research interviews. Recordings of the interviews, divided equally between high and low success rates, were acoustically analyzed. Eighteen listeners were presented with the recordings and then requested to rate them. The speech characteristics of the most effective interviewers suggest that they have more highs and lows in their voice sound, and that they use relatively short pauses. There are a number of other considerations covered, including those dealing with syllables per second, falling/rising intonations, FO mean and pitch ratings, and FO standard deviation. The article concludes that the "study indicates the need for acoustic analysis to clarify the basis for listener impressions and to specify the potential acoustic cues to account for listener behavior." The author provides twenty-seven references, with eight from the 1980s.

242. Smead, Raymond J., and James Wilcox. "Ring Policy in Telephone Surveys." *Public Opinion Quarterly* 44, no. 1 (Spring 1980): 115–16.

In a section titled "Comments and Letters," Smead and Wilcox approach the question of what an appropriate ring policy should be for research firms engaged in surveying. The Bell telephone system reported that in 1980 a call consisted of 2-second rings separated by 5 seconds of silence. A test was conducted using the members of a major university consumer panel. Calls were placed using 10 rings, with calls rotated by time of day. Three callbacks were used. There were 219 respondents reached. The average response time was 8.7 seconds, with a variance of 40.5 seconds. The results indicate that 4 rings reach 97 percent of those at home. A survey of nine national survey firms showed a range from 3 to 10 rings per call with a mean and mode equal to 6. The authors suggest that almost half of the research firms surveyed may be wasting time by going beyond the 4-ring level. No references are included.

13.2 COMPUTER-ASSISTED TELEPHONE INTERVIEWING

243. Groves, Robert M. "Implications of CATI: Costs, Errors, and Organization of Telephone Survey Research." *Sociological Methods & Research* 12, no. 2 (November 1983): 199–215.

An understanding into the nature of error structure is the first benefit with the use of computer-assisted telephone interviewing (CATI). Groves suggests that a lack of data on the magnitude of errors pre-CATI makes comparisons difficult. A further possible use of CATI is to control the pace of the interview, and to experiment with new question formats. The author cites interviewer fatigue and respondent confusion in the midst of long complex questions as examples of some of the challenges that CATI may produce. The last area of concern is the man/machine relationship. How much should the machine be permitted to do in terms of the interviewing activity, and at what point does the interviewer lose interest due to machine control of the session? There are a number of figures and tables that accompany the text. The figures show schematically the differences between non-CATI telephone survey procedures and those of the CATI procedures. The tables cover changes in measurement of costs and errors related to questionnaire facilities, administration and control features, supervisory and monitoring capabilities, and coding capabilities. No references are included.

244. Groves, Robert M., and Nancy A. Mathiowetz. "Computer Assisted Telephone Interviewing: Effects on Interviewers and Respondents." *Public Opinion Quarterly* 48, no. 1B (Spring 1984): 356–69.

Computer-assisted telephone interviewing (CATI) represents the third step in a continuum which began with personal interview surveys, progressed to telephone surveys with paper questionnaires, and has evolved to the use of computers to assist in conducting and quantifying surveys. Groves and Mathiowetz set up a research design that would compare CATI versus non-CATI interviewing. For the most part, only small differences were found. Results include: (1) the average number of minutes per CATI interview was higher than those for non-CATI interviews; (2) the interviewer variability estimates tended to be lower in the CATI interviews; and (3) the skip error problems were lower in the CATI interviews. The authors explain that the first difference offsets cost, whereas the last two concern survey error (with the last two considered benefits of CATI systems). The article discusses the differences between CATI and non-CATI in the following areas: questionnaires, performance characteristics, interviewer and respondent reactions, response differences, and interviewer differences. Five tables accompany the text, along with eight references (all of which are from the 1980s).

245. Harlow, Bernard L., Jeanne F. Rosenthal, and Regina G. Ziegler. "A Comparison of Computer-Assisted and Hard Copy Telephone Interviewing." *American Journal of Epidemiology* 122, no. 2 (August 1985): 335-40.

After comparing computer-assisted telephone interviewing (CATI) with standard hard copy methods, the authors found that CATI did not affect the overall participation rate, answers recorded as "don't know," or the "quality" of the interview as determined by the interviewer. One interesting difference described involves the range and logic checks built into the CATI system which stop the interview process when logic or range errors are detected, thus forcing the interviewer to change or verify a question that is involved. The non-CATI approach has no similar instantaneous check. Citing the works of J.M. Shanks and colleagues (Item No. 248), a number of CATI benefits are discussed. These include:

(1) the ability to use complex question branching and to modify question wording based on responses to previous questions; (2) interviewer's performance can be remotely observed from other monitors; and (3) computer data management programs permit immediate results from the survey and reduce editing and coding that would otherwise be necessary. The work of R.M. Groves and colleagues (Item No. 243) is cited when reviewing CATI disadvantages. These involve the inability of the interviewer to examine the whole questionnaire as well as other shortcomings posed by the standardization of any format for computer use. A great deal of time may be necessary, along with the requisite computer skills, to ready a survey for CATI use. Statistical packages built into computers and the ability to generate hard copy with question and response matched are seen as significant pluses for CATI use. Nine references are provided, four are from the 1980s.

246. Palit, Charles, and Harry Sharp. "Microcomputer-Assisted Telephone Interviewing." *Sociological Methods & Research* 12, no. 2 (November 1983): 169–89.

Computer-assisted telephone interviewing (CATI) in the words of Palit and Sharp adds a "third party" to the previous means of conducting the interviewer-respondent relationship in survey research. The CATI approach involves having the telephone interviewer read the questions from a computer-guided screen, with respondents' answers input into the microcomputer usually via a keyboard. The authors cite the following advantages over noncomputer approaches: (1) with large samples the computer efficiently controls the screening process; (2) answers are immediately input; (3) the system can be programmed not to accept inconsistent entries; (4) only appropriate contingency questions are asked; (5) all appropriate contingency questions are asked; and (6) data can be evaluated immediately after the last interview is concluded. Disadvantages are that the hardware and software considerations can be expensive in both time and cost. The major focus of the article deals with a CATI system developed by the Wisconsin Survey Research Laboratory (WSRL) using a time-shared computer and microcomputers at individual interviewer stations. The results are based on the experience of some twenty completed projects. The article includes three endnotes.

247. Shanks, J. Merrill. "The Current Status of Computer-Assisted Telephone Interviewing: Recent Progess [sic] and Future Prospects." *Sociological Methods & Research* 12, no. 2 (November 1983): 119–42.

Advocates of computer-assisted telephone interviewing (CATI) speak of cost efficiencies and suggest that both the quality and complexity of data produced in this manner are improved. Potential advantages of CATI systems are outlined. Ten stages of research activity using the CATI approach are discussed, starting with the preparation of the interviewer's instrument and closing with data analysis and documentation. Chilton Research Services is identified as the commercial organization to first employ the system on a large scale, beginning in the early 1970s. The company introduced CATI to the survey community at the 1974 meeting of the American Association for Public Opinion Research (AAPOR). Some additional commercial companies subsequently involved include Amrigon, Inc., MARC, Inc., and Audits and Surveys. In academia, the University of Michigan's Survey Research Center (SRC), the University of Wisconsin's Survey Research Laboratory (SRL), UCLA, and the University of California at Berkeley's Computer-Assisted Survey Methods (CSM) are mentioned. Experiments at the federal level are reviewed including work at the U.S. Department of Agriculture (DOA), the National Center for Health Statistics (NCHS), and the U.S. Bureau of the Census, which are exploring methods of "cost control through more intensive use of the telephone." Shanks covers the CATI instrument design at some length, closing with a discussion for CATI application to nontelephone surveys. The epilogue addresses cooperative CATI development. Ten cited references (five from the 1980s) are provided.

248. Shanks, J. Merrill, William L. Nicholls II, and Howard E. Freeman. "The California Disability Survey: Design and Execution of a Computer-Assisted Telephone Study." *Sociological Methods & Research* 10, no. 2 (November 1981): 123–40.

The California Disability Survey (CDS) was the first large-scale academic or government study to use computer-assisted telephone interviewing (CATI). The article reviews the use of CATI and provides explanations for some of the decisions made in designing the CDS. Issues which may be useful to others conducting large-scale studies in the area of human services are highlighted. The CDS was a large-scale telephone study of the California population, and was designed to estimate the occurrence of disability and disabling conditions for the state as a whole as well as for a number of small administrative areas.

as a whole as well as for a number of small administrative areas. Pages 131 to 138 review the impact of CATI, with a discussion of the advantages of the technology through each of the phases in which it can be used. The article also covers three disadvantages with CATI. Notes and six references conclude the article.

249. Sudman, Seymour. "Survey Research and Technological Change." *Sociological Methods & Research* 12, no. 2 (November 1983): 217–30.

Explored are possible changes in survey research methodology which may result from the increased use of computer-assisted telephone interview (CATI) systems. Under the heading of "Survey Organization," Sudman discusses dispersion or the likelihood that interviewers will be able to work from home using "free-standing" computers. Speed and cost control are reviewed—with the first increasing, and the second being maintained with the likelihood of cost reductions. Sampling issues are considered, with screening, record keeping, organization, and sample availability discussed. The author believes that surveys will rely more and more on the telephone interview. Additionally, Sudman writes that in the future more individuals will be working at home. A challenge cited is the increased sale of telephone units equipped with switches which enable users to turn off incoming calls (therefore necessitating more call-backs to reach respondents). The entire survey process is covered by Sudman, with sections reviewing interviewer selection and training, questionnaire design, interviewing, data processing, measurement of variances, response effects, and sample bias. In conclusion, the author cites the continuing need of the researcher to use skill, experience, and judgment to create high-quality questionnaires. Human interviewers will continue to be needed for all but the simplest one- and two-question surveys which can be conducted using recorded questions. No references are included.

13.3   SCHEDULING AND FOREWARNING

250.   Groves, Robert M., and Lou J. Magilavy. "Increasing Response
      Rates to Telephone Surveys: A Door in the Face for Foot-in-the-
      Door?" *Public Opinion Quarterly* 45, no. 3 (Fall 1981): 346–58.
The goal of increasing response rates in telephone surveys is addressed.
An experimental test was conducted involving a short telephone call with
two questions asked, and then later calling again for the full interview.
Because two calls are required using this technique, labeled the "foot-in-
the-door" procedure, in order to justify the approach on a cost basis, an
alternate method must provide a significant increase in the response rate.
Authors Groves and Magilavy did not achieve such an advantage when
conducting a national telephone survey. Additionally, when normal survey approaches are used, with an added effort at persuasion, the overall
response rate is increased by 7 percent. When the foot-in-the-door approach is used, along with persuasion, there does not seem to be any
added advantage over the single case method. The authors note that the
current use of callbacks for those missed initially, as well as efforts at
persuasion for those who refuse at first try, seem to be as successful as
dual contact methods. The text includes several tables and thirteen pre-
1980 references.

251.   Nuckols, Robert C. "A Study of Respondent Forewarning in
      Public Opinion Research." Ph.D. diss., Pennsylvania State
      College, 1951. 126p.+ [25 unmarked].
The purpose of the dissertation was to determine the effects of forewarning the respondents of a public opinion poll of the nature of the
interview to follow. Nuckols hypothesized that if respondents were forewarned (by letter) they would have more time to "recall and organize bits
of information" and be prepared to give "more detailed and thought-out
answers." He also suggests that the level of cooperation will be increased
and that the entire experience will be more "enjoyable" for all concerned.
The novelty of polling was still fresh in the late 1940s and early 1950s
when this dissertation was written. It had been only fifteen years since
the advent of modern polling, with perhaps much of the interviewing
still done by in-person visits. The results of the test Nuckols devised did
not show a significant difference for those forewarned. In today's
environment, with most polling being conducted by telephone,
preadvising by written means is unlikely. References are provided.

252.   Weeks, M.F., B.L. Jones, R.E. Folson, Jr., and C.H. Benrud. "Optimal Times to Contact Sample Households." *Public Opinion Quarterly* 44, no. 1 (Spring 1980): 101–14.

The article reports on a study which determined the probabilities of finding someone at home aged fourteen or older. The researchers suggest that the data should enable household survey researchers to develop good strategies to reach respondents at home, as well as to permit more accurate initial estimates as to how much the process will cost the client or research project. The authors continue this line of thought and suggest that, by using the study data, production and efficiency standards for interviewers can be developed in a more realistic manner. Summarizing the findings, overall, Saturday proved to be the best day of the week so far as finding a respondent at home, and specifically between 10 A.M. and 4 P.M. As would be expected, the late afternoon and early evening hours showed improved chances of finding a respondent at home. The study shows that it is easier to find someone at home in a rural area, as compared with the relative difficulty of finding a respondent at home in the inner city. Comparing the 1971 and 1976 data used, there is an overall downward trend in ability to find respondents at home—more pronounced in inner city areas, and less so in rural areas. Six tables, one figure, and a single reference accompany the text.

253.   Weeks, Michael F., Richard A. Kulka, and Stephanie A. Pierson. "Optimal Call Scheduling for a Telephone Survey." *Public Opinion Quarterly* 51, no. 4 (Winter 1987): 540–49.

The sample considered for this study consisted of male U.S. Army veterans who were aged thirty-two to forty-five at the time the survey was conducted from February 1985 through March 1986. The study data shows that the likelihood of getting an answer and conducting an interview on the first call are much better on weekday evenings and on weekends than they are during weekday daytime hours. Sunday has a higher interview response rate for answered telephone calls than do other calling periods examined by the researchers. The article analyzes the time-of-day and day-of-week effects on the likelihood of obtaining answers and interviews. Three tables provide breakdowns by time-of-day (from 8 A.M. until 9:59 P.M.), days of the week, first-call outcomes by time category, and the percentage of answered second calls by time of the first call. The authors recognize the limited nature of the sample selected and hesitate to generalize to other populations. The results are nevertheless consistent with previous studies designed to determine optimal calling periods. There are nine references provided.

13.4 INTERVIEWER EFFECTS AND TRAINING

254. Billiet, Jacques, and Geert Loosveldt. "Improvement of the Quality of Responses to Factual Survey Questions by Interviewer Training." *Public Opinion Quarterly* 52, no. 2 (Summer 1988): 190–211.

The study revealed differences between trained and untrained interviewers in terms of the quantity of information gathered and also with the factor of nonresponse. Those who were trained were able to obtain more information, with underreporting and nonresponses being reduced. Training was demonstrated to be particularly useful with the open question format. Those interviewers who knew that their sessions were being tape-recorded apparently performed better. The authors attribute this to the interviewers' awareness of being monitored, and therefore the interviewers followed guidelines established during training. After five half-day training sessions, the "trained" interviewers still failed to provide sufficient feedback or "spontaneous task instructions." The article includes a short description of the training, the question wording (originally conducted in Dutch), and twenty references (three in Dutch by coauthor Loosveldt).

255. Blair, Edward. "Using Practice Interviews to Predict Interviewer Behaviors." *Public Opinion Quarterly* 44, no. 2 (Summer 1980): 257–60.

The study compared interviewers' tape-recorded practice interviews (with friends or relatives as respondents) with their tape-recorded behavior in field interviews. The research data demonstrates that the practice interviews are good predictors of the field behavior of the interviewer. Blair suggests that practice interviews are therefore good screening devices when selecting interviewers, as well as in developing estimates of the frequency with which interviewers may vary from the programmed interview in the field. Special training could be supplied to reduce the percentage of deviance from the designated program, or the results of the practice could be compared with those of the field interviews. Four types of interviewer behavior were coded: nonfluencies, reading errors, probes, and feedback. All of the study interviewers were female; selection was based on a good work record. The results reported are based on a comparison between the practice interview and average behavior in field interviews for forty-one interviews. There are thirteen pre-1980 references and one table with the text.

256.   Groves, Robert M., and Lou J. Magilavy. "Measuring and Explaining Interviewer Effects in Centralized Telephone Surveys." *Public Opinion Quarterly* 50, no. 2 (Summer 1986): 251–66.

Interviewer effects occur because of the tendency of respondents to provide different answers on questionnaires depending upon who is doing the interviewing. The researchers combined the results of many studies and were able to reach generalized estimates of interviewer effects. Nine surveys from a six-year period conducted at the Survey Research Center (SRC) of the University of Michigan were used. Any conclusions drawn from the study need to be tempered by the knowledge that the interviewers were hired, trained, and supervised at SRC, and that the administration of the surveys and the response rates achieved are those of SRC. Groves and Magilavy found little difference between open and closed questions or between factual and attitudinal questions when using the data from the generalized interviewer effect measures. Small reductions in interviewer effects were found when a computer-assisted telephone interviewing (CATI) system was employed. Elderly respondents seemed to be more vulnerable to interviewer effects. The number of clearly different answers gathered in response to open questions seems to be related to the nature of interviewer differences. Behavior changes on the part of the interviewer or changes in the flow and question sequencing may aid in the reduction of interviewer effects. Several tables and a figure present study data. Nineteen references (four from the 1980s) complete the article.

257.   Singer, Eleanor, Martin R. Frankel, and Mare B. Glassman. "The Effect of Interviewer Characteristics and Expectations on Response." *Public Opinion Quarterly* 47, no. 1 (Spring 1983): 68–83.

The findings of the research show that older interviewers obtained better cooperation rates, which the authors suggest might be the product of self-confidence or perhaps by a tone of voice that is reassuring to respondents. Large interviewing assignments had a negative effect, both in screening and response rates. The interviewers' attitudes toward a questionnaire can be more important than the questionnaire itself in terms of the impact on the response rate to the survey. One interviewer characteristic, that of educational attainment, did show that those with more education tended to achieve lower item nonresponse rates. A number of inconsistencies and inconclusive findings were reached by the study. In an effort to explain why their research varied from the findings of earlier studies, the authors suggest that their work was done by telephone whereas earlier efforts used in-person interviews. It is suggested that in-person interviews provide for greater transmittal of interviewer expectations than telephone interviews. In conclusion, the authors observe that the study demonstrated that interviewer characteristics had little effect on responses to individual questions, but that the impact might have been greater if a higher response rate had been achieved. Nine references are provided, which include several items from the 1980s.

258. Tucker, Clyde. "Interviewer Effects in Telephone Surveys." *Public Opinion Quarterly* 47, no. 1 (Spring 1983): 84–95.
Eleven national polls conducted by CBS and the *New York Times* in 1980 were studied to determine the magnitude of interviewer effects. Interviewer effects were found to exist, but they were "generally quite small." An unusual element of this study was that interviewer effects for an item were examined over several polls. The effect was not consistent from poll to poll, although it is believed that the political context and variations generated by differing regions were responsible for the inconsistencies. Tucker cautions that even though the interviewer effect may be small, the "cumulative effects of intra-interviewer correlations can be substantial" over the course of large telephone surveys. Additionally, Tucker cites the need for greater research into the effects of interviewer characteristics upon specific respondents. The article begins with a review of the findings of previous studies. There is a detailed explanation of how the study was designed, followed by sections dealing with randomization and comparable distributions, and the interviewer effect. A two-page table provides data on "Intra-interviewer Correlations (P*int) for Selected Categories of Items from 1980 CBS/New York Times National Polls." There are twenty-four references and eleven footnotes included.

13.5 ETHNICITY AND RACE OF INTERVIEWER

259. Anderson, Barbara A., Brian D. Silver, and Paul R. Abramson. "The Effects of Race of the Interviewer on Measures of Electoral Participation." *Public Opinion Quarterly* 52, no. 1 (Spring 1988): 53–83.

The survey data found in the Survey Research Center (SRC) and the Center for Political Studies (CPS) of the University of Michigan's American National Election Studies (NES) is the basis for this study. The NES surveys of 1964, 1976, 1978, 1980, and 1984 were studied. The study was designed to determine the effect of the race of the interviewer on self-reported voting, actual voting, and political attitudes of black respondents. Over the twenty-year period examined, the number of black respondents who were interviewed by black interviewers declined noticeably, especially in the South. Practically all of the white respondents were interviewed by whites. The researchers found that black respondents interviewed by black interviewers were more likely to falsely report that they voted in presidential elections than black respondents interviewed by white interviewers. With the exception of the pre-Voting Rights Act election of 1964 for southern blacks, the above finding was consistent through each presidential election year studied. For many black respondents, interviewed by black interviewers in black neighborhoods, the mere experience of being interviewed may "induce changes in actual behavior"—as these respondents were more likely to actually vote. Based on these findings, the authors propose that a number of interviewer characteristics be included in the data files of the NES and the General Social Survey (GSS). These might include the race, age, education, and the number of years of experience that the interviewer has or at least the number of years with the current survey organization. Seven tables, two figures, and twenty-seven references augment the text. Twenty-one of the references are from the 1980s.

260. Anderson, Barbara A., Brian D. Silver, and Paul R. Abramson. "The Effects of the Race of the Interviewer on Race-Related Attitudes of Black Respondents in SRC/CPS National Election Studies." *Public Opinion Quarterly* 52, no. 3 (Fall 1988): 289–324.

The nature of the interview situation suggested by Schuman and Converse (1971) is confirmed, i.e., one in which black respondents alter or change their answers to avoid offending a white interviewer. Authors

Anderson, Silver, and Abramson examined the National Election Studies (NES) from 1964, 1976, 1978, 1980, 1982, 1984, and 1986 and focused on the effects of the race of the interviewer on race-related attitudes. The analysis of the data showed that blacks interviewed by whites were much more likely to express warmth and closeness toward whites than were blacks interviewed by blacks. The authors observe that there is no simple rule for predicting if there will be race-of-interviewer effects on the answers to particular questions. It is suggested that the race of the inter- viewer be included with the data file, as was the case in the 1986 NES. When dealing with the issue of government assistance to a category of the public, "aid-to-blacks" terminology seems to be more prone to effects of the race of the interviewer than "aid-to-minorities." Nine figures, ten tables, plus an appendix with two additional tables, are included in the text, along with eleven references, eight from the 1980s.

261. Campbell, B. "Race-of-Interviewer Effects Among Southern Adolescents." *Public Opinion Quarterly* 45, no. 2 (Summer 1981): 231–44.
The research by Campbell shows clear patterns of deference by both white and black respondents to opposite-race interviewers. The magni- tude of the race-of-interviewer effect observed is similar to findings in other studies. Racially oriented items are the most likely to elicit race-of- interviewer effects, and bias is most likely to occur when the item in- volves the race of the interviewer and the respondent is of the opposite race. The research shows no evidence of any race-of-interviewer effect in items which did not deal with racial questions. Campbell believes that the race-of-interviewer effect should be controlled for, but that the level of bias would not usually be sufficient to create serious misinterpreta- tions in the substance of the data. The study is based on data gathered in 1974 involving 944 Atlanta, Georgia high-school seniors. An appendix contains the item wording used. There are three tables and twelve references.

262. Cotter, Patrick R., Jeffrey Cohen, and Philip B. Coulter. "Race-of- Interviewer Effects in Telephone Interviews." *Public Opinion Quarterly* 46, no. 2 (Summer 1982): 278–84.
The study was conducted to determine the existence of a race-of- interviewer effect in telephone interviews. It was found that the race of the interviewer has little or no effect on nonracial questions. Some, but not all, social questions are affected by the race of the interviewer. When asked racial questions by a member of another race, respondents tend to

be more "deferential" to that race than are respondents interviewed by a member of their own race. The magnitude of the race-of-interviewer effect found in this study is similar to the face-to-face interview studies reported in the opening paragraph of the article. Unlike previous studies, Cotter, Cohen, and Coulter found that there was a stronger race-of-interviewer effect for white than for black respondents. A two-page table is titled "Race-of-Interviewer for Black and White Respondents for Nonracial and Racial Questions." The telephone interviews were conducted by the Capstone Poll at the University of Alabama using a two-stage random digit dialing (RDD) method for a total of 590 individuals. All three authors are associated with the University of Alabama. Two of the references are from 1980; eight are from earlier years.

263.   Reese, Stephen D., Wayne A. Danielson, Pamela J. Shoemaker, Tsan-Kuo Chang, and Huei-Ling Hsu. "Ethnicity-of-Interviewer Effects Among Mexican-Americans and Anglos." *Public Opinion Quarterly* 50, no. 4 (Winter 1986): 563–72.

The study shows that for both Mexican-Americans and Anglos an ethnicity-of-interviewer effect exists based on the results of the telephone survey conducted. Both "objective" self-reports and "subjective" attitudinal items were shown to be subject to interviewer effects. The biasing effect was not large enough to cause respondents to alter their attitudes, but responses were "shaded" depending upon who they were talking with. The authors suggest the same deference effects that exist with Hispanics were previously found for blacks by other researchers, i.e., that interviewer effects were modest among blacks when asked about blacks by black interviewers. Some contradictory and unexpected results occurred when Mexican-Americans were asked about Spanish-language print media by Anglos. These were perceived to be of greater importance when Anglo interviewers asked than when Hispanic interviewers were involved. The ethnicity of the interviewer seems to be the key to understanding issues related to deference. Hispanics were selected for the telephone sample by identification of Hispanic surnames in telephone books from cities with large Hispanic populations. Spanish-language interviews were offered to those who said they spoke some Spanish, with assistance provided to clarify words or phrases in Spanish as needed. An appendix contains questionnaire items. There are twelve references (seven from the 1980s).

264. Schaeffer, Nora Cate. "Evaluating Race-of-Interviewer Effects in a National Survey." *Sociological Methods & Research* 8, no. 4 (May 1980): 400–19.

General Social Survey (GSS) data was used to estimate the race-of-interviewer effects. Methods employed to overcome some of the problems associated with this challenge are described. The effects were significant enough with both black and white respondents to justify the practice of matching interviewer and respondent by race. The author notes that studies which attempt to analyze racial attitudes over time need to be particularly sensitive to the racial composition of the interviewing staff of each survey conducted. Race-of-interviewer effects seem to have little distorting impact on nonracial items. In her study the author examined scales of racial liberalism, and analyzed the nonracial questions of white respondents in addition to those which dealt with racial attitudes. GSS data is publicly available. The race-of-interviewer effects seem to be small for white respondents which is due to the small percentage of cross-race interviews. By contrast, the number of cross-race interviews for blacks is higher and fluctuates to a greater degree over the years that the survey was administered. There are six endnotes and fourteen pre-1980 references.

265. Weeks, Michael F., and R. Paul Moore. "Ethnicity-of-Interviewer Effects on Ethnic Respondents." *Public Opinion Quarterly* 45, no. 2 (Summer 1981): 245–49.

This article reports on a 1975 study of ethnicity-of-interviewer effects among Cubans, Chicanos, Native Americans, and Chinese. The study of these four ethnic minorities suggests that the research findings for blacks and whites can be generalized to other ethnic groups. The race of the interviewer and respondent does not appear to be an issue in nonsensitive questions. Nonethnic interviewers seemed to slightly outperform ethnic interviewers so far as response rate and field costs are concerned. The study is based on data collected in 1975 at four sites: Miami (Cubans), El Paso (Chicanos), N.E. Arizona (Native Americans), and San Francisco (Chinese). The English language proficiency of the 1,472 children was also included in the research. A table indicates the variables used and how they were coded. There are six references of which all but one are pre-1980.

13.6 CONFIDENTIALITY

266. Frey, James H. "An Experiment with a Confidentiality Reminder in a Telephone Survey." *Public Opinion Quarterly* 50, no. 2 (Summer 1986): 267–69.

Research in the area of survey confidentiality had previously covered nontelephone surveys and found that there were no significant effects on refusal rates, but that confidentiality statements may increase respondent apprehension. In the experiment, the confidentiality reminder appeared after the substantive questions, but before sensitive personal data items on data quality as indicated by item nonresponse to a telephone survey. The confidentiality reminder generated higher nonresponse rates than in the control group. The reminder may have a "sensitizing effect" that makes respondents more cautious in their responses to subsequent questions. The results confirm similar findings with mail and face-to-face interviews, suggesting that the confidentiality reminder, when placed before sensitive questions, may serve to reduce data quality. One table and five references are provided.

267. Lucas, Wayne L. "A Research Note on Compliance with Guidelines for Protection of Human Subjects in Survey Research on Drugs." *Journal of Alcohol and Drug Education* 25, no. 2 (Winter 1980): 33–37.

The issues of "informed consent" by subjects in survey research and how to avoid discouraging participation or straightforwardness by the respondents are discussed. Five procedures were implemented to both comply with mandated guidelines while at the same time maintaining the survey population size, and generating appropriate data for the study of marijuana and other drug use. These are: (1) survey respondents were informed in writing of the means through which confidentiality was maintained, and of the voluntary nature of their participation; (2) reference was made to specific guidelines which were being complied with by the study; (3) the notification in written form regarding confidentiality and the voluntary status of the respondents was brief, simple, and clearly expressed; (4) minor issues which respondents might be concerned about were considered and dealt with in the written document; and (5) respondents were advised in writing, prior to the beginning of the survey interview, that the interviewer would respond to respondents' questions about the purpose of the research. Three pre-1980 references are included.

268. Orwin, Robert G., and Robert F. Boruch. "RRT Meets RDD: Statistical Strategies for Assuring Response Privacy in Telephone Surveys." *Public Opinion Quarterly* 46, no. 4 (Winter 1982): 560–71.

The concern that has fostered this research is that of confidentiality of the telephone respondents' answers, and thereby the degree to which respondents are willing to be forthcoming when asked sensitive questions. A number of measures have been employed in face-to-face interviews (through statistical privacy procedures) to alleviate concerns of respondents. The authors demonstrate that privacy procedures can be used in telephone interviews. One such technique, developed in 1965 by Stanley Warner, is known as the related question randomized response technique and is described in this article, along with the variations that have been developed since it was proposed. Discussion follows about the various methods available to achieve randomized response, including respondent-supplied randomizers and researcher-supplied randomizers. Alternatives to randomized response are presented, including innocuous traits as proxy randomizers and as sources of statistical noise. A table compares the characteristics of various proxy randomizers. Thirty-four references are supplied, with three references from the 1980s.

13.7 INFORMED AND PARENTAL CONSENT

269. Kearney, Kathleen A., Ronald H. Hopkins, Armand L. Mauss, and Ralph A. Weisheit. "Sample Bias Resulting from a Requirement for Written Parental Consent." *Public Opinion Quarterly* 47, no. 1 (Spring 1983): 96–102.

At issue is the impact on survey results of obtaining written parental permission to conduct research with minor-aged student respondents. The consequence of the consent form is to reduce the potential sample to about half the size, with a disproportionately larger number of white students, with blacks and Asian-Americans underrepresented. Gender sample bias was not evident, and bias related to academic factors was mixed. The authors suggest a number of implications for future research with school-aged respondents. These include: (1) a racially biased sample is likely to be generated when written parental consent is tailoring request forms to differing groups might achieve more positive results; (3) finding alternative means to meet "informed consent" in another fashion is highly desirable; and (4) further research is required to devise forms that will yield higher response rates and an increased percentage of parental consents. The results are based on a survey of students in grades four through twelve with an eligible sample size of 1,618. The questionnaire dealt with alcohol and drugs. There are nine pre-1980 references.

270. Singer, Eleanor, and Martin R. Frankel. "Informed Consent Procedures in Telephone Interviews." *American Sociological Review* 47, no. 3 (June 1982): 416–26.

The findings of the experiment undertaken suggest that, while it may be important what is said during the introduction about the telephone survey, experimental findings do not show any variables which might lead to large variations in the response. The research found that interviewer characteristics play a larger role in achieving initial cooperation than the survey undertaken. Depending upon what is said about certain issues during the survey introduction, the quality of the responses can be influenced significantly, such as with the issue of confidentiality. Those assured of "absolute confidentiality" were significantly more likely to respond to sensitive questions than those who were given partial or no assurance of confidentiality. The researchers in this case went further and disclosed the purpose of the telephone survey as part of the introduction. Singer and Frankel determined that this "appeared to affect adversely the acknowledgment of sensitive behavior." In conclusion, the authors note that requesting a signature on a consent document, announcing the topic, and length of the interview may affect the respondent's initial decision as to whether or not to participate. Eleven references include three from the 1980s.

271. Sobal, Jeffery. "The Content of Survey Introductions and the Provision of Informed Consent." *Public Opinion Quarterly* 48. no. 4 (Winter 1984): 788–93.

The norms of the contents of introductions were found to vary among survey researchers. The author believes that the issue of respondent burden and an increasing reluctance on the part of the public to be respondents contribute to the need, along with methodological and ethical reasons, for standards about survey introductions to be developed and disseminated. The author used a questionnaire to sample 172 American Association for Public Opinion Research (AAPOR) members. A total of

108 questionnaires were returned; 78 (or 45 percent) of the original mailing were useable. Table 1 reveals the following types of information disclosed in survey introductions: research organization, 85.9 percent; interviewer, 82.1 percent; research topic, 80.8 percent; sponsor, 44.9 percent; confidentiality, 42.3 percent; anonymity, 25.6 percent; purpose, 25.6 percent; future data use, 24.4 percent; sampling technique, 20.5 percent; survey length, 12.8 percent; participation voluntary, 10.3 percent; sample size, 3.8 percent; and consent signature, 3.8 percent. Mail surveys provided greater disclosure than telephone or personal interviews. Thirty references are provided (six from the 1980s).

272. Sobal, Jeff. "Disclosing Information in Interview Introductions: Methodological Consequences of Informed Consent." *Sociology and Social Research: An International Journal* 66, no. 3 (April 1982): 348–61.

Two issues are addressed in the research conducted by Sobal. First, are there methodological reasons or benefits in keeping disclosure to the minimum during the interview introduction? Second, what is the impact on refusal rates? The research indicates that there are no methodological "benefits" gained by withholding information about the interviewer, the interview, or the research. Refusals did not increase in relation to the length of the introduction, but a significant impact was seen when respondents were informed that the interview would take twenty minutes rather than "a few minutes." In this case refusal numbers increased. The basis for the questions posed goes beyond the costs of the added length of the interview, and potentially the additional number of respondents needed. The crux of the issue is the ethical consideration toward the respondent—and the view of those calling for fuller disclosure, that these considerations override any methodological challenges. Some view fuller disclosure as a means of developing higher standards and upgrading social research. A sixty-item, pre-1980 list of references is included.

273. Thompson, Teresa L. "A Comparison of Methods of Increasing Parental Consent Rates in Social Research." *Public Opinion Quarterly* 48, no. 4 (Winter 1984): 779–87.

The challenge of gaining written parental consent from parents to permit their child(ren) to participate in research is the focus of this article. Previous studies indicate that the requirement of the written consent reduces the sample size by half and generates overrepresentation of whites and underrepresentation of blacks. Four different methods were tried: incentive to the child; incentive to the parents; communication with the child; and communication with the parent. The most effective approach was communication with the parents themselves through telephone calls. White parents were almost unanimous in granting permission. There was "very high participation" from black parents. Of the four methods, the latter was the most time-consuming. The incentive to the child involved a picture of themselves, which served as a motivating tool to increase the chances that the permission request slip would arrive home and receive the parents' attention. All the methods researched succeeded in increasing the consent rates. Incentives to parents increased the consent rates more for white students than for black students. Incentives and communication with the children achieved consent rates for both racial groups which were somewhat similar. Without other intervention, a follow-up letter produced a consent rate of about 40 percent—higher for whites than blacks. There are twelve references (three from the 1980s) and two tables.

13.8 COMPARATIVE STUDIES

274. Booth, Alan, and David R. Johnson. "Tracking Respondents in a Telephone Interview Panel Selected by Random Digit Dialing." *Sociological Methods & Research* 14, no. 1 (August 1985): 53–64.

Various approaches used in tracking a panel of respondents over a three-year period are reported. Of the original 2,032 respondents, 78 percent were reinterviewed three years later. The study used random digit dialing (RDD) and sought to compare those findings with earlier, traditional approaches. Citing a Groves and Kahn study (*Surveys by Telephone: A National Comparison with Personal Interviews*, 1979), it is observed that telephone interviewing is "as reliable as personal interviews and much less costly." Booth and Johnson found that the attrition rate encountered using the telephone method described is similar to studies using personal interviews. The authors advocate frequent—at least annually—tracking, employing a combination of mail and telephone follow-ups. Obtaining the names of blood relatives who would know the respondent's whereabouts in the event of relocation was found to be very useful in maintaining the integrity of the sample. Certain categories were found to show attrition: females 14–24 years of age in 1980 (the year of initial interviewing), blacks, Spanish-speaking individuals, two-person households, renters, those not graduating from high school, and metropolitan residents. These categories correspond to the "same categories of individuals that are lost in longitudinal studies using personal interviews." There are seven pre-1980 references.

275.   Herzog, A. Regula, and Willard L. Rodgers. "Interviewing Older Adults: Mode Comparison Using Data from a Face-to-Face Survey and a Telephone Resurvey." *Public Opinion Quarterly* 52, no. 1 (Spring 1988): 84–99.

The basic finding is that there was little difference between respondents sixty years of age and older versus those under sixty so far as interview mode in a reinterview is concerned. The sixty years and older respondents did answer "don't know" (DK) disproportionately higher on the telephone. The researchers used the results from a 1984 face-to-face sample survey of 1,491 residents of the Detroit metropolitan area, and a reinterview of a random subset of these respondents by telephone. The initial sample contained an oversample of older adults. The telephone reinterview yielded a lower response rate for older than for younger respondents with an overall rate of 90 percent. The authors conclude that the telephone mode is suitable as a reinterview method with older respondents. About 17 percent of the original respondents were lost in the telephone follow-up survey. Half the loss was due to respondents with unlisted telephone numbers or no telephone, while the rest was due to nonresponse or unwillingness to list a telephone number. Two tables provide the data on response distributions and indexes by mode of interview and age of respondent. Six examples of questions used in the Study of Michigan Generations are provided. There are twenty-four references, with nine from the 1980s.

276.   Herzog, A. Regula, Willard L. Rodgers, and Richard A. Kulka. "Interviewing Older Adults: A Comparison of Telephone and Face-to-Face Modalities." *Public Opinion Quarterly* 47, no. 3 (Fall 1983): 405–18.

Originally presented as three separate papers at the 33rd Annual Meeting of the Gerontological Society, San Diego, November 1980, the present paper is an abbreviated and revised version. It examines telephone interviewing of older adults and then compares the data with face-to-face interviews. The researchers sought to address three issues. These include: (1) examining the differences in age distribution between the samples of face-to-face and telephone modes; (2) providing explanations for such differences; and (3) determining differences in demographic characteristics of the adults reached by the two modes as well as studying the response quality. In the article summary, the authors note that telephone surveys tend to underrepresent older adults; those that do participate are disporportionately well educated. However, the authors maintain that this does not appear to introduce systematic biases. They continue by stating that it is as possible to conduct studies of the elderly as it is for the general population. Apparently older adults perceive telephone interviews to be lengthier than face-to-face interviews. The issue of the social responsibility of minimizing the burden on respondents is raised. Three of the references are from the 1980s; eighteen are from earlier years.

277. Jordan, Lawrence A., Alfred C. Marcus, and Leo G. Reeder. "Response Styles in Telephone and Household Interviewing: A Field Experiment." *Public Opinion Quarterly* 44, no. 2 (Summer 1980): 210–22.

A field comparison of telephone and household interviewing was conducted to evaluate whether the data collected by each approach was comparable. The authors found that the telephone sample had more missing data on family income, more acquiescence, evasiveness, and extremeness response bias, as well as an increased number of somewhat contradictory answers to checklist questions. The telephone data was not as good as the face-to-face interview data, even though the two samples were sociodemographically essentially the same. The telephone sample was created through the random digit dialing approach, while the face-to-face sample was the product of the area probability method. One technical difference between the way certain questions were asked is discussed. Face-to-face interviews can simultaneously employ several flash cards, thus showing the answer options to the respondent. Telephone respondents asked the same question can respond only after the question options have been serially read over the telephone. Additionally, the interviewers missed the visual cues—those which aid in the decision as to when to probe or pause for a more complete response—that are available in face-to-face interviews. There are three tables. Twenty-seven references are provided, with one from 1980.

278. Kemper, Raymond Alfred. "Secret Ballots, Open Ballots, and Personal Interviews in Opinion Polling." Ph.D. diss., Columbia University, 1951. 148p.

The methodology for this dissertation consisted of using a sample of fifteen hundred adults. The sample was divided into three comparable subsample groups: one subsample was interviewed face-to-face; a second group used secret ballots and sealed ballot-boxes; and the third group was polled employing "open ballots" which were returned to the field-worker once the respondent had completed the form. Twenty "fact questions" and thirteen "opinion questions" were used. Three comparisons were then made based on the results. The face-to-face data was compared with the secret ballot data, and with the open ballot. The open ballot results were compared with those of the secret ballot. When the three methods of polling were examined, differences were found with seven of the twenty fact questions and with nine of the thirteen opinion questions. References are provided.

13.9 TEXTBOOK

279. Gorden, Raymond L. "Sample Surveys." Chap. 11 in *Interviewing: Strategy, Techniques, and Tactics*, 233–72. 3rd ed. The Dorsey Series in Sociology. Homewood, IL: Dorsey Press, 1980.

The volume is intended for use as a textbook for both undergraduates and graduate students, for supervisors and trainers of interviewers, and for professionals currently engaged in the practice of interviewing. Many sections of the volume contain information which would be useful for interviews, with chapter 11 specifically addressing the needs of survey researchers. The basic types of sample surveys are discussed, including considerations of cross-sectional versus longitudinal surveys and also approximating longitudinal surveys. Basic sampling strategies are reviewed with simple random, systemic, multistage, and stratified sampling covered. Modes of surveys are outlined, with mailed and personally administered questionnaires presented, along with telephone and face-to-face formats. The chapter also includes sections on how to gain access to the respondent, the format of the interview schedule or questionnaire, and some suggestions for creating a good format for the interview schedule.

14. Responses

14.1 RESPONSE EFFECTS

280. Bradburn, Norman M. "Response Effects." Chap. 8 in *Handbook of Survey Research*, edited by Peter H. Rossi, James D. Wright, and Andy B. Anderson, 289–328. Quantitative Studies in Social Relations, consulting editor Peter H. Rossi. New York: Academic Press, 1983.

The empirical evidence for response effects is Bradburn's concern in this chapter. The nature and size of these effects, which occur during the process of questioning in data collection, are focused upon. The author is not considering refusals to be interviewed or the failure to answer individual questions as response effects. Rather, he refers the reader to Anderson, Basilevsky, and Hum's chapter in the *Handbook* (Item No. 155) for treatment of the aforementioned problems. Bradburn summarizes three types of errors: (1) deliberate or motivated errors; (2) memory errors; and (3) communications errors. Presented is a model for conceptualizing the factors that affect responses. A twenty-four-page section follows which reviews the literature on the empirical studies of response effect; the longest part is under the heading "Task Variables." Shorter sections discuss interviewer variables and respondent variables. The literature review summarizes what the author perceives to be the major sources of response effects, which includes those for behavior and attitude variables. The administrative elements of the task—namely the interview; question order; open versus closed questions; question length and wording; and memory factors—seem to contribute to the greatest degree in producing response effects. In citing literature which is indecisive on the matter, Bradburn allows that characteristics of the interviewer and the respondent may also play a role in response effects. There are 190 references provided at the end of the chapter.

281.   Kiesler, Sara, and Lee S. Sproull. "Response Effects in the Electronic Survey." *Public Opinion Quarterly* 50, no. 3 (Fall 1986): 402–13.

The electronic survey is conducted using a text processing program to self-administer a computer-based questionnaire. Survey costs can be reduced using this approach, as the raw data can be transferred automatically into computer-readable form. Kiesler and Sproull suggest that communities or organizations with access to computers will be the likely users. They maintain that these groups will be well educated, urban, white-collar, and technically sophisticated. The authors found that electronic surveys can achieve good response rates, with quicker turnaround time, and with a smaller number of item incompletions than with regular mail surveys. The electronic survey has certain advantages over the mail survey in that open-ended questions which may need long answers can be asked, along with the ease of making corrections. Branching questions and question sequencing possibilities are further benefits available through the electronic format. The study sample using the electronic survey generated a larger number of socially undesirable responses than in the paper survey. The explanation may be that respondents are more "self-absorbed and uninhibited when they communicate using a computer." Answers also tend to be more extreme when using the electronic survey than when responding to a paper survey. A table charts, by percentages, the socially desirable responses. There are twenty references, ten from the 1980s.

282.   Krosnick, Jon A., and Duane F. Alwin. "An Evaluation of a Cognitive Theory of Response-Order Effects in Survey Measurement." *Public Opinion Quarterly* 51, no. 2 (Summer 1987): 201–19.

A theory to explain response order effects is discussed. A 1984 General Social Survey (GSS) was used as the basis for an experiment to test for response-order effect using a measure of values. Respondents were asked questions designed to measure adult values for child qualities. The researchers found that the values selected by respondents were, in part, determined by the order in which response choices were offered. By systematically varying response order, the study demonstrated that if an item was placed in the first three on a list of choices, the likelihood was increased that it would be selected as one of the most important qualities for a child to have. Response marginals were altered by as much as 17 percent by this response effect. Krosnick and Alwin describe this as "substantial in absolute terms, as well as in relative terms, compared to size of wording, form, and context effects typically observed." The study analysis leads the authors to conclude that respondents with less cognitive sophistication are more likely to be influenced by changes in response order. Suggestions to reduce these effects include increasing respondent motivation as a means to increase concentration and shortening the list of offered alternatives. Five tables are included, along with fifty references (fourteen from the 1980s).

283. Krosnick, Jon A., and Howard Schuman. "Attitude Intensity, Importance, and Certainty and Susceptibility to Response Effects." *Journal of Personality and Social Psychology* 54, no. 6 (June 1988): 940–52.

The research described examines whether changes in survey-question form, wording, and context have a greater impact on responses from individuals with attitudes that are weak, unimportant, or held with uncertainty. Two types of form effects, two types of wording effects, and two types of order effects were tested. As the authors report, the "only reliable negative relation between attitude intensity and importance and response effects appeared in comparisons between questions that offer middle alternatives and those that do not." Holders of nonintense attitudes disporportionately seek out the middle alternative when it is available. The authors believe that the psychological mechanisms in the many reliable response effects already known need to be further understood as the next appropriate research step. Krosnick and Schuman report the results of twenty-seven experiments which were part of national telephone surveys conducted by the University of Michigan's Survey Research Center (SRC) between September 1974 and April 1984. These experiments on measures of attitude intensity, importance, and certainty were found "not to differentiate individuals who show response effects from those who do not." Eight tables accompany the text. One-third of the sixty references represent research from the 1980s.

14.2   NO OPINION/DON'T KNOW

284. Bishop, George F., Alfred J. Tuchfarber, and Robert W. Oldendick. "Opinions on Fictitious Issues: The Pressure to Answer Survey Questions." *Public Opinion Quarterly* 50, no. 2 (Summer 1986): 240–50.

Respondents apparently provide opinions on fictitious issues partly because of the pressure to answer—a situation that is created by both the form of the question and the manner in which "don't know" (DK) responses are handled by the interviewer. Blacks and less well educated respondents are more willing to offer opinions on fictitious issues. People who are less well informed on a subject are more easily pressured into giving an opinion. This may be because the less the person knows about a subject the more easily confused the person tends to be about it. The authors write that the survey researcher can eliminate most of the problem by providing a specific "no opinion" category or by using a filter question. This option could result in losing from 20 to 25 percent of the cases on some public affairs issues. The authors suggest that "probing" into what a respondent meant when a DK answer was provided assumes that there is, in fact, an answer waiting to be heard—when actually there may be none. Probing and DK answers are brought into question, with the suggestion that they be reexamined. Several tables show the responses received by the survey study. An appendix provides the questions used in the different formats. There are nine references, three from the 1980s.

285. Duncan, Otis Dudley, and Magnos Stenbeck. "No Opinion or Not Sure?" *Public Opinion Quarterly* 52, no. 4 (Winter 1988): 513–25.

The issue addressed in this study is whether different kinds of noncommital responses are interchangeable in a survey. The authors maintain that based on a study of the 1956, 1958, and 1960 American Panel Surveys, they found that the response options "no opinion" and "not sure" are not interchangeable. The other options available to respondents were: "strongly agree," "agree," "not sure, it depends," "disagree," and "strongly disagree." A small number of responses were marked as "don't know," although respondents were not told that this was an option. Most of the article consists of a statistical analysis and interpretation of the results of the surveys indicated above. In the conclusions, the authors write that they found "evidence of nonrandom response consistency in the use of 'No opinion' response and in the choices between it and the only nominally equivalent 'Not sure, it depends' response." They also found no evidence of a persistence of response to a single question over the period of the surveys. Duncan and Stenbeck believe that the panel design is particularly useful to researchers studying the response processes leading to inconsistent and noncommital answers to opinion questions. Fourteen references, seven from the 1980s, complete the article.

286. Leigh, James H., and Claude R. Martin, Jr. "'Don't Know' Item Nonresponse in a Telephone Survey: Effects of Question Form and Respondent Characteristics." *Journal of Marketing Research* 24 (November 1987): 418–24.

The background literature is discussed, along with the theoretical basis and hypothesis formulation—in particular the 1981 threshold model of Schuman and Presser (Item No. 182). The effects of question form and respondent factors are reviewed. A study is described involving 398 adults who were asked a sixty-six question survey. The discussion of the study methods includes sections on experimental treatments, focal attitude questions, measures of item nonresponse, and predictor variables. Tables show the study data and include: (1) "ANOVA and ANCOVA results of percentage item nonresponses"; (2) "ANOVA and ANCOVA results of percentage item nonresponses for subsample of respondents with item nonresponse"; and (3) "Percentage complete response to general and specific attitude items." The study confirmed the Schuman and Presser threshold model. A split-ballot experiment was used in a survey which concerned attitudes on banking. Experienced or involved respondents and those respondents with little experience or involvement were found to differ in the variation of item nonresponse in relation to the number of scale points and question specificity. Sixteen references, six from the 1980s, are provided.

287. Poe, Gail S., Isadore Seeman, Joseph McLaughlin, Eric Mehl, and Michael Dietz. "'Don't Know' Boxes in Factual Questions in a Mail Questionnaire: Effects on Level and Quality of Response." *Public Opinion Quarterly* 52, no. 2 (Summer 1988): 212–22.

In their conclusion the authors state that they prefer self-administered (mailed) questionnaires without "don't know" (DK) boxes. They cite the following reasons: (1) more answers are provided with more information yielded; (2) there is a reduced need to adjust for missing data; (3) the inclusion of DK boxes changes the response distributions; (4) error rate remains much the same, with or without DK boxes; (5) lack of DK boxes did not affect return vote; and (6) absence of DK boxes made the questionnaire shorter and easier to read. The survey population was composed of relatives of recently deceased persons. The authors suggest that similar experiments on different groupings would be useful in order to examine the findings in a study of "self rather than proxy respondents." Three tables show: (1) the results of the mailing with and without DK boxes; (2) the rate of substance responses shown according to percentage-point differences; and (3) the items with significant differences in distribution of substantive responses. There are seven references.

14.3   RANDOMIZED RESPONSE

288.   Edgell, Stephen E., Samuel Himmelfarb, and Karen L. Duchan. "Validity of Forced Responses in a Randomized Response Model." *Sociological Methods & Research* 11, no. 1 (August 1982): 89–100.

S.L. Warner introduced the randomized response technique (RRT) as a way to eliminate evasiveness and untruthful responses to questions of a sensitive or potentially embarrassing nature. The original RRT was statistically inefficient and required large sample sizes to achieve an acceptable degree of accuracy. A modification, described in the introduction, is referred to as the Directed Response RRT. It is this method that the researchers Edgell, Himmelfarb, and Duchan chose to investigate. In the follow-up telephone interview, 91 percent of the respondents contacted said that the Directed Response RRT approach led them to believe that their responses were more confidential; 90 percent suggested that the approach would make people more willing to admit to socially unacceptable behavior. Discussion is provided concerning the so-called sensitive attribute, and the percentages of the respondents who did not answer questions as directed. On some questions, when directed to answer "yes" when the real answer was "no," many individuals tried to communicate the real answer to the interviewer by giggles, smiles, or other body language—as with the question: "Have you ever had a homosexual experience?" There are sixteen references, two from the 1980s.

289. Fox, James Alan, and Paul E. Tracy. *Randomized Response: A Method for Sensitive Surveys.* Sage University Paper series on Quantitative Application in the Social Sciences, edited by John L. Sullivan, and Richard G. Niemi, 07-035. Beverly Hills, CA: Sage Publications, 1983. 80p.

The Sage University Paper discusses sources of error in surveys, particularly with responses to sensitive, socially disapproved or incriminating behaviors and attitudes. A review of traditional methods for protecting the anonymity of respondents and the confidentiality of responses follows, with rejoinders to the effect that these approaches are either limited or at least are so perceived by respondents. The focus of the volume is on randomized response (RR) as a means of "effectively and efficiently" protecting survey respondents and thus reducing survey bias. Strategies, design considerations, an alternate strategy, polychotomous measures, quantitative measure, subgroup comparison, measures of association, and disclosure control are all covered in the second section of the book. Section 3 considers application of RR methods, and includes information on substantive applications, comparison studies, and validation research. The appendix is titled "Instructions to Respondents" and contains several different formats. Sixty-nine references (with fifteen from the 1980s) complete the paper.

290. Stem, Donald E., Jr., and R. Kirk Steinhorst. "Telephone Interview and Mail Questionnaire Applications of the Randomized Response Model." *Journal of the American Statistical Association* 79, no. 387 (September 1984): 555–64.

With cost in the forefront of their minds, authors Stem and Steinhorst suggest several less expensive methods of generating randomized response studies. Since personal interview approaches are expensive, as alternatives the authors devised a self-administered mail questionnaire using a two-part spinner to generate the randomization, and a telephone method using the respondents' local telephone directory as the randomization device. The telephone technique experienced a 12.7 percent dropout rate during the randomized response model (RRM) section of the questionnaire. The overall dropout ratio was 21 percent—a high nonresponse rate. The authors acknowledge that more work is needed to bring the nonresponse rate to an acceptable level. The approach was successful in generating appropriate randomization and in protecting actual privacy as well as perceived privacy of the respondents. RRM techniques are used when attempting to reduce measurement error in studies dealing with sensitive or nonnormative behaviors. Outlined are characteristics deemed necessary when employing the RRM methodology. These include: (1) simple instructions should be used which do not introduce response bias or cause excessive nonresponse; (2) the randomization device should provide appropriate distribution for answers, as well as the generation of surrogate answers; (3) instructions should be clear as to when to use surrogate answers; (4) privacy (actual and perceived) should be provided; and (5) devices used should be readily available or easily mailed. Fifteen references (two from the 1980s) accompany the article.

291. Tamhane, Ajit C. "Randomized Response Techniques for Multiple Sensitive Attributes." *Journal of the American Statistical Association* 76, no. 376 (December 1981): 916–23.

The randomized response (RR) technique was developed to deal with untruthful response or noncooperation by respondents when asked about sensitive or stigmatizing attributes. The RR technique avoids the "evasive answer bias," but is designed to deal with a single sensitive attribute. The author writes about a technique which enables the social researcher to study several sensitive attributes together. Tamhane provides a review of the literature concerning the multiple attributes problem and describes a new RR technique for dealing with the problem. The results of an actual application are provided as a demonstration of the way that RR can be used. The author discusses the measurement of respondent jeopardy, provides a comparison with competing techniques, describes the application of the "M" technique (the multiple RR trials technique), and discusses the results. The article contains mathematics at an advanced level. There are seventeen references.

292. Tracy, Paul E., and James Alan Fox. "The Validity of Randomized Response for Sensitive Measurements." *American Sociological Review* 46, no. 2 (April 1981): 187–200.

Researchers Tracy and Fox determined that the randomized response (RR) method outperformed the traditional direct-question approach. They believe that the RR technique is useful for the study of sensitive phenomena, such as research on attitudes toward minorities, illegal or deviant behaviors, mental illness, and the array of sexual behaviors. The results of the comparison tests described here indicate that the RR method is considerably less vulnerable to systematic response bias relative to the direct-question approach. In the RR method the interviewer does not know what question the respondent is answering. The interviewer records the response to a random question, or as the authors phrase it, the approach uses "indeterminate questions...and thus maintains the anonymity of the responses." The test mechanism employed compared the self-reported arrests for two interview methods (namely, RR and direct question) with the corresponding documented scores appearing in police arrest files. This study was designed to provide field-validation of a quantitative RR model. Six tables deal with the following: randomizing device; a summary of the arrest data; response error; regression of response error; sources of response error; and mean square error comparisons. There are nineteen references, with one from the 1980s.

14.4 LYING, NONATTITUDES, AND UNINFORMED RESPONSES

293. Hawkins, Del I., and Kenneth A. Coney. "Uninformed Response Error in Survey Research." *Journal of Marketing Research* 18, no. 3 (August 1981): 270–74.

As early as 1947 (*Tide*, p. 72), it was known that the general public would provide opinion on topics on which they had no information (S.N. Gill was the researcher). Hawkins and Coney wanted to determine what percentage of the population would express a view on a fictitious public policy issue. Also explored were three other questions: (1) What is the impact of the "don't know" (DK) category? (2) Do questions which surround the fictitious issue effect the response to it? and (3) Are specialized groups that "should" have an interest in the fictitious issue more likely to voice an opinion than the general public? Five hundred members of the general public and five hundred lawyers were the subjects for the mail survey. The findings showed that respondents will provide opinions on matters about which they have no knowledge. The DK option reduces uninformed responses, and a fictitious issue surrounded by actual issues is more likely to draw a response. The specialized group (i.e., the lawyers) showed a similar response rate to that of the general public in relation to the fictitious issue. A table provides the percentages of surveys returned, along with the percentages of responses to the fictitious issue. Seventeen references are included (two from the 1980s).

294. Lewis, I.A., and William Schneider. "Is the Public Lying to the Pollsters? A Question of Truth." *Current* 245 (September 1982): 25–35. Also in *Public Opinion* 5, no. 2 (April/May 1982): 42–47.

The authors explore the issue of whether the public is really lying or perhaps whether other factors might be responsible for what appears to be lying. Apparently people misrepresent the truth in order to conform to their impressions of social acceptability. Examples of invalidity are described, with a view to determine the magnitude of the problem. The issue of different interviewing techniques is highlighted. Nonattitudes are discussed along with the differentiation of respondents into two groups— the stable and the random (with less than 20 percent of the total sample having "real and stable attitudes on any given issue"). Questions which call for respondents to reconstruct past experiences run the risk of misreporting. Those that misrepresent are examined; misrepresentations are higher among nonwhites, young people, and lower income groups. Finally, the issue of the difference between what people say they believe, and what their actual behaviors are, is reviewed. As the authors suggest, a respondent may be providing a true opinion, but actual behavior "simply cannot be predicted from their attitudes." No references are included.

295. Murphy, John H. "Methodological Problems Related to the Use of Fictitious or Obscure Issues to Investigate 'Uninformed Response' in Survey Research." *Advances in Consumer Research* 11 (1984): 52–55.

The issue this study seeks to respond to is whether or not it is useful to use fictitious and/or obscure issues to examine the degree to which respondents who lack valid information will respond to the questioners' requests for attitudinal data. Murphy determined that the employment of fictitious and obscure issues "may be of questionable value in understanding the uninformed response phenomenon." He discusses a research project conducted by Weber and Cook (*Psychological Bulletin*, 1972) in which they identified four possible role models for subjects: the good subject, the faithful subject, the negativistic subject, and the apprehensive subject. The good subject responds in a way he thinks will support the researcher's hypothesis; the faithful subject follows instructions scrupulously; the negativistic subject either provides no useful information or answers in a manner he believes is counter to the hypothesis of the researcher, the so-called screw you effect referred to by Masling (*Nebraska Symposium on Motivation*, 1966); and the apprehensive subject attempts a positive manner, viewing the researcher as a type of "evaluator." It is clear for a number of reasons that subjects will respond to questions about which they know little or nothing. An alternative to fictitious issues is asking in-depth questions as follow-ups, after actual issue questions have been asked to determine subjects' knowledge on an issue. Twelve references (four from the 1980s) accompany the article.

296. Schneider, Kenneth C. "Uninformed Response Rates in Survey Research: New Evidence." *Journal of Business Research* 13, no. 2 (April 1985): 153–62.

The relationship between uninformed responses and a number of factors (such as type of question, presence or absence of an "unsure" option, level of pressure used to get answers, and the method of communication used) is investigated. Uninformed response as defined by Schneider is "the tendency of respondents to 'guess at' answers when they lack sufficient knowledge to provide an informed response." Using the "don't know" or "unsure" option significantly reduces—but does not eliminate—uninformed responses. Schneider poses a number of questions which he believes arise from these issues, and attempts to answer some of them. His findings include the observation that uninformed responses are considerably greater when gauging opinions and attitudes than when measuring recall and other factually based questions. Schneider believes that "unsure," "don't know," or "no opinion" options should always be provided. He suggests that uninformed responses arise from a fear of embarrassment rather than from a desire to be of assistance to the poll-taker. Some techniques used to increase the response rate may, in fact, make the problem of the uninformed responses greater. Ten references (four from the 1980s) complete the article.

297. Smith, Tom W. "Nonattitudes: A Review and Evaluation." Chap. 8 in *Surveying Subjective Phenomena*, edited by Charles F. Turner, and Elizabeth Martin, vol. 2, pt. 3, 215–55. Panel on Survey Measurement of Subjective Phenomena, Committee on National Statistics, Commission on Behavioral and Social Sciences and Education, National Research Council. New York: Russell Sage Foundation, 1984.

The chapter is divided into sections, beginning with one titled "Converse's Nonattitudes." Instrument error is covered in another section which is divided into the following subsections: "Concept"; "Are There Hidden Nonattitudes?" "Are DK's Nonattitudes?" "Distribution of Nonattitudes"; "Correlates of Nonattitudes"; and "Evidence of Instrument

Error." The last two sections are "True Change" and "Implications." Smith believes that instrument error and nonattitudes are present in "appreciable amounts" in many opinion questions, and that they contribute to low consistency. Converse is cited as being of the view that individuals with nonattitudes should stop providing random responses to interviewers, while others maintain that the approach of choice is to improve the questions that are asked. Smith suggests that true change should be the focus of greater attention as a possible source of survey data inconsistencies. The author concludes by observing that the study of individuals (rather than aggregates) may provide a better grasp of the error structure of opinion questions, attitude change, and potentially even insights into how the human mind operates. There are several tables, twenty-three notes, and five pages of references provided.

14.5   RESPONDENT ANONYMITY

298. Kaplowitz, Stan A., Edward L. Fink, Dave D'Alessio, and G. Blake Armstrong. "Anonymity, Strength of Attitude, and the Influence of Public Opinion Polls." *Human Communication Research* 10, no. 1 (Fall 1983): 5–25.
In order to seek responses to six statements on public issues, 113 subjects (all undergraduate students) were administered questionnaires. Some of the issues were designed to generate views showing strong commitment; others were selected in areas where the subjects had no commitment or knowledge. Subjects were differently advised, i.e., some believed their responses would be anonymous, while others believed that their responses would be available to the public. Each questionnaire had a bogus distribution of responses from the students at the university. Each statement of interest was supported by the bogus majority in one questionnaire form, and rejected by it in the other form. On low-commitment issues, the students were influenced toward the bogus majority. With high-commitment issues, the bogus majority made no appreciable difference. An appendix table shows the "Variance–Covariance Matrix Analyzed Via LISREL." A discussion of the findings concludes the article, along with notes and several pages of references.

299. Kearney, Kathleen A., Ronald H. Hopkins, Armand L. Mauss, and Ralph A. Weisheit. "Self-Generated Identification Codes for Anonymous Collection of Longitudinal Questionnaire Data." *Public Opinion Quarterly* 48, no. 1B (Spring 1984): 370–78.

The challenge is to find a way in which respondents can remain anonymous, but at the same time be available at different times for additional data which can then be linked. The researchers found that the self-generated identification (ID) code (even more effective when combined with the "off-one" matching procedure) provides a solution to collecting longitudinal data while maintaining respondent anonymity. Earlier research indicated that incorrectly linked cases created some sample bias. One solution to this problem is the off-one matching method in which pairs of codes that were different on any one of the seven elements (including missing elements) were matched. The authors did not link data from codes with more than one different element due to the increased risk of mismatching and thereby linking incorrect data. The study results indicated that 92 percent of the samples were linked over a one-month "interest" interval, and 78 percent of the possible cases were successfully linked over a one-year interval. Less than 2 percent were incorrectly linked in either sample. The article contains several tables and fourteen references (one from the 1980s).

300. Malvin, Janet H., and Joel M. Moskowitz. "Anonymous Versus Identifiable Self-Reports of Adolescent Drug Attitudes, Intentions, and Use." *Public Opinion Quarterly* 47, no. 4 (Winter 1983): 557–66.

The study is a test of the view that in order to achieve success in a survey which is designed to measure potentially incriminating information, a completely anonymous survey environment is necessary. The research findings suggest that identifiable drug surveys of adolescents do tend to show less current drug use on such surveys, but that the bias is dependent upon the subject's grade and sex, and the item sensitivity. Overall, the researchers believe that confidence can be placed in the drug surveys. A technique known as the "bogus pipeline" is discussed. Using this technique, the experimenter tries to persuade the survey participants that false answers can be detected through (usually) bogus physiological measures which are taken along with the self-report measure. This approach can complicate matters as it uses deception in an environment in which prevention or treatment programs rely on honesty and truthfulness between participants and assistance providers. In sum, there was a lack of significant differences found between the self-reporting of the anonymous versus the identifiable respondents. An appendix contains the questionnaire items and the response formats. There are ten references, two from the 1980s.

14.6   ADDITIONAL STUDIES

301.   Bachman, Jerald G., and Patrick M. O'Malley. "Yea-Saying, Nay-Saying, and Going to Extremes: Black-White Differences in Response Styles." *Public Opinion Quarterly* 48, no. 2 (Summer 1984): 491–509.

The data used by the researchers was collected from approximately 130 high schools, generating approximately 17,000 respondents each year, with an 80 percent response rate of all the seniors sampled. The surveys began in 1975, along with follow-up surveys which are mailed to a subset of each senior class. The surveys are conducted by the Institute for Social Research (ISR) at the University of Michigan. The study examines the differing styles of response between black respondents and white respondents when faced with Likert-type questionnaire items. The researchers found that blacks are more likely than whites to choose the extreme response categories—especially the positive end of agree-disagree scales. The sex, family socioeconomic level, educational accomplishments, and aspirations of respondents do not seem to generate consistent differences in response styles. Southern students of both races seem to have stronger agreement tendencies, but controlling for geography only marginally alters the overall black-white differences. The text includes four tables. There are eighteen references (eight from the 1980s).

302.   Bishop, George F., Robert W. Oldendick, Alfred J. Tuchfarber, and Stephen E. Bennett. "Pseudo-Opinions on Public Affairs." *Public Opinion Quarterly* 44, no. 2 (Summer 1980): 198–209.

The researchers examined the frequently suspected tendency of survey respondents to provide answers to questions on subjects which they have given little or no thought. The authors tested the issue by inserting a nonexistent "Public Affairs Act" into the Greater Cincinnati Survey. They found that a substantial number of respondents claimed to have an opinion on the fictitious act. These respondents tended to be "black, less educated, less interested in politics, and less trusting of others." The survey indicated that respondents willing to provide opinions on the fictitious act were, in general, in favor of the "liberal" or progovernment position on domestic issues. The general failure of public opinion surveys to eliminate such respondents through an appropriate filter questions or a dummy item of the kind used in this experiment is noted. In closing, the authors observe that although they may have received opinions on an act that does not exist, the opinions received nevertheless represent "enduring (personality) dispositions" and may therefore be of significant interest. Additionally, these opinions raise the question of validity, e.g., "What is it that we are trying to measure?" Fifteen references (one from 1980) complete the article.

303. DeMaio, Theresa J. "Social Desirability and Survey Measurement: A Review." Chap. 9 in *Surveying Subjective Phenomena*, edited by Charles F. Turner, and Elizabeth Martin, vol. 2, pt. 3, 257–82. Panel on Survey Measurement of Subjective Phenomena, Committee on National Statistics, Commission on Behavioral and Social Sciences and Education, National Research Council. New York: Russell Sage Foundation, 1984.

Social desirability is viewed as a major source of response bias in survey research. Explained in simple terms, social desirability is "a tendency on the part of respondents to give favorable impressions of themselves." It is not clear, however, what the source of respondents' views on the subject is. DeMaio divides the chapter into the following sections: "Personality or Item Characteristic?"; "What is 'Desirability'?"; "Who Sets the Standards of Desirability?"; "Substantive Results"; and "Discussion." The explanations provided in the chapter do not really define social desirability, but they do incorporate several common elements, such as the idea that some things are good and some are bad, and that respondents seek to be perceived as "good" and answer accordingly. The author suggests the effort to define social desirability is an ongoing problem; nevertheless survey researchers can employ the knowledge that responses to survey questions are influenced by what we perceive to be socially desirable. There are fourteen notes which are nonbibliographic in nature, and over a page of references.

304. Dwyer, F. Robert. "Response Errors in Survey Research." *California Management Review* 23, no. 1 (Fall 1980): 39–45.

The consideration of response errors in survey research begins with a review of the accuracy of self-reports. The thrust of the article concerns methods which can be used to improve research practice. Sections discuss mixed designs, a systems approach to error management, design creativity, and improving response accuracy. The intent of the article is to review the range of response errors. A figure presents "A Randomized Response Model." There are fifteen pre-1980 references provided.

305. Fox, Richard J., Melvin R. Crask, and Jonghoon Kim. "Mail Survey Response Rate: A Meta-Analysis of Selected Techniques for Inducing Response." *Public Opinion Quarterly* 52, no. 4 (Winter 1988): 467–91.

The researchers found that six of nine factors examined successfully increased the response rates on average. These factors include university sponsorship, prenotification by letter, stamped return postage, postcard follow-up, first-class outgoing postage, and questionnaire color. The most effective factor, that of university sponsorship as opposed to private business, is of course, not generally a controllable factor. Small cash incentives with the questionnaire have a positive effect on response rate on average. The emphasis here is on small monetary incentives, as it appears that increasing the amount is counterproductive. Previous studies using the regression approach found little or no effect with prenotification. The meta-analysis approach utilized by researchers Fox, Crask, and Kim found an 8 percent increase when using a postcard prenotifying the respondents of an upcoming survey. The authors state that the form of meta-analysis used "clearly defines the individual impact of each of the factors examined." The appendix compiles the previous twenty-five years of published materials on mail survey response rate effects, including the significant coverage in the *Journal of Marketing Research, Public Opinion Quarterly*, and the *Journal of Applied Psychology*. There are sixteen references, eleven from the 1980s.

306. Keene, Karlyn H., and Victoria A. Sackett. "An Editors' Report on the Yankelovich, Skelly and White 'Mushiness Index.'" *Public Opinion* 4, no. 2 (April/May 1981): 50–51.

The "Mushiness Index," developed by the firm of Yankelovich, Skelly and White at a cost of $150,000, is designed to ascertain the firmness of opinion in the areas of foreign and domestic issues. "Mushiness" is the term used to describe the relative degree of volatility and changeability in the views held by the public. The company is careful to distinguish between volatility and intensity of opinion. The technique uses a favor/oppose question followed by four six-point scale questions, and is applicable to the whole range of interview formats available, including in-person, telephone, and self-administered. The first nationwide test of the product was conducted in December 1980. Domestic issues were found to yield opinions less mushy than those in the foreign policy domain. Charts show responses to a particular issue, as well as firm, very mushy, and mushy responses to public policy issues. No references are included.

307. Mellinger, Glen D., Carol L. Huffine, and Mitchell B. Balter. "Assessing Comprehension in a Survey of Public Reactions to Complex Issues." *Public Opinion Quarterly* 46, no. 1 (Spring 1982): 97–109.

The study shows that, even for those individuals with less than a high-school education, the majority of the respondents were able to make "meaningful and consistent discriminations" regarding the risks, benefits, and other factors presented in the "vignettes." (A sample vignette appears at the end of the article). For those respondents with pre-high-school education levels, the interviewer employed visual aids explaining the major concepts which were to be covered in the interview. These individuals did show difficulty with the more complex and abstract vignettes. The authors maintain that the study results indicate that cross-sectional samples of the general public can be successfully surveyed with the use of careful interview strategy and with an "educational sequence" of questioning, visual aids, and other procedures for those who need special assistance due to a lack of knowledge on the subject and/or issues involved. The researchers were attempting to develop procedures for household interviewing in the area of determining the public's judgments about ethical issues in biomedical research. Described are the mechanisms utilized to increase respondent comprehension and the development of a composite comprehension index based on three types of information from the interview. There are five references and one figure with the text.

308.   Sharp, Laure M., and JoAnne Frankel. "Respondent Burden: A Test of Some Common Assumptions." *Public Opinion Quarterly* 47, no. 1 (Spring 1983): 36–53.

The Office of Management and Budget (OMB) was assigned the responsibility of administering regulations concerning what OMB called "respondent burden"—referring to the time needed for the completion of forms. For survey research this meant the amount of time that the respondent needed to complete interviews or self-administered interviews. In 1976 OMB generated a rule that no data-gathering endeavor could take more than thirty minutes (except under very exceptional circumstances). In light of these circumstances, the authors undertook a study to investigate the issue of respondent burden for survey research. The finding is that Sharp and Frankel do not believe that it is a major issue, and that respondents did not refuse to participate because of overly frequent requests to participate in surveys in the past. The researchers did find that about one-third of the respondents questioned did not believe that answering surveys is of benefit to them or that responding will assist or be of influence in government decisions. A similar proportion believe that too many surveys were being conducted, and that too many personal questions were being asked—and yet they nevertheless agreed to participate. Of the variables tested, the length of the questionnaire was the only one which produced statistically significant differences in burden perception. Thirteen pre-1980 references are provided.

309.   Wood, Nancy Lee. "An Exploration of the Internal Stability of Public Opinion Holding Using 'The Mushiness Index'." Ph.D. diss., University of Colorado at Boulder, 1985. 165p.

The instability of public opinion is addressed in this dissertation, with opinion researchers and policy makers the beneficiaries of the research. It is suggested that weak opinion holding is based on the lack of attentiveness to public issues. The study presented is a secondary analysis using data collected by the firm of Yankelovich, Skelly, and White, Inc. This firm developed a filtering device called "The Mushiness Index" which enabled Wood to examine a number of elements concerning opinion stability. Wood describes the research as inductive and exploratory, focusing on four aspects of opinion holding: "types of questions which generate firm opinions; demographic subgroups who emerge as firm opinion holders; the phenomena of nonsubstantive responses; and social and response characteristics that impact opinion holding." The results of the study show that questions on "domestic policy, unloaded queries, questions containing additional information and aggressive stance queries generate relatively firm opinions." Conversely, questions on "foreign policy, unloaded queries..., and conciliatory stance queries elicit the most nonsubstantive responses." Wood believes the findings show the means by which polling techniques can be improved. References are provided.

15. Data Collection

310. Dooley, David. "Survey Data Collection: Issues and Methods in
      Sample Surveys." Chap. 10 in *Social Research Methods*, 233–64.
      Englewood Cliffs, NJ: Prentice-Hall, 1984.
This textbook is designed for students in their first course on social
science methods. While other chapters cover areas of interest to survey
researchers, chapter 10 specifically addresses survey research, discussing
the major areas of design, error, sampling, and data collection. The
chapter opens with a review of the *Literary Digest* Poll of 1936, then
continues with descriptions of various survey types including panel and
trend surveys, cross-sectional and cohort designs, and face-to-face,
telephone, and mail approaches. Random error, bias, and total survey
error are reviewed next. Sampling terminology and sampling designs
including probability and nonprobability are discussed along with random
sample error. The treatment of data collection incorporates the issues of
interviewer effects and training and questionnaire construction. The topics
of completion rates and bias related issues are also covered. The chapter
includes a summary, several exercises, and a forty-nine-entry glossary. A
cumulative reference list of ten pages is provided at the end of the book,
along with a glossary, and name and subject indexes.

311. Mangione, Thomas W., Ralph Hingson, and Jane Barrett. "Col-
      lecting Sensitive Data: A Comparison of Three Survey
      Strategies." *Sociological Methods & Research* 10, no. 3 (February
      1982): 337–46.
The challenges addressed by the authors concerned how to reach respondents who did not own a telephone and how to deal with geographic areas
which did not match telephone exchange boundaries. The study found
that a combined telephone/field strategy to be a viable alternative to in-
person interviewing, i.e., using in-person interviews as backups when
telephone numbers were unavailable. Another option tested involved the

"drop-off/pick-up, self-administered questionnaire." This approach did not yield substantially improved data and generated significantly different distribution outcomes on a number of sensitive measures. The self-administered method provided the researchers with more middle category responses. The above approaches were compared with in-person interviewing, which appears to be considered by respondents to be the most "enjoyable" of the options reviewed. Conducted in Boston in 1977, the major focus of the study was drinking behavior. Several tables show the comparisons between the data for each of the options discussed. Four references conclude the article.

312.   Weinberg, Eve. "Data Collection: Planning and Management." Chap. 9 in *Handbook of Survey Research*, edited by Peter H. Rossi, James D. Wright, and Andy B. Anderson, 329–58. Quantitative Studies in Social Relations, consulting editor Peter H. Rossi. New York: Academic Press, 1983.

The goal of data collection is to gather the information needed in a "uniform and reliable way." The process should be completed in the designated time and within the available budget. The management of data collection involves the determination of priorities, the maintenance of appropriate levels of quality and quantity work, and the continual review of the process to ensure that the objectives of the survey are being addressed within the limits of the budget. Most of Weinberg's chapter concerns how to meet these goals, with sections on planning; recruitment and training; the selection of the appropriate data collection method; the recruitment and selection of interviewers; the training of interviewers; interviewer manuals; and the management of data collection. There are many subsections within these areas, all designed to focus on the numerous aspects which constitute the requirements that lead toward successful data collection. There are five pre-1980 references provided.

16. Statistical Analysis

16.1 MODELS

313. Berk, Richard A. "Applications of the General Linear Model to Survey Data." Chap. 13 in *Handbook of Survey Research*, edited by Peter H. Rossi, James D. Wright, and Andy B. Anderson, 495–546. Quantitative Studies in Social Relations, consulting editor Peter H. Rossi. New York: Academic Press, 1983.

The general linear model (GLM) is described by Berk as one of the most popular statistical tools for analyzing survey data. The GLM includes multiple regression, analysis of variance, and analysis of covariance as special cases. The chapter provides an overview of the GLM. Berk discusses the topic in the following sections in the chapter: "The Two-Variable Regression Model"; "The Multivariate Model"; and "Some Common Problems with the Multivariate Model." The chapter is designed for readers with advanced mathematical skills. To quote the author, "This chapter assumes that the reader has at least a nodding acquaintance with multiple regression and elementary statistical concepts at about the level of Blalock [*Social Statistics*, 1972] or Hayes [*Statistics for the Social Sciences*, 1973]." Blalock and Hayes refer to entries in the Berk chapter bibliography; both appear to be textbooks for social science statistics. Seventy references follow the chapter, with about 70 percent drawn from the 1970s.

314. Clogg, Clifford C. "Some Statistical Models for Analyzing Why Surveys Disagree." Chap. 11 in *Surveying Subjective Phenomena*, edited by Charles F. Turner, and Elizabeth Martin, vol. 2, pt. 4, 319–66. Panel on Survey Measurement of Subjective Phenomena, Committee on National Statistics, Commission on Behavioral and Social Sciences and Education, National Research Council. New York: Russell Sage Foundation, 1984.

The inadequacies of the linear model as a tool in analyzing response distributions that occur when measuring subjective phenomena are discussed. The value of association models and the latent-class model developed by Paul Lazarsfeld are considered as viable alternatives to the linear model. A simultaneous latent-class model for across-group comparisons is defined, with an example provided as to how to estimate models simultaneously. Contingency-table methods are used throughout the chapter. The log-multiplicative association model is considered for its use in the estimation of category scores for discrete ordinal variables. There are twenty tables included along with numerous advanced statistical calculations using symbol language understood by statisticians and those with advanced statistics coursework. References are found at the end of the chapter.

315. Taylor, D. Garth. "Analyzing Qualitative Data." Chap. 14 in *Handbook of Survey Research*, edited by Peter H. Rossi, James D. Wright, and Andy B. Anderson, 547–612. Quantitative Studies in Social Relations, consulting editor Peter H. Rossi. New York: Academic Press, 1983.

The key concepts and techniques of qualitative data analysis are discussed at an advanced level, along with other areas which are not covered in introductory works. The mathematical skills required to fully appreciate the chapter contents include—but are not limited to—matrix algebra, design matrices, and the capability to deal with the general linear model for contingency table analysis. Subjects discussed include hierarchical modeling, latent structure analysis, log linear modeling, and the regression analysis of percentages in contingency tables. There are 123 references with approximately 66 percent of the references from the 1970s, 15 percent from the 1960s, and the balance from pre-1960 years.

16.2   MISSING/INCOMPLETE DATA

316. Anderson, Andy B., Alexander Basilevsky, and Derek P.J. Hum. "Missing Data: A Review of the Literature." Chap. 12 in *Handbook of Survey Research*, edited by Peter H. Rossi, James D. Wright, and Andy B. Anderson, 415–94. Quantitative Studies in Social Relations, consulting editor Peter H. Rossi. New York: Academic Press, 1983.

In many instances data which is missing in a random fashion can be treated in a manner which prevents the loss of information and/or eliminates possible sources of bias. If the data is missing in a nonrandom fashion, the difficulties are more significant. In the words of the authors, with the least problematic case of random nonresponse, "we can fix it," whereas with nonrandom nonresponse, "the standard methods are not appropriate." The last line conveys the summary of the chapter's three authors: "The only real cure for missing data is not to have any." The review of the literature consists of an analysis of experimental design models using incomplete data, missing data in survey samples, regressive analysis with incomplete observations, and the consideration of other multivariate models. Advanced mathematics is used throughout the chapter. There are 278 references at the end of the chapter, covering works primarily from the 1960s and 1970s.

317. Kalton, Graham. *Compensating for Missing Survey Data*. Research Report Series. N.p. [Ann Arbor?]: Institute for Social Research, The University of Michigan, 1983. 157p.

Kalton deals with the means by which missing data in surveys is handled, with efforts centered on the 1978 and 1979 Research Panel surveys of the Income Survey Development Program (ISDP). There are five chapters, with multiple tables and diagrams. Numerous complex mathematical formulae accompany the text and would suggest an advanced knowledge of mathematics or statistics as a prerequisite to a useful understanding of the text. Chapter 1 deals with the types of nonresponse and nonresponse bias. Chapter 2 considers general issues for missing data compensation procedures. Weighting adjustments, used mostly to compensate for total nonresponse, are covered in the third chapter. Imputation is the subject of chapter 4, with methods identified and two simulation studies discussed. Chapter 5 covers miscellaneous topics including multiple imputations and weighted data. An appendix written by Leslie Kish is titled "Repeated Replication Imputation Procedure (RRIP)." There is a twenty-page bibliography at the end of the volume, followed by an unnumbered page of additional ISR Research Reports.

318. Madow, William G., Harold Nisselson, and Ingram Olkin, eds. *Incomplete Data in Sample Surveys*. Vol. 1, *Report and Case Studies*. Panel on Incomplete Data, Committee on National Statistics, Commission on Behavioral and Social Sciences and Education, National Research Council. New York: Academic Press, 1983. 495p.

The Panel on Incomplete Data was organized in 1977 to conduct a comprehensive review of the literature and to examine ways of improving the methods used to deal with incomplete data. William G. Madow served as the study director, coordinating all the panel's activities and projects. Ingram Olkin served as chair of the panel. Volume 1 (of a three-volume set) is divided into two parts. Part 1 is titled "Report" and has five chapters covering introductory material and recommendations, problems of incomplete data, measuring and reporting nonresponse, and one chapter each for a review of case studies and the review of theory. An appendix provides biographical sketches of panel members and staff. Two pages of references are included at the end of part 1. Part 2, "Case Studies," begins with an overview of the ten case studies which follow in succeeding chapters. In order the chapters are: "Employment Cost Index"; "Livestock Inventory Surveys"; "Surveys of Consumer Attitudes"; "Office Equipment Survey"; "Annual Survey of Manufacturers"; "Survey of Consumer Finance"; "National Longitudinal Survey"; "Readership of Ten Major Magazines Survey"; "Center for Health Administration Studies"; and "Health and Nutrition Examination Survey." The volume closes with an author index and approximately six pages of subject indexing.

319. Madow, William G., Ingram Olkin, and Donald B. Rubin, eds. *Incomplete Data in Sample Surveys*. Vol. 2, *Theory and Bibliographies*. Panel on Incomplete Data, Committee on National Statistics, Commission on Behavioral and Social Sciences and Education, National Research Council. New York: Academic Press, 1983. 579p.

There are seven parts to this volume. These include: "Introduction"; "Selected Topics in Data Collection"; "Nonresponse and Double Sampling"; "Weighting and Imputation Methods"; "Imputation Methodology: Total Survey Error"; "Superpopulation Models for Nonresponse"; and "Bibliographies." The bibliographies include a sixty-page annotated bibliography on incompete data, with lengthy multiparagraph entries, and an eighty-six page unannotated "Bibliography on Nonresponse and Related Topics." The twenty-two chapters and two bibliographies represent the contributions of twenty-three authors, some of whom provided more than one chapter. (It should be noted that six contributors are from outside the United States.) The theoretical presentations in volume 2 are primarily within the framework of simple random sampling. The report is dedicated to William Gemmell Cochran who wrote the chapter titled "Historical Perspective." Cochran's contribution covers fifty years research in incomplete data in sample surveys—the years in which he was personally active in this area of research. The volume contains both author and subject indexes, as well as an extensive contents section which includes the sections of each chapter in outline form.

320. Madow, William G., and Ingram Olkin, eds. *Incomplete Data in Sample Surveys*. Vol. 3, *Proceedings of the Symposium*. Panel on Incomplete Data, Committee on National Statistics, Commission on Behavioral and Social Sciences and Education, National Research Council. New York: Academic Press, 1983. 413p.

About 25 percent of the participants in this symposium were from outside the United States. The *Proceedings* volume is divided into eight sessions, with a total of fifteen numbered chapters (Session VIII does not use chapter numbers). The Sessions are titled "Background"; "Aspects of Design"; "Theory I"; "Computer Methods Assuming Likelihoods"; "Theory II"; "A Model and Adjustment Procedure"; "Issues in Imputation and Public Policy Experiments"; and "Hot-Deck Methods and Inference." This volume of proceedings, along with the previous two volumes in the set, is designed to represent a comprehensive review of the literature on survey incompleteness in sample surveys, as well as to provide a forum in which to explore improving the methods of responding to it. Much of the material includes advanced mathematics, with knowledge of advanced statistics taken for granted by the authors. In ten places in the volume there are sections titled "Discussion." Here a writer other than the chapter writer provides observations on the material—these are critical and evaluative in nature. Rejoinder remarks are also included, as are responses to the observations. The Symposium on Incomplete Data was held by the Panel on Incomplete Data in Washington, D.C. on 10-11 August

1979 and was designed to include current research into the review of incomplete data. The Symposium was also arranged to provide a forum for interested nonpanel members.

16.3   MISCELLANEOUS

321.   Alwin, Duane F., and Richard T. Campbell. "Continuity and Change in Methods of Survey Data Analysis." *Public Opinion Quarterly* 51, no. 4, pt. 2 (Winter 1987): S139–S155.
The origins of modern methods of survey data analysis are discussed with considerable attention directed to the Lazarsfeld paradigm. Regression methods are reviewed with sections focusing on path analysis, structural equation models, and partial correlation. The next area covered deals with the causal approach to measurement error with a section on linear structural relations (LISREL) and LISREL models. Categoric methods are considered next with a discussion of log-linear models. The final section discusses panel data. In their conclusion, the authors observe that despite the presence of sophisticated techniques such as causal analysis, the most widely used survey data interpretation and presentation is through the use of univariate and bivariate tables. A list of 105 references is provided. The list is essentially a historical bibliography of survey data analysis.

322.   Cordray, Sheila Mary. "The Problem of Attrition in Longitudinal Survey Research." Ph.D. diss., The University of Oregon, 1982. 187p.
The impact of respondent loss in longitudinal survey research is the main subject of this dissertation. Cordray suggests that the representativeness of the respondents, in relation to the original population, is the most significant issue. Such a view contrasts with the existing research literature which seeks to compare nonrespondents or late respondents to other respondents and make evaluations concerning response bias by examining the differences between the two groups. The research data for the study is from a fifteen-year, multiwave study of a group of young men in Oregon. The dissertation includes a review of comparisons between the data from the retained samples and those from the original

group. Statistical and substantive bias of the samples is determined. Cordray found that the impact of attrition is dependent upon the extent of the loss, the composition of the original group, and the method of analysis attempted. References are provided.

323. Glenn, Norval D. "Replications, Significance Tests and Confidence in Findings in Survey Research." *Public Opinion Quarterly* 47, no. 2 (Summer 1983): 261–69.

Glenn describes a procedure for calculating the statistical significance of an array of parameter estimates from two or more replications. The possible originator of the method was the pioneer survey researcher Samuel Stouffer. A table shows the critical values needed for quick application of the "Stouffer method." The purpose is to be able to use comparable data from two or more samples to combine the probabilities from two or more replications. The author researched the data available from the General Social Surveys (GSS) from 1972 to 1978 and 1980 and did not find any reports which included "properly computed significance tests for an array of parameter estimates from replicate analyses." The author was surprised at this finding since the demographic and background variables were the same for all of the GSS considered, which among other variables, provides the opportunity for replications. Three additional tables accompany the text, along with thirteen references—four from the 1980s.

324. Lee, Eun Sul, Ronald N. Forthofer, and Ronald J. Lorimor. "Analysis of Complex Sample Survey Data: Problems and Strategies." *Sociological Methods & Research* 15, nos. 1-2 (November 1986): 69–100.

The analysis of complex sample survey data is discussed with special emphasis on the effect of sample designs in statistical inference. Three examples are given to illustrate challenges with complex survey design: a typical community survey, a two-stage design in the surveys of mental hospitals, and a highly complex design in the National Health and Nutrition Examination Survey I (NHANES I). The authors suggest that complex survey data may require techniques beyond regular statistical methods in order to achieve appropriate inferences. They maintain that "more appropriate methods" are called for—those which incorporate sample design and selection probability. Secondary analysis of large-scale survey data has become more commonplace in the discipline of sociology and in the areas of social and health sciences in general. Multivariate statistical approaches are in greater use. Some of the causes which have led to these solutions include unequal selection probabilities, stratification, and clustering which may arise in social surveys involving complex sample design. The article contains three tables, each associated with one of the three examples discussed. There are ninety-eight references, about one-third from the 1980s.

325. Piazza, Thomas. "The Analysis of Attitude Items." *American Journal of Sociology* 86, no. 3 (November 1980): 584–603.

The author suggests new approaches to solving an old survey problem, i.e., how to select the best question from a group of questions designed to determine attitude. The results from the selected questions are combined to create a single index or scale which becomes the indication of the attitude. Piazza maintains that the usual techniques employed to create the scale are inadequate. The article covers an analysis of interim covariation, specific analytic procedures (including proportionality of correlations), and canonical correlation, with a comparison of the last two mentioned methods. Piazza maintains that the procedures of item analysis permit the measurement of an attitude, provide refinement in the definition of what has been measured, and determine whether or not the items are related to other variables of interest in a consistent way. The text includes five tables, one figure, and a six-item pre-1980 list of references.

17. Results

17.1 QUALITY AND VARIATION

326. Borrelli, Stephen, Brad Lockerbie, and Richard G. Niemi. "Why the Democrat-Republican Partisanship Gap Varies from Poll to Poll." *Public Opinion Quarterly* 51, no. 1 (Spring 1987): 115–19.

Examining poll results from 1980 and 1984, the authors found that the point spread between Democratic and Republican identifiers was as much as twenty. The findings indicated that polls which only sampled voters, polls which were taken near election day (for the 1984 samples), and polls which stressed the words "today" or the present in their question wording, produced results which favored the party that was leading in the presidential race at the time of the poll. The researchers used a total of fifty-one polls from the last four months prior to the elections of 1980 and 1984. There are several tables which show how the polls were scored as well as the effects of methods variables on the poll reports of the Democratic-Republican partisanship gap. Three references are provided.

327. Groves, Robert. "Research on Survey Data Quality." *Public Opinion Quarterly* 51, no. 4, pt. 2 (Winter 1987): S156–S172.

The review of the subject begins with the author noting the absence of a unifying theory in survey research, and that as such survey research is not an academic discipline. Rather, the field has grown as a result of contributions from statisticians, psychologists, political scientists, sociologists, and others. The next section deals with the components of survey quality, and discusses coverage error, nonresponse error, and sampling error. The topic of measurement error follows, with discussions of measurement error arising from the interviewer, the respondent, the questionnaire, and the mode of data collection. Underemphasized properties of survey quality are reviewed, including the cost complications of error reduction and interrelationships of error sources. The last part of the article considers the requirements needed to develop a theory of surveys, which Groves defines as "a set of linked concepts and propositions that can be used to guide a particular survey design to achieve maximum cost efficiency." The phrase "cost efficiency" is explained to mean that "survey quality is maximized given the costs available for the survey." Many disciplines would contribute to such a theory including cognitive psychology, psycholinguistics, the study of social interaction, and the sociological study of intergroup relations. There are forty-nine references.

328.   Lipset, Seymour Martin. "Different Polls, Different Results in 1980 Politics." *Public Opinion* 3, no. 4 (August/September 1980): 19–20, 60.

The varying reasons as to why poll results differ are explained in simple terms. Lipset begins by observing that the eight public national surveys do not use the same definition to describe the prospective voter. Different screening methods are used leading Gallup poll results to be based on 75 percent of all those interviewed in contrast to the Harris method which includes 54 percent. Definitions of sample eligibility also vary; one such definition is "likely voters." Analytic methods account for some of the differences. Interviewing techniques are a factor, with possible short-comings with telephone surveys caused by the approximately 10 percent who may not have a home telephone. Telephone surveys also miss 25 to 40 percent of those called for the first time. Weighting formulas are mentioned, with the note that these are not public information. Probability error is reviewed, along with a reminder to be aware of the actual date the survey was conducted. The use of survey results as indicators of trends is highlighted. The practice of polling organizations to increase their sample sizes as election day draws near receives comment. This practice has the impact of reducing possible error range. No references are included.

329. Turner, Charles F. "Why Do Surveys Disagree? Some Preliminary Hypotheses and Some Disagreeable Examples." Chap. 7 in *Surveying Subjective Phenomena*, edited by Charles F. Turner, and Elizabeth Martin, vol. 2, pt. 3, 159–214. Panel on Survey Measurement of Subjective Phenomena, Committee on National Statistics, Commission on Behavioral and Social Sciences and Education, National Research Council. New York: Russell Sage Foundation, 1984.

The examination of the literature and extensive discussions of examples leads Turner to three conclusions: (1) discrepancies in comparisons involving survey estimates are made by all types of research organizations; (2) nonsampling artifacts in the measurement of subjective phenomena go beyond univariate response distributions; and (3) no one explanation will be suitable for all of the observed discrepancies. Turner believes that a reexamination of the social psychological phenomena which are fundamental to survey research is necessary in order to more adequately understand the nature of the interpersonal exchange which occurs during the survey interview. Also, the survey analyst needs to better understand the "meaning" of survey questions to interviewees along with clarifying how respondents "experienced the reality of the interview situation." Ten tables and eight figures accompany the text. A significant portion of the text discusses four examples in detail. Thirty-seven notes and a reference section are provided at the end of the chapter.

17.2 ACCURACY

330. Converse, Philip E., and Michael W. Traugott. "Assessing the Accuracy of Polls and Surveys." *Science* 234, no. 4780 (28 November 1986): 1094–98.

The article explains the differences in results of similar polls seeking to provide opinion positions on the same subjects. Further, it reviews several sources of variability and fixed bias which attempt to explain how to better evaluate different data for the same issue or subject. Topics covered include sampling error; comparing products of different survey houses; variability in sample composition; measurement variability—interviewers; and measurement variability—the questionnaire. In conclusion, the authors state that often there is no question as to what procedures would be best, but that constraints of money and/or time have influence which therefore have a direct bearing on the precision of the polls and surveys. The authors also point out that steps deleted in the effort to keep costs down are not stated along with the results, thus leaving the consumer unable to adjust error margins accordingly. The author lists fourteen 1980s references and nine pre-1980 references.

331. Max, Alfred. "Basic Factors in the Interpretation of Public Opinion Polls: An Attempt at Assessing the Degree of Reliance to be Placed upon Figures Released by Private Polling Agencies on Current Social and Political Issues." Ph.D. diss., The American University, 1941. 239p.

Almost fifty years ago, Max suggested that sociological applications, rather than political ones, would be the "most promising" uses of the "new science" of public opinion polling employing scientific samples. The dissertation was written only five years after George Gallup's pioneering work and presents the issues of the evolving discipline. One area of consideration was the relationship between "commercial organizations" and "scientific institutions." A call is made for cooperation, shared knowledge, and peaceful coexistence. The concept of a board controlled by the government merging nonprofit and commercial polling organizations is suggested. The 1940s was a time in the United States in which government boards were being instituted for a wide variety of social concerns. Instead, the National Opinion Research Center (NORC) was established, and continues to this day. Most of the dissertation covers the qualitative concept of cross section, with additional chapters devoted to question wording, interviewing techniques and their impact on poll validity, and the qualitative approach to opinion measurement. References are provided.

332. Presser, Stanley. "Is Inaccuracy on Factual Survey Items Item-Specific or Respondent-Specific?" *Public Opinion Quarterly* 48, no. 1B (Spring 1984): 344–55.

The earliest large-scale test to address the question of whether survey research questionnaires generate truthful answers was the 1949 Denver Community Study (Survey). The Denver Study remains one of the most extensive examinations designed to test the validity of survey data. There was an assumption that reporting errors were uncorrelated across survey items. The Denver Survey showed that respondents who were asked seven questions on electoral behavior, and provided inaccurate responses to one of them, were disproportionately inaccurate on each of the other six. Inaccuracy on seven questions dealing with unrelated subjects was found to be item-specific. The inaccuracy with the electoral behavior questions tended to be higher with those respondents who expressed higher political interest. The author reports that either the interest in politics was exaggerated and/or the association between interest and participation was overestimated in past research. Presser cites research indicating that interest in politics is related to political participation (in this case the issue relates to whether a person actually voted). Using the data from the Denver Survey, Presser examined the issue of uncorrelated errors by constructing a measure of validity for each of the fourteen questions asked. Five tables provide analyses of the data. Nineteen references complete the article, with two from the 1980s.

333. Roper, Burns W. "Are Polls Accurate?" In *Polling and the Democratic Consensus*, edited by L. John Martin, 24–34. *Annals of the American Academy of Political and Social Science*, edited by Richard D. Lambert, vol. 472. Beverly Hills, CA: Sage Publications, 1984.

Burns W. Roper has worked in opinion research for over four decades. He is currently chairman of the board of the Roper Organization as well as the Roper Public Opinion Research Center. The title accurately summarizes the quest of the article—to look at the accuracies and inaccuracies of polls. The opening section deals briefly with examples of accurate polls, followed by a section describing some inaccurate polls. In looking at factors which lead to accuracy, Roper observes that polls on basic beliefs or subjects which the respondent has thought about for some time are more accurate than polls where the knowledge level is low. Ego or prestige questions in which the person thinks that there is a "correct answer" tend to produce less accurate poll results—a situation known as the right-answer bias. Although sampling error is often cited, Roper maintains that the major source of survey error arises from question wording. Timing of the question plays a role, as does response bias, specifically nonresponse bias, perhaps highest among mail surveys. Data interpretation and the context in which a question is asked are further possible sources of error. Lastly, Roper considers some pitfalls that can arise with what on the surface seems to be an easy question type—the factual one. He demonstrates how easily some oversights can skew poll data. No references are included.

334. Siwolop, Sana. "Excuse Me, What's the Pollsters' Big Problem? The Answer Is Accuracy. But They're Refining Their Art." *Business Week*, no. 2985 (16 February 1987): 108.

Polls and market surveys are described by Siwolop as being "a black art." Citing a 1984 panel of experts from the National Research Council (NRC), the following observation is made about survey designers: they "simply do not know much about how respondents answer questions." It is suggested by Judith Tanur that the problem may be because questionnaire construction is not "guided by a framework or a theory." Polling has become very big business; in 1986 the combined revenues of the top forty-four U.S. polling companies were greater than $1.5 billion. Various high technology approaches are being tried to assist in boosting the accuracy of poll results. The Gallup Organization Inc. has invested in a company which builds devices that measure eye movement. These devices are used to monitor people watching television and viewing print advertising. Other efforts concern how questions are answered and the time delay of answers. Public refusal to participate is up to 40 percent, perhaps because of the increasing incidence of requests. No references are included.

17.3   SECONDARY ANALYSIS AND CONTEXT

335. Dodd, Sue A., and Patricia M. Rector. "A User's Approach to Harris Public Opinion Survey Data." *Social Science Information Studies* 3 (April 1983): 81–93.

Polls are discussed in this article for their value in providing data for secondary analysis. With many questions repeated in different polls, the data can be examined to observe social changes over time. Issues such as racial tension, abortion, and gun control offer examples of topics with which such changes can be noted. The Dodd and Rector article covers the Harris data, accessible through the Louis Harris Data Center (established in 1965) at the University of North Carolina at Chapel Hill. By 1983 there were over four hundred data files. There is a computerized question retrieval system in place which in 1983 had the completed text of approximately thirteen thousand questions from 121 national surveys conducted between 1963 and 1976. The article describes Harris as the "father of modern election-night early projections." Having developed a key precinct sampling system that was first used in 1958, CBS used the approach in 1964 to predict and analyze the elections. Harris polls are said to contain more in-depth questioning on issues, as well as averaging about one hundred questions per survey—a number and depth considered greater than most polls. Characteristics, sample designs, the computerized retrieval system, and finding aids receive consideration. Also noted are press releases, processing Harris data, data formats, and how to order Harris data. The paper was presented at the annual conference of the International Association of Social Science Information Service and Technology (IASSIST), San Diego, 27–30 May 1982. Twenty-four references (four from the 1980s) complete the article.

336. Milbrath, Lester W. "The Context of Public Opinion: How Our Belief Systems Can Affect Poll Results." In *Polling and the Democratic Consensus*, edited by L. John Martin, 35–49. *Annals of the American Academy of Political and Social Science*, edited by Richard D. Lambert, vol. 472. Beverly Hills, CA: Sage Publications, 1984.

Five specific recommendations are provided when conducting polls. These are: (1) do not assume that as the pollster you know the dominant social paradigm (DSP) of your population; (2) be cautious when considering questions to avoid assuming that the respondent has a belief paradigm which may not be present; (3) be wary of polls that assume a DSP without questioning it; (4) do not expect to find consensus in public opinion; and (5) do not expect a close tie between opinion and action. The paradigm referred to above is the social paradigm—a model composed of underlying societal beliefs. These paradigms are often taken for granted, but change occurs, and this can impact on the way public opinion is manifested and measured. Milbrath suggests that modern industrial societies are now undergoing a paradigm shift. Table 1 highlights the contrasts between a new environmental paradigm and DSP. Table 2 shows the types of actors in social change. Figure 1 is a graphic showing the "Spatial Representation of Postures Toward the Environment." The conclusion focuses on the issue of the context in which questions are asked. Milbrath is concerned that myths not be generated through the inappropriate continuance of foregone DSPs. There are eleven footnotes.

18. Comparative Studies and Special Topics

18.1 COMPARATIVE STUDIES

337. Bromer, Richard Frank. "A Comparison of Three Methods of Opinion Polling." Ph.D. diss., Purdue University, 1948. 109p. + 13 numbered appendix pages.

The author compares and contrasts three methods of opinion polling: depth interviews, straight interviews, and secret ballots. The depth interview, as explained by Bromer, is an in-person interview in the respondent's home in which the respondent is encouraged to speak at length on the questions asked. The interviewer "copies down the gist of what the respondent has to say." The straight interview is one in which the respondent is given a choice of two or three answers to each question. Bromer uses the form "agree," "disagree," and "undecided." The secret ballot spoken of here is one which the respondent completes in private. The respondent can then drop the ballot in a "locked ballot box" carried from house to house by the interviewer. In the forty years since this research was completed, it is easy to see how the nature of these formats has changed. The amount of time—and therefore money—required to pursue a "depth interview" with an appropriately sized scientific sample would be prohibitive in the 1980s. Also, the America of the 1940s was a more trusting and safer place than today when fewer individuals are willing to open their homes to strangers. The telephone format is not considered here, as all interviews for the study were conducted at the respondent's home. In the Bromer study only one question yielded a highly significant difference between the total results through each of of the three approaches—and this may have been generated by who the respondents thought the interviewer represented. References are provided.

338.   Cureton, Robert D. "A Methodological Comparison of Telephone and Face-to-Face Interviewing for Political Public Opinion Polling." Ph.D. diss., Southern Illinois University, 1976. 111p.

The approach used by Cureton was to employ a ten- to twenty-minute questionnaire either by telephone or in person, followed by a one- to two-minute debriefing questionnaire. In the summary and conclusions chapter it is stated that "telephone interviewing generally produces results as useful for measurement of political attitudes and prediction as does face-to-face [interviewing]." Several areas in which the face-to-face interview may be sought are those involving long interviews and those requiring any kind of visual aid. This dissertation was written at a time when the Gallup Organization used "the face-to-face technique almost exclusively for nationwide polls." Cureton writes that telephone interviewing in political polling had become "quite popular." It is fair to say that the subsequent years have changed the climate of data gathering rather drastically since Cureton did his research. The cost of in-person interviewing has gone skyward, and computer dialing and modern telecommunications technology have made the telephone approach the standard mode for the late 1980s. References are provided.

339.   Smith, Tom W. "House Effects and the Reproducibility of Survey Measurements: A Comparison of the 1980 GSS and the 1980 American National Election Study." *Public Opinion Quarterly* 46, no. 1 (Spring 1982): 54–68.

Through a collaborative experiment between the National Opinion Research Center (NORC) and the Center for Political Studies (CPS)/Survey Research Center (SRC) at the University of Michigan, identical items were asked by both organizations in the 1980 General Social Survey (GSS) and the 1980 American National Election Study (NES) respectively. Significant differences were shown to exist between the results of the two "houses," with the greatest and most systematic differences found in the area of nonresponse. The Michigan surveys record more "Don't Know's" (DK) than the NORC survey. The result difference is caused by varying survey treatments of item nonresponse. The author suggests that this variation could probably be eliminated by standardizing interviewer training and instruction. Overall, Smith concludes that surveys are capable of measurements which are both reliable and reproducible. Although identical wording was used by the organizations participating in this experiment, a number of other factors were more difficult to equalize, namely those of timing and the context in which the questions were asked. There are two appendixes, one table, and nine references with four from the 1980s.

340. Snyder, Robin V. "The Two Worlds of Public Opinion: Media Opinion and Polled Opinion on the Abortion Issue." Ph.D. diss., Rutgers University, 1985. 228p.

Snyder covers the means by which decision makers or government officials determine current public opinion. The two main approaches examined include the mass media and public opinion polls. The abortion issue is used as the case study, with the "CBS Evening News" and the *Washington Post* serving as representatives of mass opinion. The similarities and differences between the poll and media versions are examined. The study reveals that the mass media and the polling results indicate "different interpretations of public sentiment on the abortion issue to political influentials." Polls show that the majority of Americans support "at least a limited right to abortion, media opinion suggests that anti-abortion views are more prevalent." The advantages and shortcomings of both mass media and public opinion polls are discussed, with the consequences for contemporary democracy examined. References are provided.

18.2   ETHNIC/MINORITY POPULATIONS

341. Bowman, Phillip J. "Significant Involvement and Functional Relevance: Challenges to Survey Research." *Social Work Research & Abstracts* 19, no. 4 (Winter 1983): 21–26.

Minority populations in the United States pose special challenges for survey researchers. The last two decades have seen an increasing cynicism toward surveys by Black Americans, Mexican Americans, Native Americans, and other "high-risk" groups who "suffer from socially structured inequalities." Bowman examines the existing literature dealing with the way that survey researchers have provided strategies to adapt to the changing environment. The most ardent critics call for "community control" and demonstrated "relevance to the community needs." The adaptive strategies fall into four categories: indigenous interviewers, community consultants and groups, trade-off and exchange arrangements, and relevance to community needs. Bowman suggests that research among racial minorities must be guided by two principles, significant involvement and functional relevance. Significant involvement refers to the group being studied playing a central role throughout the research process. Functional relevance means that needs and perspectives of the study group should be promoted by the research. An example of these principles successfully incorporated into the planning conceptualization, development of the questionnaire, data collection, and analysis is described. The research was conducted in 1979 and 1980, and the project was titled the National Survey of Black Americans. Two of the twenty-five references are from the 1980s.

342. Hill, Robert B. "The Polls and Ethnic Minorities." In *Polling and the Democratic Consensus*, edited by L. John Martin, 155–66. *Annals of the American Academy of Political and Social Science*, edited by Richard D. Lambert, vol. 472. Beverly Hills, CA: Sage Publications, 1984.

The major contribution of polling in the last forty years in relationship to minorities has been the determination that there has been a "dramatic decline in intolerant racial attitudes among whites in all regions of this nation." The major flaw has been that the focus of the polls has centered around white attitudes toward blacks. Blacks have been treated as a whole group without any breakdown into subgroups. Hispanics, Asians, Native Americans, and other minorities have received little or no attention as far as their polled attitudes are concerned. Hill suggests that telephone polling of certain minorities fails to recognize the financial limitations of some who are without telephones, thus skewing the results toward the higher-income persons. Hill argues for more face-to-face interviews for minorities, in order to ensure greater accuracy in data collection, and for some questions relating attitudes and actions. He cites a typology developed by Robert K. Merton (*Sociological Ambivalence and Other Essays*, New York, Free Press, 1976) which is based on "the premise that prejudicial attitudes vary independently with discriminatory behavior." It is recommended that this tool be used when dealing with efforts to determine changing positions in these two areas. The confusion with the terms, attitudes, and beliefs is reported, with some operational definitions provided and explained. There are thirty-seven footnotes.

343. Smith A. Wade. "Problems and Progress in the Measurement of Black Public Opinion." *American Behavioral Scientist* 30, no. 4 (March/April 1987): 441–55.

Smith believes that survey analysts have oversimplified many of the differences among black Americans, with the apparent underlying assumption that blacks think alike. The article begins with a historical overview of the survey measurement of black public opinion. Next, Smith observes that after fifty years of survey research, the early 1980s indicate little change in the way blacks are treated in surveys. One of the problems cited is that few studies of blacks have been undertaken in the most recent thirty-year period, and that the study of racial issues has not been applied to the small number of black respondents usually found in modern surveys. The author maintains that this has led to the "statistically 'invisible' man," the "statistically 'inscrutable' man," to unreliable information on race problems, and to the handicapping of the national leadership. The article continues by providing an update of the methodological developments in surveying blacks, with intergenerational research, the challenge of finding blacks for surveys, and telephone sampling of blacks discussed. While the techniques described were developed for nationwide surveys, the author believes that the approach can be used in regional, state, and local studies. Of the thirty-three references, about one-third represent literature of the 1980s.

18.3 ADDITIONAL STUDIES

344. Namenwirth, J. Zvi, Randi Lynn Miller, and Robert Philip Weber. "Organizations Have Opinions: A Redefinition of Publics." *Public Opinion Quarterly* 45, no. 4 (Winter 1981): 463–76.

The basic tenet of the article is that organizations do, in fact, have opinions, and that these opinions can be ascertained by asking spokespersons standard public opinion questions using methods employed for individuals. It is the view of the authors that the failure to determine the views of organizations may lead to a misrepresentation of the total reality of public opinion. The introduction examines the historical attempt to define "public opinion," with proponents that have maintained that opinion is (and can only be) individually held, and that therefore consideration of supposed public opinion held by organizations does not enter the picture. The authors explore, through a series of experiments, the belief that organizations will respond to opinion polling questions, that opinions are held by organizations, and that they differ materially from the opinions of individuals on a small number of standard public opinion questions. In the discussion section of the paper, the authors explain the importance of the opinions held by organizations by suggesting that they are more influential than individuals, that they have more resources and information, and are better able to convert opinions into effective collective action. A number of tables compare organizational opinions versus individual opinions. A twenty-eight-item list of references concludes the article; one is from the 1980s.

345. Orton, Barry. "Phony Polls: The Pollster's Nemesis." *Public Opinion* 5, no. 3 (June/July 1982): 56–60.

The "pseudo-poll" or phony poll is discussed in its varying formats and purposes. Beginning with the most powerful—in terms of sheer numbers potentially affected—AT&T's 900 DIAL-IT service is covered. For a fee, callers may express their opinion to the network. The first such use was by ABC News on 28 October 1980. There are obvious shortcomings with this approach to opinion gathering, such as in political cases, the problem or possibility of organized multiple voting, and the issue of the charge to place one's opinion [notwithstanding the issue of the fact that the audience is self-selected]. Other pseudo-polls discussed include the straw polls making a resurgence in popular magazines, and the pseudo-polls appearing in a wide variety of journals which are really used to mask fund-raising appeals. Warner-Amex Corporation's "Qube" system is covered. This system employs two-way cable television technology which has been used by NBC News and Cable News Network (CNN) in their news programming. Attempts have been made by the American Association for Public Opinion Research (AAPOR) Standards Committee to have the media refer to "straw vote," "call-in-vote," or "media-based balloting" when reporting pseudo-polls. No references are provided.

346. Schroedel, John G. "Analyzing Surveys on Deaf Adults: Implications for Survey Research on Persons with Disabilities." *Social Science and Medicine* 19, no. 6 (1984): 619–27.

The article focuses specifically on the experience of researchers in dealing with the challenges of surveying the deaf. The author also discusses the implications of the research to the broader group of individuals with disabilities other than hearing loss. Definitions of disability vary, and Schroedel cautions against comparing studies since many definitions only serve the specific purposes of a particular study. Further, care needs to be taken when examining the terms deafness, deaf population, and deaf community. The deaf community consists of those who are sign language users while the deaf population includes many geriatrically deafened persons who do not sign. Schroedel reports on forty-one studies on deaf adults in the United States and Canada which were conducted between 1959 and 1981. These reports were analyzed to evaluate how rates of response are affected by three methods of data collection, degree of verification efforts, scope of the sample, and sociodemographic characteristics of those in the survey populations. The results of these surveys guide social policies which influence health care, education, and social services for the deaf. Interview surveys generate a higher mean rate of response as compared with mail or "convenience" methods. The author suggests that a handbook for survey researchers on how to conduct surveys with the deaf would be a useful addition to the literature. A list of the survey reports used is included along with fifty-one references.

19. Cross-Disciplinary Research

347. Bodenhausen, Galen V., and Robert S. Wyer, Jr. "Social Cognition and Social Reality: Information Acquisition and Use in the Laboratory and the Real World." Chap. 2 in *Social Information Processing and Survey Methodology*, edited by Hans-J. Hippler, Norbert Schwarz, and Seymour Sudman, 6–41. Recent Research in Psychology. New York: Springer-Verlag, 1987.

One dozen postulates in social cognition are presented with evidence for and against. Each postulate is presented as a single underlined sentence in the text, followed by a discussion, a review of the research in the area, and a section titled "Applicability." The use in the real world of each postulate is discussed. The survey research use of these postulates is not always clarified. In the last section of the text of the chapter, Bodenhausen and Wyer acknowledge the complaints of researcher Neisser concerning the need to conduct research in natural settings, rather than in the laboratory. The authors argue that while laboratory work is certainly not irrelevant, studies are needed which document laboratory findings in "naturalistic research settings." There are ninety-eight references provided in the last five pages of the chapter.

348. Hippler, Hans-J., Norbert Schwarz, and Seymour Sudman, eds. *Social Information Processing and Survey Methodology*. Recent Research in Psychology. New York: Springer-Verlag, 1987. 223p.

The volume is designed to continue the dialog between cognitive psychologists and survey researchers. It is intended for both the users and developers of survey methods, as well as those interested in how humans process social information. The editors believe that cognitive psychologists may be able to improve the quality of survey responses, and at the very least contribute to the understanding of what is possible to ask respondents and the justifications as to why. In keeping with the parameters selected for this annotated bibliography—namely, that only American authors are considered—a number of European writers who have contributed to the Hippler volume await a future bibliography for inclusion. As a result of this caveat, six of the eleven chapters were selected, including the following:

Chapter 2:   Social Cognition and Social Reality: Information Acquisition and Use in the Laboratory and the Real World (Bodenhausen and Wyer—Item No. 347).

Chapter 3:   Information Processing Theory for the Survey Researcher (Hastie—Item No. 357).

Chapter 4:   Bipolar Survey Items: An Information Processing Perspective (Ostom—Item No. 359).

Chapter 8:   Attitude Measurement: A Cognitive Perspective (Tourangeau—Item No. 352).

Chapter 10:   Context Effects on Self-Perceptions of Interest in Government and Public Affairs (Bishop—Item No. 195).

Chapter 12:   Perspectives for Future Development (Sudman—Item No. 351).

349.   Jabine, Thomas B., Miron L. Straf, Judith M. Tanur, and Roger Tourangeau, eds. *Cognitive Aspects of Survey Methodology: Building a Bridge between Disciplines.* Report of the Advanced Research Seminar on Cognitive Aspects of Survey Methodology. Committee on National Statistics, Commission on Behavioral and Social Science and Education, National Research Council. Washington, DC: National Academy Press, 1984. 176p.

The Advanced Research Seminar on Cognitive Aspects of Survey Methodology (CASM) had two meetings: the first was held on 15–21 June 1983 in St. Michaels, Maryland; the second follow-up meeting took place 12–14 January 1984. The seminar was a cross-disciplinary collaboration among professionals in sociology, political science, statistics, anthropology, psychology, business administration, and many representatives who also serve with survey research organizations. The seminar considered the following topics: surveys as a vehicle for cognitive research improving survey methods; issues for the national health interview survey; and how to translate ideas into action. The presentation of the seminar overview constitutes about 14 percent of the report. Approximately 30 percent of the volume covers the outcomes of the project, including research plans and activities developed by the participants after the initial meeting. At least twelve authors contributed to the follow-up articles. About 55 percent of the report is comprised of four appendixes and the index. Appendix A provides three background papers by Roger Tourangeau, Norman Bradburn and Catalina Danis, and Kent Marquis, and are titled "Cognitive Sciences and Survey Methods," "Potential Contributions of Cognitive Research to Survey Questionnaire Design," and "Record Checks for Sample Surveys," respectively. The three appendixes that follow cover the organization and structure of the seminar, background materials for the seminar, and biographical sketches of the participants. There is a six-page subject index at the end of the report.

350. Loftus, Elizabeth F., Stephen E. Fienberg, and Judith M. Tanur. "Cognitive Psychology Meets the National Survey." *American Psychologist* 40, no. 2 (February 1985): 175–80.

The collaborative efforts between cognitive psychologists and survey researchers are described. A major concern for survey designers is the degree to which respondents accurately remember events and report them to interviewers. People sometimes deliberately fail to mention incidents—that is, they lie. Lying may be to the interviewer or to themselves. These issues relate to the study of memory and have important consequences for survey researchers. A criticism by Neisser (*Memory Observed: Remembering in Natural Contexts*, 1982) is discussed. Neisser believes that "interesting or socially significant" research has been overlooked in favor of theoretical laboratory settings. Neisser wishes psychologists to pursue "naturalistic settings." It is suggested that one of the ways to achieve this end is through the collaboration between social researchers and cognitive psychologists. Such a dialog between these professionals is cited in the Loftus article to have been initiated in 1980 when a two-day workshop was convened by Albert Biderman of the Bureau of Social Science Research (BSSR) with assistance from the U.S. Bureau of the Census and the U.S. Bureau of Justice Statistics. The article discusses how existing surveys can be used to provide information on cognitive processes, outlines new surveys which are to be developed to establish norms for cognitive abilities, and considers ways in which survey methods can be improved. There are twenty-five references provided, fifteen from the 1980s.

351.   Sudman, Seymour. "Perspectives for Future Development." Chap.
       12 in *Social Information Processing and Survey Methodology*,
       edited by Hans-J. Hippler, Norbert Schwarz, and Seymour
       Sudman, 212–19. Recent Research in Psychology. New York:
       Springer-Verlag, 1987.

Sudman identifies some priorities for research and suggests likely future
developments. The author suggests that researchers in the applied social
science of survey research are more likely to be interested in the discipline of cognitive psychology than these psychologists will be in the
study of survey research. It is nevertheless hoped for by survey
researchers that those in the basic science of cognitive psychology will
utilize more natural task tests to investigate theories. The author cites
the natural questions and natural populations of the survey researcher as
the major distinguishing elements between the two disciplines.
Linguistics is another area in which survey researchers may look for
insights. Under the heading "Future Prospects," Sudman suggests the
following: (1) the development of the mathematical theorems of
impossibility will be applied to both cognitive psychology and survey
research; (2) further work in both disciplines will be conducted by
obtaining protocols from respondents on how they retrieved the
information that was requested; (3) priming and cueing methods will see
increased use; (4) new knowledge and technology will permit
individualized cues, anchors, or other stimuli to fit the characteristics of
the individual, thus obtaining the best information possible; and (5)
cognitive psychologists will do more experiments with natural
phenomena and general population samples. Three references are
provided.

352.   Tourangeau, Roger, "Attitude Measurement: A Cognitive
       Perspective." Chap. 8 in *Social Information Processing and Sur-
       vey Methodology*, edited by Hans-J. Hippler, Norbert Schwarz,
       and Seymour Sudman, 149–62. Recent Research in Psychology.
       New York: Springer-Verlag, 1987.

The chapter is divided into four parts. The first examines the nature of
the problems that can arise in attitude surveys. Response effects are
considered with several examples included. Parts 2 through 4 consider the
major steps involved in answering attitude questions, outline a view of
the structure of attitudes, and provide examples in an attempt to explain
response effects. Tourangeau describes his presentation as being of scant
comfort to survey researchers in that it is demonstrated just how difficult
it is to reduce or eliminate response effects, as they are part of the

underlying attitudes or nonattitudes. The analysis does suggest, however, that response effects may be limited to some issues and some respondents. In determining how a respondent interprets a given item, the usefulness of random probe techniques is emphasized by Tourangeau. As a suggestion for further research, the author believes that a means to identify the vacillators who held a number of "scripts" weakly, rather than one strongly, would be very useful. Nineteen references are provided of which eight are from the 1980s.

20. Models and Theories

353. Brody, Charles J. "Things Are Rarely Black and White: Admitting Gray into the Converse Model of Attitude Stability." *American Journal of Sociology* 92, no. 3 (November 1986): 657–77.

In 1964, Philip Converse proposed a model of the nature of political attitude holding among the mass public—the black-and-white (BW) model of attitude stability designed to describe "over-time responses to repeated questions." This model treated "no opinion" responses as nonopinion holders and combined this group with estimated nonattitudes. Such an approach leads to high levels of nonattitudes. Brody reasons that nonsubstantive responses should be treated probabilistically. The new data categories call for a model of the BW format with Brody suggesting that a black-gray-white (BGW) model is more appropriate. Nonattitude estimates in the BGW model are "markedly lower" than with the BW model. Brody reviews the literature on the reaction to the Converse model and analysis, provides a presentation of the data and methods used to evaluate the modified model/analysis, and discusses the results. Five tables showing an analysis of the data are given (with the appendix containing the questions asked). There are twenty-seven references; five represent research from the 1980s.

354. Crane, Ben M. "The Silence Effect in Public Opinion." Ph.D. diss., University of Wisconsin, Madison, 1979. 268p.

The "silence effect" referred to here concerns the "tendency of individuals to refrain from publicly expressing their views when those views are perceived to be in the minority or losing support." Crane's study considers the "quasi-statistical sense" mechanism by which individuals are suspected of gaining awareness of public opinion. The author tested the effect with a cross-sectional telephone survey of Madison, Wisconsin residents and found that the silence effect was "consistently observed across three types of dependent measures and two different public issues." Chapter 1, a review of the literature, contains sections dealing with the quasi-statistical sense, conformity pressures, the silence effect, the spiral effect, the unshakable minority, and the notion of involvement. The rest of the dissertation includes chapters on theory, method, results, and conclusions. Crane repeatedly credits Elisabeth Noelle-Neumann's empirical research into the individual basis of public opinion as the foundation for his efforts—which he suggests is to "seek to inspect, clarify, replicate, and extend her work." Appendixes supply the interviewer with instructions and the research instruments. There are thirty-one pages of references.

355. Glynn, Carroll J., and Jack M. McLeod. "Implications of the Spiral of Silence Theory for Communication and Public Opinion Research." Chap. 3 in *Political Communication Yearbook*, edited by Dan Nimmo, Lynda Lee Kaid, and Keith Sanders, vol. 1, 43–65. Carbondale, IL: Southern Illinois University Press, 1985.

The contributions made by Elisabeth Noelle-Neumann and her "spiral of silence" theory are the focus of this chapter. Noelle-Neumann has a particular way of viewing what public opinion is, namely, "the views one can express in public without isolating oneself" and the ideas one expresses "without fear of sanctions" and as a "pressure to conform." Elements of the theory based on this view of public opinion are presented, along with a test of the theory. In reviewing the implications of the theory to public opinion research, the authors point to the treatment of public opinion by Noelle-Neumann as a process-oriented phenomenon, as contrasted with the view that public opinion is stable and in a fixed state. The chapter writers cite the difficulties in public opinion research with definitional confusions, and suggest that until common ground is achieved on the theoretical level significant advances are in jeopardy. Questions which arise from the authors' study suggest that a number of lines of research might be pursued, including examining whether public opinion polls overestimate change, and also whether polls influence individuals' perceptions of the opinions held in their environment. Chapter 3 contains no footnotes, endnotes, or references within the chapter, but a cumulative "Selected Bibliography" appears on pages 315 to 358 and includes references made from chapter 3.

356. Glynn, Carroll J., and Jack M. McLeod. "Public Opinion du Jour: An Examination of the Spiral of Silence." *Public Opinion Quarterly* 48, no. 4 (Winter 1984): 731–40.

Glynn and McLeod discuss, test, and confirm Elisabeth Noelle-Neumann's theory, called the "spiral of silence." The spiral of silence theory states that "one's perception of the distribution of public opinion motivates one's willingness to express political opinions. This act of self-expression then changes the global environment of opinion, altering the perceptions of other persons, and ultimately, affecting their willingness to express their own opinions." The authors also found that "individuals perceiving support for a certain candidate would be more likely to express a preference for that candidate." Another Noelle-Neumann finding is reported in the discussion section. At issue is the so-called hardcore—those who are less influenced by campaign discussions, where voting is less influenced by campaign talk, and who are more concerned by the candidates' stands on issues and their personal qualities. Stated another way—these individuals are not moved by public opinion. The study conducted was by telephone and involved ninety-eight voters. Respondents were telephoned twice before, and once following the 1980 presidential election. There are seven references, four from the 1980s.

357. Hastie, Reid. "Information Processing Theory for the Survey Researcher." Chap. 3 in *Social Information Processing and Survey Methodology*, edited by Hans-J. Hippler, Norbert Schwarz, and Seymour Sudman, 42–70. Recent Research in Psychology. New York: Springer-Verlag, 1987.

A list of general principles is presented which summarizes the essentials of information processing theory. The list includes discussions of information, memory structures, spreading activation, transforming symbolic information, the executive monitor, independent memories, and limited resources. Further consideration is provided for the areas of processing errors. An example of the measurement of political beliefs and knowledge is given. The final section deals with the limitations of information processing theories. Ten diagrams accompany the text. The author has sought to make the reader aware of both the gains and the losses associated with information processing theories. Some of the limitations of information processing theory suggested by Hastie include: small consideration of motivational factors, absence of sophisticated measurement theories or scaling techniques, the limitations inherent in any laboratory derived analysis of perception, memory, and reasoning processes (that being the need for application testing in the real world by survey researchers). Sixty-three references are found on the last three pages of the chapter.

358. Noelle-Neumann, Elisabeth. "Toward a Theory of Public Opinion." Chap. 13 in *Surveying Social Life. Papers in Honor of Herbert H. Hyman*, edited by Hubert J. O'Gorman, 289–300. Middletown, CT: Wesleyan University Press, 1988.

Noelle-Neumann quotes Hyman's 1957 article in which a definition of public opinion is given as "the views of the electorate on the controversial issues of the day." Hyman continued to write that "We need concepts and corresponding research on what is both fundamental or deep and also common to a group or society. The study of values...would enrich current theories of opinion formation and broaden what is at present an unduly narrow psychological emphasis." From this framework Noelle-Neumann discusses developments since the earliest approaches toward a theory in 1932, including her own work, and suggests where efforts may be going in the future. The issue as to whether universities are willing to fund public opinion research leading to theories of public opinion that would have "scholarly validity" has been brought into question. It is suggested that there seems to be "grave doubt" as to whether such a theory is attainable. Primary emphasis is placed on work conducted during the decades of the 1960s, 1970s and 1980s. Literature from the 1980s is cited seven times. There are forty-three references in total.

359. Ostrom, Thomas M. "Bipolar Survey Items: An Information Processing Perspective." Chap. 4 in *Social Information Processing and Survey Methodology*, edited by Hans-J. Hippler, Norbert Schwarz, and Seymour Sudman, 71–85. Recent Research in Psychology. New York: Springer-Verlag, 1987.

The discussion centers around survey items which are designed to measure bipolar subjective responses (such as likes/dislikes, beliefs/disbeliefs, and judgments of similarity/dissimilarity). The author cites researchers who theorize that people naturally think in bipolar terms. The chapter compares and contrasts two alternative conceptual approaches toward understanding how respondents answer bipolar items. The first approach considered is the "dimensional," followed by the recent and more complex approach called "information processing." The dimensional approach is concerned with identifying beliefs on the response continuum, whereas the information processing approach emphasizes the structural interrelation among the beliefs. Special attention is given to two item formats—the two category format and the continuous rating scale format. In the two category format section the author reviews the details of the activation and matching process. The continuous rating scale is described by the author as one in which the respondent chooses to make a mark on an unbroken line or where there is a set of categories to choose from which has enough options to allow the respondent to communicate all important subjective discriminations (which can be as few as seven to nine categories). There are twenty-seven references at the end of the chapter.

Addendum

360. Bainbridge, William Sims. *Survey Research: A Computer-Assisted Introduction.* Belmont, CA: Wadsworth Publishing Company, 1989. 370p. Includes diskette.

361. Begin, G., and M. Boivin. "Comparison of Data Gathered on Sensitive Questions via Direct Questionnaire...." *Psychological Reports* 47 (December 1980): 743–50.

362. Bohrnstedt, G.W. "An Empirical Study of the Reliability and Stability of Survey Research Items." *Sociological Methods & Research* 15, no. 3 (1987): 171–76.

363. Brown, K.W. "Survey Research: Determining Sample Size and Representative Response." *Business Education Forum* 40 (1986): 31–34.

364. Bugher, Wilmer. *Polling Attitudes of Community on Education: Manual,* edited by Willard Duckett. Bloomington, IN: Phi Delta Kappa, 1980. lv. (various pagings).

365. California. Legislature. Senate. Select Committee on Citizen Participation in Government. *Network Projections and the Use of Exit Polls in Coverage of Election Returns: Testimony Received at the Hearing of the Senate Select Committee on Citizen Participation in Government, December 12, 1985 [1984].* Sacramento, CA: Joint Publications Office, 1984. 32p.

366. Crespi, Irving. *Public Opinion, Polls, and Democracy.* Boulder, CO: Westview Press, 1989.

367. De la Garza, Rodolfo O., ed. *Ignored Voices: Public Opinion Polls and the Latino Community.* 1st ed. Austin, TX: Center for Mexican American Studies, University of Texas at Austin, 1987. 224p.

368. Duncan, Otis Dudley, and Howard Schuman. "Effects of Question Wording and Context: An Experiment with Religious Indicators." *Journal of the American Statistical Association* 75, no. 370 (June 1980): 369–75.

369. Dutka, Solomon, Lester R. Frankel, and Irving Roshwalb. *How to Conduct Surveys.* New York: Audits & Surveys, 1982. 197p.

370. Evans, S.S., and J.E. Scott. "Effects of Item Order on the Perceived Seriousness of Crime: A Reexamination." *Journal of Research in Crime and Delinquency* 21 (May 1984): 139–51.

371. Fairbourn, E. LeGrand. "Validity of Participant Report of Causal Factors in Value Judgments." Ph.D. diss., Brigham Young University, 1983. 89p.

372. Field, Mervin D. "Political Opinion Polling in the United States of America." Chap. 10 in *Political Opinion Polling: An International Review,* edited by Robert M. Worcester, 198–228. New York: St. Martin's Press, 1983.

373. Fienberg, S.E., and J.M. Tanur. "Combining Cognitive and Statistical Approaches to Survey Design." *Science* 243 (24 February 1989): 1017–22.

374. Fowler, Floyd J. *Survey Research Methods.* Rev. ed. Applied Social Research Methods Series, vol. 1. Newbury Park: CA: Sage Publications, 1988. 159p.

375. Freeman, Howard E., K. Jill Kiecolt, William L. Nicholls II, and J. Merrill Shanks. "Telephone Sampling Bias in Surveying Disability." *Public Opinion Quarterly* 46, no. 3 (Fall 1982): 392–407.

376. Frey, James H. *Survey Research by Telephone.* 2nd ed. Sage Library of Social Research, vol. 150. Newbury Park, CA: Sage Publications, 1989.

377. Golden, Gary. *Survey Research Methods.* ACRL Continuing Education Program, CE 503. Chicago, IL: Association of College and Research Libraries, 1982. 69p.

378. Goyder, John. *Silent Minority: Nonrespondents in Sample Surveys.* Boulder, CO: Westview Press, 1987. 232p.

379. Greenberg, Hinda Feige. "Survey Research Resources Directory." *Journal of Reading, Writing and Learning Disabilities International* 1, no. 4 (1985): 51–58.

380. Hartman, B.W., D.R. Fuqua, and S.J. Jenkins. "Problems of and Remedies for Nonresponse Bias in Educational Surveys." *Journal of Experimental Education* 54 (1985): 85–90.

381. Landecker, W.S. "The Use of Survey Research in the Sociology of Knowledge." *Knowledge: Creation, Diffusion, Utilization* 4, no. 1 (1982): 73–94.

382. Lepkowski, James Michael. "Design Effects for Multivariate Categorical Interactions." Ph.D. diss., The University of Michigan, 1980. 329p.

383. Lindenmann, Walter K. *Attitude and Opinion Research: Why You Need It, How to Do It.* 3d ed. Washington, DC: Council for Advancement and Support of Education, 1983. 121p.

384. McCall, Chester H. *Sampling and Statistics Handbook for Research.* Ames, IA: Iowa State University Press, 1982. 340p.

385. Marquis, K.H., et al. *Response Errors in Sensitive Topics Surveys: Estimates, Effects, and Correction Options.* Santa Monica, CA: Rand Corporation, 1981. 174p. [R-2710/2-HHS]

386. Mishler, Elliot George. *Research Interviewing: Context and Narrative.* Cambridge, MA: Harvard University Press, 1986. 189p.

387. Munger, G.F., and Loyd, B.H. "The Use of Multiple Matrix Sampling for Survey Research." *Journal of Experimental Education* 56, no. 4 (1988): 187–91.

388. Rossi, Peter H., and Nock, Steven L., eds. *Measuring Social Judgments: The Factorial Survey Approach.* Beverly Hills, CA: Sage Publications, 1982. 255p.

389. Rubin, Donald B. *Handling Nonresponse in Sample Surveys.* Princeton, NJ: [Prepared for the Census Bureau under contract number BC-80-SAC-66229], 1980. 158p.

390. Rugg, William Donald. "A Study of the No Opinion Vote in Public Opinion Polls." Ph.D. diss., Princeton University, 1941. 129p.

391. Schiffman, Susan S., M. Lance Reynolds, Forrest W. Young, with contributions from J. Douglas Carroll, et al., with a foreword by Joseph B. Kruskal. *Introduction to Multidimensional Scaling: Theory, Methods, and Applications.* New York: Academic Press, 1981. 413p.

392. Schneider, K.C."Uninformed Response Rate in Survey Research—New Evidence." *Journal of Business Research* 13, no. 2 (1985): 153–62.

393. Singer, M. "Toward a Model of Question Answering: Yes–No Questions." *Journal of Experimental Psychology: Learning, Memory and Cognition* 10 (April 1984): 285–97.

394. Skinner, S.J., et al. "Impact of Humor on Survey Responses." *Industrial Marketing Management* 121 (April 1983): 139–43.

395. Stewart, Alva W. *Public Opinion Polls, Benefits and Dangers: A Brief Checklist.* Public Administration Series—Bibliography P-2641. Monticello, IL: Vance Bibliographies, 1989. 10p.

396. Stinchcombe, Arthur L., Calvin Jones, and Paul Sheatsley. "Nonresponse Bias for Attitude Questions." *Public Opinion Quarterly* 45, no. 3 (Fall 1981): 359–75.

397. Tillinghast, Diana Stover. "Direct Magnitude Estimation Scales in Public Opinion Surveys." *Public Opinion Quarterly* 44, no. 3 (Fall 1980): 377–84.

398. Van Houton, Therese and Harry P. Hatry. *How to Conduct a Citizen Survey.* Planning Advisory Service report, no. 404. Chicago, IL: American Planning Association, 1987. 24p.

399. Viladas, Joseph M. *The Book of Survey Techniques.* Greenwich, CT: Havemeyer Books, 1982. [277p.] Loose-leaf.

400. Walker, John E. "Local Opinion Polling—the Benefits of Polls and How to Conduct them." *Journal of Educational Public Relations* 9, no. 4 (Spring 1987): 10–14.

401. Weaver, R., and T.L. Glasser. "Survey Research for Legislative Relations." *Public Relations Review* 10, no. 2 (1984): 39–48.

402. Withey, Stephen Bassett, and Richard M. Jaeger. *Study Guide for Survey Research Methods in Education.* Alternative Methodologies in Educational Research. Washington, DC: American Educational Research Association, [1980?] E-1–E-13p.

403. Yankelovich, Skelly and White, Inc. *The Mushiness Index: A Refinement in Public Policy Polling Techniques.* N.p. 1981. 77p.

404. Yates, Frank. *Sampling Methods for Censuses and Surveys.* 4th ed. New York: Macmillan, 1981. 458p.

405. Yeric, Jerry L., and John R. Todd. *Public Opinion: The Visible Politics.* 2d ed. Itasca, IL: F.E. Peacock Publishers, 1989. 257p.

Appendix A

ACRONYMS

AAPOR	American Association for Public Opinion Research
ACRL	Association of College and Research Libraries
ANCOVA	Analysis of Covariance
ANOVA	Analysis of Variance
AP	Associated Press
APOI	*American Public Opinion Index*
APSA	American Political Science Association
ASA	American Statistics Association
BGW	Black-Gray-White Model
BSSR	Bureau of Social Science Research
BW	Black-and-White Model
CASM	Cognitive Aspects of Survey Methodology
CASRO	Council of American Survey Research Organizations

CATI	Computer-Assisted Telephone Interviewing
CDS	California Disability Survey
CNN	Cable News Network
CPS	Center for Political Studies
CSM	Computer-Assisted Survey Methods
DJN	Distinctive Jewish Names
DK	Don't Know
DOA	U.S. Department of Agriculture
DSP	Dominant Social Paradigm
ES	Effect Size
EST	Eastern Standard Time
GLM	General Linear Model
GOP	Grand Old Party (Republican)
GSS	General Social Survey
HC	*Hartford Courant*
IASSIST	International Association of Social Science Information Service and Technology
ISDP	Income Survey Development Program
ISR	Institute for Social Research
LISREL	Linear Structural Relations (computer program)
M technique	Multiple Random Response Trials Technique

NCHS	National Center for Health Statistics
NCPP	National Council on Public Polls
NCS	National Crime Survey
NES	National Election Studies
NHANES I	National Health and Nutrition Examination Survey I
NORC	National Opinion Research Center
NRC	National Research Council
NYT	*New York Times*
OMB	Office of Management and Budget
PSU	Primary Sampling Unit
RDD	Random Digit Dialing
RRIP	Repeated Replication Imputation Procedure
RR	Randomized Response
RRT	Randomized Response Technique
RSR	*RSR Reference Services Review*
SMSA	Standard Metropolitan Statistical Area
SRC	Survey Research Center
SRL	Survey Research Laboratory
TDM	Total Design Method
WSRL	Wisconsin Survey Research Laboratory

Appendix B

LIST OF JOURNALS

Appendix C

DISSERTATIONS

Britton, Gary L. "A History of Some Recent Applications of Survey Sampling for Human Populations." Ph.D. diss., University of Northern Colorado, 1983. 202p. (Item No. 11).

Bromer, Richard Frank. "A Comparison of Three Methods of Opinion Polling." Ph.D. diss., Purdue University, 1948. 109p. +13 numbered appendix pages. (Item No. 337).

Cordray, Sheila Mary. "The Problems of Attrition in Longitudinal Survey Research." Ph.D. diss., University of Oregon, 1982. 187p. (Item No. 322).

Cureton, Robert D. "A Methodological Comparison of Telephone and Face-to-Face Interviewing for Political Public Opinion Polling." Ph.D. diss., Southern Illinois University, 1976. 111p. (Item No. 338).

Crane, Ben M. "The Silence Effect in Public Opinion." Ph.D. diss., University of Wisconsin, Madison, 1979. 268p. (Item No. 354).

Fairbourn, E. LeGrande. "Validity of Participant Report of Causal Factors in Value Judgments." Ph.D. diss., Brigham Young University, 1983. 89p. (Item No. 371).

Hawver, Carl Fullerton. "The Congressman's Conception of His Role: Based on a Study of the Use of Public Opinion Polls by Members of the United States House of Representatives." Ph.D. diss., American University, 1963. 311p. (Item No. 82).

Kemper, Raymond Alfred. "Secret Ballots, Open Ballots, and Personal Interviews in Opinion Polling." Ph.D. diss., Columbia University, 1951. (Item No. 278).

Koch, Nadine Sue. "Perceptions of Public Opinion Polls." Ph.D. diss., The Ohio State University, 1985. 239p. (Item No. 63).

Lepowski, James Michael. "Design Effects for Multivariate Categorical Interactions." Ph.D. diss., The University of Michigan, 1980. 329p. (Item No. 382).

Lickteig, Carl W. "Informational Salience Effects on Attitudinal Inference and Expression: Context Effects in Survey Research." Ph.D. diss., University of Louisville, 1984. 139p. (Item No. 200).

Max, Alfred. "Basic Factors in the Interpretation of Public Opinion Polls: An Attempt at Assessing the Degree of Reliance to be Placed upon Figures Released by Private Polling Agencies on Current Social and Political Issues." Ph.D. diss., The American University, 1941. 239p. (Item No. 331).

Nelson, Allan D. "Political Implications of Modern Public Opinion Research." Ph.D. diss., University of Chicago, 1962. 489p. (Item No. 86).

Nuckols, Robert C. "A Study of Respondent Forewarning in Public Opinion Research." Ph.D. diss., Pennsylvania State College, 1951. 126p.+ (Item No. 251).

Patrick, William Lawrence. "Network Television and Public Opinion Polls." Ph.D. diss., Ohio University, 1975. 421p. (Item No. 114).

Rinaldo, Matthew J. "The Use of Questionnaires and Public Opinion Polls by U.S. Congressmen to Determine Constituency Attitudes." Ph.D. diss., New York University, 1978. 176p. (Item No. 87).

Rugg, William Donald. "A Study of the No Opinion Vote in Public Opinion Polls." Ph.D. diss., Princeton University, 1941. 129p. (Item No. 390).

Shapiro, Leopold J. "The Opinion Poll." Ph.D. diss., The University of Chicago, 1956. 202p. (Item No. 56).

Snyder, Robin V. "The Two Worlds of Public Opinion: Media Opinion and Polled Opinion on the Abortion Issue." Ph.D. diss., Rutgers University, 1985. 228p. (Item No. 340).

Wood, Nancy Lee. "An Exploration of the Internal Stability of Public Opinion Holding Using 'The Mushiness Index.'" Ph.D. diss., University of Colorado at Boulder, 1985. 165p. (Item No. 309).

Appendix D

MONOGRAPH SERIES NAMES

Appendix E

BASIC BIBLIOGRAPHIC SOURCES

ABC Pol Sci. A Bibliography of Contents: Political Science and Government

Bibliographic Index

Book Review Digest

Book Review Index

Business Periodicals Index

CIS/Index to Congressional Publications and Public Laws

Communication Abstracts

Cumulative Book Index

Current Contents/Social and Behavioral Sciences

Current Index to Journals in Education

Dissertation Abstracts International

Education Index

Historical Abstracts

Index to Legal Periodicals

Magazine Index

Monthly Catalog of U.S. Government Publications

National Union Catalog

Psychological Abstracts

Public Affairs Information Service

Public Opinion Quarterly Index

Readers' Guide to Periodical Literature

Resources in Education

Shelflist of the Library of Congress

Social Sciences Citation Index

Social Sciences Index

Sociological Abstracts

Statistical Reference Index

Subject Guide to Books in Print

Subject Guide to Forthcoming Books

United States Political Science Documents

Appendix F

INDEXING AND ABSTRACTING RESOURCES*

ABC Pol Sci. A Bibliography of Contents: Political Science and Government. 1969-. 5/yr. ABC-Clio Information Services, 2040 Alameda Padre Serra, Box 4397, Santa Barbara, CA 93140-4397.

This international current awareness journal covers approximately three hundred periodicals alphabetically by title. *ABC Pol Sci* reproduces edited tables of contents and has an annual index. The journal covers political science, government, and associated areas. Languages include English, French, Italian, and German, with items appearing in the original language. The annual index is divided into the following sections: subject; author; list of periodicals showing year, volume, and issue number; and a periodical address directory. Main access points include polls (with an average of fifteen citations per year) and surveys (with an average of forty-five citations per year).

American Public Opinion Index. 1981-. Annual. Opinion Research Service, PO Box 70205, Louisville, KY 40270.

The Index provides access to the results of hundreds of opinion surveys conducted in the United States. The volume includes questions as well as the responses. An accompanying microfiche set, *American Public*

---

* This material appeared previously as "Polling Indexes and Abstracts" in an article titled "Public Opinion Polls: A Guide to Accessing the Literature." *RSR Reference Services Review* 16, no. 4 (1988): 65–74 [Item No. 7]. Permission has been granted by Pierian Press. (*Current Index to Journals in Education* entry was not found in the original.)

Opinion Data, contains the response data as well as the exact question wording and detailed information about the polling methodology used. The index is divided into two sections. Section one is the alphabetical subject index to the polls, with headings such as family, health; and Reagan, Ronald. For example, under the heading Reagan, Ronald—Age appears the question [p. 860, 1985] "at 78 when he completes his term (he is too old to be president, his age doesn't matter all that much) ABC Jul." This refers us to the source of the response data, that of the ABC News Polling Unit in section two. Page 1246, section two, informs us that it was a national telephone poll with 1506 in the sample; also provided is the full address and telephone number for the ABC unit. The 1985 volume has over one hundred different polling sources, many of which are not well known by the general public.

> *Business Periodicals Index.* 1958-. Monthly except August. H.W. Wilson, 950 University Ave., Bronx, NY 10452. Formerly *Industrial Arts Index.*

The index covers over three hundred English-language periodicals. Some of the major periodicals indexed during the last five years that include articles dealing with polling are *Advertising Age, American Demographics, Broadcasting, Business Week, Journal of Advertising Research, Journal of Consumer Research, Monthly Labor Review,* and *Sales and Marketing Management*. Major access points include public opinion polls, surveys, and opinion polls. "See also" references are suggested for the subject of interest and surveys, that is, educational surveys, telephone surveys, consumer surveys, and so on. Similar references are made with opinion polls: employees—opinion polls; newspapers—opinion polls; physicians—opinion polls; and so on. Additional terms to consider are election forecasting, questionnaires, consumers' preference, audience research, and United States—foreign opinion. *Business Periodicals Index* is available online through WILSONLINE and is also available on CD-ROM.

> *Communication Abstracts: An International Information Service.* 1978-. Quarterly. Sage Publications, 275 S. Beverly Dr., Beverly Hills, CA 90212.

Political campaign coverage is well represented. The title abstracts about two hundred international English-language journals (listed in issue number three of each year) as well as books and book chapters. Abstracts average about 150 words, half a page in the small format used for this title. The major resources indexed here include *Annals of the American*

Academy of Political and Social Science, Journalism Quarterly, Newspaper Research Journal, and *Public Opinion Quarterly.* The indexers favor grouping access under the word polling, with some entries found under surveys, questionnaires, and polls. Specifically under polls or polling, there is an average of seven entries a year.

Current Index to Journals in Education (CIJE). 1979-. Monthly. Oryx Press, 2214 North Central at Encanto, Phoenix, AZ 85004.
CIJE selects, indexes, and abstracts approximately 740 education and education-related journals, including some foreign titles. It is part of the ERIC system, a national information network for providing access to education literature. Citations are arranged by educational journal (EJ) number under sixteen major subject headings. There are subject, author, and journal contents indexes. Major access points are surveys, public opinion, and questionnaires. The source is valuable for polling and survey topics because of the large number of interdisciplinary social and behavioral education-related journals considered that are not normally retrieved through political science, business, and social science indexes. CIJE can be searched online through DIALOG or BRS; it is available on ERIC CD-ROM (1969–1987).

PAIS Bulletin. 1915-. Semi-monthly. Public Affairs Information Service, Inc., 11 W. 40th St., New York, NY 10018-2693.
This source covers over one thousand periodical titles per year from which selected articles are indexed. Additionally, six thousand or more books are scanned; reports, pamphlets, proceedings, government documents, and newspaper articles are also selectively indexed. The subject areas covered are the social sciences including business, government, political science, and other related disciplines. Although all the materials indexed are in English, the literature is gathered globally. There is a cumulative subject index for the years 1915 to 1947 published by Carrollton Press. Significant titles indexed are *American Behavioral Scientist, American Demographics, Business Week, Campaigns & Elections, The Journal of Political Action, Congressional Quarterly Weekly Report, The Economist, National Journal, Public Opinion, Public Opinion Quarterly,* and *The Wall Street Journal.* The main access points include public opinion polls and surveys. As with other indexes considered, additional entries can be found under the specific type of survey (i.e., telephone surveys, consumer surveys, business surveys, and so on). Formal subject headings (travel—surveys; teachers—surveys; directories—surveys; and so on) are also used. Additional entry points to

consider include sampling; directories—public opinion polls; and market research—telephone interviews. *PAIS Bulletin* is available online through BRS and DIALOG, and is also available on CD-ROM.

> *Public Opinion Quarterly Index.* New York: Elsevier Science
> Publishing Co., 1984.

This volume provides indexing to the first forty-six volumes of the *Public Opinion Quarterly* (1937–1982). One previous cumulative index covered volumes one through thirty-one (1937–1967). Several thousand published articles are indexed in this source. There are author, subject, and book review indexes. Polling literature is indexed under the following subject headings: newspapers—polls; polls; polls—Congress; polls—elections; polls—*Public Opinion Quarterly*; and prediction. Direct access to a particular subject area can also be achieved by searching the index using appropriate key words.

> *Social Sciences Citation Index* (SSCI). 1966-. 3/yr with annual
> and quinquennial cumulations. Institute for Scientific Information,
> 3501 Market St., Philadelphia, PA 19104.

SSCI indexes fully 1,400 periodical titles, and approximately 3,300 titles selectively; some 250 books are also indexed. Twenty-two categories within the social sciences are covered on a worldwide basis. This is the most comprehensive printed index available for the social sciences. The set contains four indexes: source, permuterm subject, corporate author, and citation. The latter index contains entries that are arranged by cited author. For example, if one wishes to locate authors who have used George Gallup's book, *Pulse of Democracy*, as a footnote, one would consult the citation index for each year since 1966 under the heading Gallup, George. Polling literature is indexed in the permuterm subject index. The Institute for Scientific Research indexing system permits access to this subject via any keyword in the title. There are four five-year cumulative indexes. The index is available online through BRS and DIALOG.

> *Social Sciences Index.* 1974-. Quarterly. H.W. Wilson, 950
> University Ave., Bronx, NY 10452. (Formerly *International Index*
> 1907–1965, and *Social Sciences and Humanities Index* 1965–
> 1974).

About 350 English-language periodical titles are scanned. Some of the key journals indexed are *American Journal of Political Science, American Sociological Review, Annals of the American Academy of Political and*

Social Science, The Economist, Foreign Affairs, Journal of Applied Behavior Science, The Journal of Politics, Psychology Today, Public Opinion, Public Opinion Quarterly, and *Western Political Thought.* Access points include public opinion polls, surveys, and attitudes. As with *Business Periodicals Index,* the subject is linked with surveys or attitudes (i.e., social surveys, market surveys, mental health surveys, political attitudes, war attitudes, and so on). Some additional terms are election forecasting and telephone in social surveys. *Social Sciences Index* is available online through WILSONLINE and is also available on CD-ROM.

> *Statistical Reference Index.* 1980-. Monthly with annual cumulations. Congressional Information Service, 4520 East-West Hwy., Bethesda, MD 20814.

Each annual edition is published in two volumes, index and abstracts. The index volume is divided into the following sections: subjects and names; categories (geographic breakdowns, economic breakdowns, etc.); issuing sources; titles; and guide to selected standard classifications. The abstract volume is divided into broad categories such as associations, state governments, and universities. Access points include opinion and attitude surveys, consumer surveys, elections, methodology, and political attitudes. Over ninety percent of the publications covered in *SRI* are included in the *SRI* Microfiche Library.

> *United States Political Science Documents.* 1976-. Annual. University of Pittsburgh, NASA Industrial Applications Center, 823 William Pitt Union, Pittsburgh, PA 15260.

This bibliography is the published version of a computer-based information system for political science developed by the University Center for International Studies. It indexes more than 150 major journals in the areas of political science and related disciplines, all of which are published in the United States. This publication includes about thirty-five hundred abstracted articles per year. There are five indexes: author/contributor, subject, geographic area, proper name, and journal. Part one comprises Indexes; part two: Document Descriptions. Polling literature is indexed under the following subject headings: mass public opinion, political poll, public opinion indicator, public opinion survey, and survey research. The bibliography is available online through DIALOG.

Appendix G

ORGANIZATIONS

Academy of Political Science
2852 Broadway
New York, NY 10025
(212) 866-6752

American Association for Public Opinion Research
P.O. Box 17
Princeton, NJ 08542
(609) 924-8670

American Political Science Association
1527 New Hampshire Avenue N.W.
Washington, DC 20036
(202) 483-2512

American Psychological Association
1200 17th St. N.W.
Washington, DC 20036
(202) 955-7600

American Sociological Association
1722 N St. N.W.
Washington, DC 20036
(202) 833-3410

American Statistical Association
1429 Duke St.
Alexandria, VA 22314
(703) 684-1221

Council of American Survey Research Organizations
Three Upper Devon Belle Terre
Port Jefferson, NY 11777
(516) 928-6954

International Survey Library Association
Roper Center
P.O. Box 440
Storrs, CT 06268
(203) 486-4440

National Council on Public Polls
205 E. 42nd St.
New York, NY 10017
(212) 986-8262

World Association for Public Opinion Research
c/o Prof. Valerie Lauder
School of Journalism
CB-3365, Howell Hall
University of North Carolina
Chapel Hill, NC 27599
(919) 962-4078

Appendix H

SELECTIVE KEY WORD INDEX STOP LIST

Change

Data

Example

Finding

Individual

Information

In-house

Investigator

Issue

Item

Knowledge

Method

Methodology

Opinion

Poll

Problem

Project

Public opinion

Public opinion poll

Researcher

Result

Statistics

Student

Survey

Survey research

United States

Use

Variable

Author Index

A

Abrams, F. 127
Abramson, P.R. 259, 260
Adler, K.P. 210
Advanced Research Seminar
on Cognitive Aspects of
Survey Methodology 349
Aiken, L.R. 227
Aldrich, J.H. 170
Allen, D.E. 32
Allen, D.F. 152
Alpern, D.M. 57, 70
Alreck, P.L. 21
Altschuler, B.E. 71
Alwin, D.F. 154, 176, 282,
321
Anderson, A.B. 43, 155, 316
Anderson, A.B., ed. 13, 23,
24, 43, 145, 153, 155,
158, 161, 163, 215, 234,
280, 312, 313, 315, 316
Anderson, B.A. 259, 260
Anderson, J.F. 1
Andrews, F.M. 156
Arafat, I. 32
Armenakis, A.A. 157
Armstrong, G.B. 298
Asher, H.B. 8
Assael, H. 233
Assembly of Behavioral and
Social Sciences 164

B

Atkin, C.K. 101
Atkins, F.C. 228

Babbie, E.R. 26, 27
Bachman, J.G. 148, 301
Backstrom, C.H. 28
Bainbridge, W.S. 360
Baker, H. 113
Balter, M.B. 307
Barrett, J. 311
Barry, J.M. 5
Basilevsky, A. 155, 316
Beal, R.S. 72
Becker, J.F. 80
Becker, K.M. 77
Bedeian, A.G. 157
Begin, G. 361
Benjamin, G., ed. 90
Bennett, S.E. 302
Benrud, C.H. 252
Berdie, D.R. 1
Berg, M. 136
Bergsten, J.W. 237
Berk, R.A. 313
Bickman, L. 124
Billiet, J. 254
Bishop, G.F. 183, 189, 190,
195, 196, 197, 198, 204,
284, 302
Blair, E. 255

Selective Key Word Index

(See Appendix H for stop word list.)

A

AAPOR Standards Committee 345
ABC 118, 129, 133, 345
ABC/Harris 142
ANCOVA 286
ANOVA 286
AT&T 345
Abortion 335, 340
Abuses 164, 165
Academic 38, 43, 104, 133, 173, 248
Academy of Political Science 90
Accuracy 30, 52, 75, 95, 135, 178, 186, 192, 228, 232, 288, 304, 330, 333, 334, 350
Acoustic 241
Acquiescence 277
Activation process 359
Additive recursive causal models 163
Administer 22
Administered 148
Administration 49, 152, 243, 256
Admissibility 100
Adolescent(s) 261, 300
Advances in Experimental Social Psychology 55

Adversaries 126
Advertising 334
Afternoon hours 252
Age 82, 112, 186, 214, 216, 259, 275
Age of Dealignment 142
Agenda-setting 67, 114, 197
Aggregate estimation 49
Aggregate value preferences 154
Agree-disagree scales 301
Akron Area Survey 201
Alabama 174
Alaska 134, 136
Alcohol 269
Almond, Gabriel 210
Altruistic thoughts 150
Ambiguity format 170
Ambivalence 111, 184
American Association for Public Opinion Research 16, 31, 45, 64, 76, 106, 108, 112, 147, 172, 247, 271, 345
American Journal of Sociology 2
American Newspaper Publishing Association 20
American Panel Surveys 285
American Political Science Association 62

C

Q

R

U

V